高等院校旅游专业系列教材

旅游企业岗位培训系列教材

旅游饭店英语

（第二版）

张翠玲　黄中军　主编

李秀霞　鄢莉　副主编

U0360216

清华大学出版社

北京

内 容 简 介

本书结合国际旅游饭店业发展的新特点，依照旅游饭店岗位服务场景、工作流程和职业技能要点，系统介绍了房间预订、礼宾服务、接待、问讯、外币兑换与收银、客房整理、维修与安保、餐厅服务、酒吧服务、商务中心、购物、康乐中心、会议服务等旅游饭店英语基本知识，并通过指导学生实训的形式，以强化学生的技能培养。

本书构思独特，结构严谨，内容翔实，突出实用性，并注重旅游饭店英语服务全过程应用能力的培养。本书既可作为普通高等院校本科旅游管理专业的教材，同时又兼顾普通高校专接本、高职、高等教育自学考试、成人教育旅游管理教学，也可用于旅游饭店从业者的在职岗位培训，参加旅游英语资格取证考试提供辅导。

图书在版编目（CIP）数据

旅游饭店英语 / 张翠玲，黄中军主编. —2 版. —北京：清华大学出版社，2023.2
高等院校旅游专业系列教材　旅游企业岗位培训系列教材
ISBN 978-7-302-51314-8

Ⅰ．①旅…　Ⅱ．①张…　②黄…　Ⅲ．①旅游饭店－英语－高等学校－教材　Ⅳ．①F719.3

中国版本图书馆 CIP 数据核字（2018）第 223836 号

责任编辑：杜　星
封面设计：常雪影
责任校对：王凤芝
责任印制：宋　林

出版发行：清华大学出版社
　　　　网　　　　址：http://www.tup.com.cn, http://www.wqbook.com
　　　　地　　　　址：北京清华大学学研大厦 A 座　　　　邮　　编：100084
　　　　社　总　机：010-83470000　　　　　　　　　　邮　　购：010-62786544
　　　　投稿与读者服务：010-62776969，c-service@tup.tsinghua.edu.cn
　　　　质 量 反 馈：010-62772015，zhiliang@tup.tsinghua.edu.cn
印 装 者：三河市铭诚印务有限公司
经　　销：全国新华书店
开　　本：185mm×260mm　　　印　　张：20.25　　　字　　数：460 千字
版　　次：2009 年 9 月第 1 版　　2023 年 4 月第 2 版　　印　　次：2023 年 4 月第 1 次印刷
定　　价：59.00 元

产品编号：069471-01

旅游系列教材编审委员会

序 言

随着我国改革开放进程加快和国民经济的高速发展，交通与通信技术的不断进步，旅游景区（点）维护、旅游文化挖掘及宾馆酒店设施设备的不断完善，居民收入和闲暇时间的增多，旅游正日益成为现代社会人们主要的生活方式和社会经济活动，大众化旅游时代已经快速到来。

旅游作为文化创意产业的核心支柱，在国际交往、文化交流、扶贫脱贫、拉动内需、解决就业、丰富社会生活、促进经济发展、构建和谐社会、弘扬中华文化等方面发挥着巨大作用，旅游已成为当今世界经济发展最快的"绿色朝阳产业"。

2021 年 5 月，文化和旅游部印发《"十四五"文化和旅游市场发展规划》，规划确定了"十四五"时期旅游业发展的总体思路、基本目标、主要任务和保障措施，是未来我国旅游业发展的行动纲领和基本遵循，为我国的旅游业发展指明了方向。

随着全球旅游业的飞速发展，旅游观念、产品、营销方式、运营方式及管理手段等都发生了巨大变化，面对国际旅游业激烈的市场竞争，旅游行业的从业员工急需更新观念、提高服务技能、提升业务与道德素质，旅游行业和企业也在呼唤"有知识、懂管理、会操作、能执行"的专业实用型人才。加强旅游经营管理模式的创新、加速旅游经营管理专业技能型人才培养已成为当前亟待解决的问题。

针对我国高等职业教育旅游管理专业知识老化、教材陈旧、重理论轻实践、缺乏实际操作技能训练等问题，为满足社会就业发展和日益增长的旅游市场需求，我们组织多年从事旅游教学实践的国内知名专家教授及旅游企业经理共同精心编撰了本套教材，旨在迅速提高大学生和旅游从业者专业素质，更好地服务于我国旅游事业。

本套教材根据大学旅游管理专业教学大纲和课程设置，融入旅游管理的最新实践教学理念，坚持以习近平新时代中国特色社会主义思想为指导，力求严谨，注重新发展理念，依照旅游活动的基本过程和规律，全面贯彻国家新近颁布实施的旅游法规及各项管理规定，按照旅游企业用人需求，结合解决学生就业，注重校企结合，贴近行业企业业务实际，强化理论与实践的紧密结合，注重管理方法、实践技能与岗位应用的培养，并注重教学内容和教材结构的创新。

本套教材的出版，对帮助学生尽快熟悉旅游操作规程与业务管理，毕业后能够顺利走上社会就业具有特殊意义。

牟惟仲

2021 年 10 月

前　言

旅游作为文化创意产业的核心支柱，在国际交往、文化交流、拉动内需、解决就业、丰富社会生活、促进经济发展、构建和谐社会、弘扬中华文化等方面发挥着越来越大的作用，旅游业已成为我国服务经济发展的重要产业，在我国经济发展中占有极其重要的位置。为了加快推动旅游业的发展，国务院发布了《关于加快发展旅游业的意见》，于2013年颁布实施了新的《旅游法》，这是党中央和中国政府的伟大战略决策。

外语是涉外服务工具，也是对外交流的重要手段，英语作为国际旅行的通用语言和主要交际工具，旅游从业人员的英语应用水平直接影响着我国旅游业的发展速度与服务质量；为了满足日益增长的旅游市场需求、培养社会急需的既有丰富的旅游专业知识又有过硬外语水平的专业人才，我们组织全国多所高等院校长年从事旅游饭店英语教学和实践活动的专家教授，共同精心编写了此教材，旨在迅速提高大学生和旅游饭店从业者的专业英语应用水平，更好地服务于我国的旅游事业。

本书作为普通高等教育旅游管理专业的特色教材，自2009年出版以来，因写作质量好、实用性强而多次重印，很受全国各高等院校师生欢迎。此次再版坚持科学发展观，严格按照教育部"加强职业教育、突出实践技能培养"的要求，针对大学旅游饭店服务英语教学要求和职业能力培养目标，结合模块化组合和实例教学，注重强化听力、口语等实际应用训练。作者审慎地对原教材内容进行了反复论证、精心设计、深入推敲、细心写作。本书再版对帮助学生尽快熟悉旅游饭店英语服务业务要求，走上社会顺利就业，从事旅游饭店职业岗位工作具有特殊意义。

旅游饭店英语是大学本科旅游管理专业的核心课程，也是旅游饭店从业者必须掌握的关键技能。全书共分16个单元，以学习者应用能力培养为主线，根据国际旅游饭店业发展越来越注重全方面服务的新特点，结合旅游饭店英语岗位服务操作规范和职业技能要点，系统介绍了房间预订、礼宾服务、接待、问讯、外币兑换与收银、客房整理、维修与安保、餐厅服务、酒吧服务、商务中心、购物、康乐中心、会议服务等旅游饭店英语基本知识。

本书融入了旅游饭店英语的最新实践教学理念，力求严谨，注重与时俱进，具有理论适中、知识系统、案例鲜活、贴近实际、实用性突出等特点，并注重旅游饭店英语服务全过程应用能力的培养。本书可以作为普通高等院校本科旅游管理专业的首选教材，同时兼顾普通高校专接本、高职、高等教育自学考试、成人教育教学，也可以作为旅游饭店从业者在职岗位培训用书、旅游英语资格取证考试辅导用书。

本书由李大军总体筹划并具体组织，由张翠玲和黄中军主编，由张翠玲统改稿，由鄢莉、李秀霞为副主编，由杨昆教授审定。作者编写分工如下：牟惟仲（序言），邹蓉（第1单元），黄中军（第2单元），李秀霞（第3单元、第5单元），陈永生（第4单元、第6单元），鄢莉（第7单元、第8单元、第15单元），张翠玲（第9单元、第11单元、第14单元），梁艳智（第10单元、第16单元），张凤霞（第12单元），谭明华（第13单元），王乃换、蔡丽伟（附录），李晓新（文字和版式修改、制作教学课件）。

　　在本书修订再版过程中，我们参阅了大量旅游饭店英语的最新书刊和网站资料，精选了优质案例和图片，并得到了有关专家教授的具体指导，在此一并致谢。为方便教学，本书配有电子课件，读者可以从清华大学出版社网站（www.tup.com.cn）免费下载。因作者水平有限，书中难免存在疏漏不足，恳请专家和广大读者给予批评指正。

编者

目 录

Unit 1

Hotel Basics

 Learning Objectives

After this unit, you will be able to:

➤ know the basic hotel services and amenities
➤ tell the hotel departments and their duties
➤ use courtesy English when serving guests
➤ publicize the new concept of "Green Hotel"

 Warming Up

I. Look at the symbols of hotel services below and identify each service that hotels can offer. Use the words from the list.

24-hour airport shuttle bus	Meeting facilities	Indoor swimming pool
Laundry service	Exercise facilities available	Valet parking
24-hour room service	Restaurant on premises	Satellite or cable TV

1_____

2_____

3_____

4＿＿＿＿＿＿   5＿＿＿＿＿＿   6＿＿＿＿＿＿

7＿＿＿＿＿＿   8＿＿＿＿＿＿   9＿＿＿＿＿＿

II. **Working in a hotel, you have to know your hotel services and amenities very well, which can make you serve guests more efficiently and professionally. Now have a brainstorming to collect as many words or phrases as possible according to the following classification.**

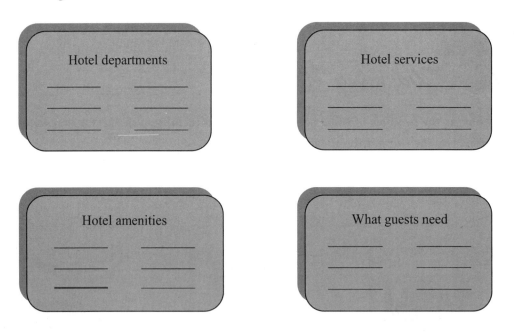

 *Situational Conversations*

Pre-questions

Suppose you are a clerk in a hotel.

1. What is Service?

2. What requirements are necessary to be a successful staff member in a hotel?

3. How should we address a guest if we do not know the name or title?

4. What are courtesy English when serving guests?

5. What can you do if you wish most guests to be repeat guests in your hotel?

Conversation 1   The Sense of Service

Zhou Wang, a fourth-year student majoring in Hotel Service and Management in a tourism institute, is doing his internship in Crown Plaza Shenzhen. The training manager is talking to him about the sense of service.

(M: The Hotel Training Manager   Z: Zhou Wang)

M: Good morning, Mr. Zhou. Welcome to our hotel. You're going to spend 3 months on having your operations intern here. Are you ready for that?

Z: Yes, Sir. I'm so excited and a bit upset.

M: That's for sure. After all, it's your first full-time job. Could you tell me why you choose Hotel Service and Management as your major?

Z: I enjoy dealing with people. In a hotel, we can meet and serve people from all walks of life and I have a real liking for guests and a warm desire to them.

M: That's great. Then, could you tell me what makes you feel uneasy?

Z: I don't have much experience to communicate with strangers.

M: Great! I understand. Take it easy. I will tell you what you can do, but before that, please tell me how you think of the hotel business.

Z: A hotel is an establishment that provides paid lodging, usually on a short-term basis, and it is also a home away from home for all the travelling guests.

M: Good idea. Then, what about hotel service?

Z: I think hotel service is a very decent and honorable occupation, and it is understanding, anticipating and fulfilling needs of others.

M: Right. Good service is a blending of courtesy and efficiency without either familarity or servility. Do you happen to know what the word "SERVICE" stands for?

Z: Sorry, Sir. What do you mean?

M: Actually, service is the SERVICE. As you can see, each of its letters is rich in meaning. S stands for smiling, E for excellent, R for ready, V for viewing, I for inviting, C for creating and the last E for Eye. In other words, we should keep smiling all the time, everything we do should be excellent, be ready to treat every guest with hospitality, view every guest as a special, invite guests to return, create a warm atmosphere and show our care with eye contact.

Z: Oh, I see. You are telling me how to treat the guests. Well, I'll regard every guest as a VIP.

M: Good. I do hope you can bear in mind our hotel's mission — Crown Plaza is the business hotel that focuses on delivering the important services and facilities for formal and informal meetings consistently and completely. In addition, pay particular attention to your behavior and language, as well as be aware of the cultural diversity.

Z: Thank you, Sir. We did have such training courses for courtesy English, and service etiquette.

M: Terrific! Besides, remember we are one business, and we all work as a team to lead and win.

Z: Yes, I'll try my best to be a good team player.

Conversation 2   Choosing Your Hotel

Li Yang will have a business trip to Canada, but she doesn't have any idea about how to choose a proper hotel. Robert Goldfield, a Canadian hotel manager, is giving Li Yang some advice.

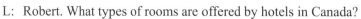

(*L: Li Yang   R: Robert*)

L: Robert. What types of rooms are offered by hotels in Canada?

R: In Canada, hotel guest rooms are usually divided into two kinds — a room and a suite. The specific room types offered are as the following: single room designed for one person; double room, containing one king-size or queen-size bed; twin room, with two single beds; triple room, containing three single beds or a standard room with an additional single bed. While a suit is subdivided into several types as follows: Standard Suite, also named junior suite or family suite, Deluxe Suite, Executive Suite and Presidential Suite, which usually is the best accommodation in a hotel. However, if you want to find a single room, you should always check through whether you're booking into a hotel that has a shared bathroom, because some people are very uncomfortable doing that.

L: Can I get any discount if I make a room reservation on hotel's website?

R: It depends on the time you go. I mean the full price "rack rates" can vary from peak season to off-season.

L: What is the "rack rates"?

R: A hotel's rack rate, or its brochure rate, is usually the maximum room charges published by hotels when occupancy is high. In fact, I think that to get the best hotel room rate is over the telephone. You have to telephone the hotel directly, and you need to be very aggressive about asking what the specials are, what the discounts are, and if there are any special rates for membership.

L: Good idea. My next question is whether there are the standard rules for tipping hotel personnel. You know tipping is not popular in China.

R: Tipping is always at the discretion of the traveler. However, generally speaking, you should tip the doorman, the bellman and the person who valet parks your car. I think a $2 tip is probably appropriate.

L: It's very kind of you, Robert. I do appreciate your information.

Key Words & Expressions

aggressive	[ə'gresiv]	*adj.*	主动的
behavior	[bi'heivjə]	*n.*	行为
colleague	['kɔli:g]	*n.*	同事
courtesy	['kə:təsi]	*n.*	礼貌
etiquette	['etiket]	*n.*	礼仪
occupation	[,ɔkju'peiʃən]	*n.*	职业
personnel	[,pə:sə'nel]	*n.*	员工
sincerity	[sin'serəti]	*n.*	真诚
bear in mind		记住	
off-season		淡季	
operations intern		学生实习	
peak season		旺季	
rack rates		门市价	
valet park		代客泊车	
The Sense of Service		服务意识	

Additional Useful Expressions

1. Meeting and Greetings

  a. Good morning, Sir/Madam.

  b. Good afternoon/evening, welcome to our hotel.

  c. How are you today, Sir?

  d. Did you have a nice trip?

  e. Nice to meet you, Sir.

f. What can I do for you?

g. May I have your name, please?

h. May I have your signature, Sir? …here please.

i. May I be of service, Madam?

j. May I recommend our…, Sir?

k. Is there anything else I can do for you, Madam?

2. Best wish

a. We look forward to your arrival.

b. Have a pleasant stay at our hotel, Sir.

c. Have a pleasant stay with us, Madam.

d. Have a nice day!

e. Have a pleasant evening.

f. Enjoy your stay.

g. Have a nice trip.

h. Have a safe trip.

3. Extending thanks

a. Thank you very much.

b. Thank you for telling us.

c. Thank you for your compliment.

d. Thank you for waiting.

e. Thank you for being so understanding.

f. That's very kind of you. I really appreciate what you have done for me.

4. Responding to one's appreciation

a. You are welcome.

b. It's my pleasure.

c. My pleasure.

d. Glad to be of service. Please feel free to contact us anytime.

5. Expressing "sorry" and apologizing

a. Excuse me.

b. I'm awfully sorry.

c. I beg your pardon, Sir.

d. Sorry to have bothered you.

e. Excuse me for interrupting.

f. I'm very sorry. There could have been a mistake. I do apologize.

g. I'm sorry to have kept you waiting, Sir.

6. Responding to one's apologizing

a. That's all right.

b. It doesn't matter.

c. Take it easy.

7. Positive answer

a. Certainly, Sir. I will do it right away.

b. Very good, Sir. I'll be glad to help.

c. Certainly, Madam. I'll be happy to do it.

d. Yes, certainly, just leave it to us, Sir.

8. Negative answer

a. I'm sorry. There is no discount.

b. I'm sorry, Madam. I'm afraid we can do nothing.

9. Saying farewell

a. Good-bye, and have a nice trip.

b. Thank you for coming.

c. We all look forward to serving you again.

d. Hope you enjoyed staying with us.

Classroom Activities

__ Listening Practice __

I. Listen to the recording and complete the following passage.

Welcome to the Holiday Inn DIAMOND BAR

With a breathtaking view overlooking the San Gabriel Mountains our hotel's 1._____ is near Anaheim, downtown Los Angeles and a number of attractions and businesses making it the premier place to stay for business and 2._____ travelers.

Leisure travelers love that our hotel is near Disneyland and many other local 3._____ including the Big League Dreams sports park and outdoor activities like golf and tennis. In addition, we are close to a variety of shops at the Ontario Mills which easily can meet all of your 4._____ needs.

Corporate guests of our hotel enjoy being near Anaheim businesses and appreciate the 24-hour business center that has fax, copy, 5._____ and print services. In addition, over 5,000 square feet of meeting space is available for our guests. Feel free to 6._____ one of our 13 rooms and take advantage our technical amenities and helpful 7._____ who can ensure that your next meeting or social event is a success.

Whether you're looking for hotels near Disneyland and Los Angeles or those near local corporations, we are the perfect choice. You'll feel right 8._____ here as you relax by our outdoor pool and soak up the sun or as you burn off some steam in the fitness center. And, when it's time for a meal, you can eat right on our property at the on-site restaurant, DB's Bar and Grill, where kids eat free! Choose us—the name you can trust.

II. Listen to the recording and answer the questions.

1. Why will George work in a hotel?

2. How long will George work in the hotel?

3. Which department will George start to work?

4. What will George do as a Front Office clerk?

5. What is the second department which George will work for?

6. What is PA cleaner?

7. What will George want to do in the F and B department?

8. What does George think about his work in the hotel?

 __ *Communicative Practice* __

Role Play

Work in pairs or groups and create conversations according to the given situations.

Situation 1: A brief introduction of hotel service and amenities

A guest of a hotel is calling the Front Office for the information of hotel service and amenities. A Front Office clerk is answering the phone. Use the given information to help you.

Services and Amenities

-Hilton honors program-earn points and miles

-Complimentary hot breakfast

-Free high speed wireless internet throughout the hotel

-Complimentary beverage area 24 hours a day

-Great Room with 42" TV and fireplace

-Indoor heated swimming pool with atrium and patio

-24 hour front desk service

-ATM machine

-Baggage storage

-Safety deposit box

-State-of-the-art fitness center

-Handicapped rooms available

-Non-smoking rooms available

-Business services including fax, copying, express mail

-Free newspapers

-Cribs, high chairs and rollaway beds available

-Courtesy transportation to airport

Situation 2: A job interview

Mr. Lee wants to find a job in a 3-star hotel. Now he is attending a job interview. The hotel HR manager is asking Mr. Lee some questions about hotel and hotel service. Use the given information to help you.

- why the applicant wants to work in a hotel

- which department he prefers

- tell the applicant which department is in need of hands

- if the applicant has work experience in a hotel

- tell him the decision will be made until next Friday.

Situation 3: How to be a good hotel staff

Mark and his classmates get together. They discuss how to be a good staff in hotel industries.

 *Reading*

Pre-reading questions

1. Do you wash your towel and bed sheet every day?

2. If you stay in a hotel, do you want your towel and bed sheet washed and changed every day? And why?

3. Do you have any good ideas to help hotels to save energy, and protect natural resources?

"Green" Hotels and "Green" Hotels Association

Hotels are extremely large-volume users of water, detergent, cleansers and other chemicals that can be detrimental to our environment, and hotel managers must be aware of the hotel's impact on our life resources. "Green" Hotels are eco-friendly properties whose managers are eager to institute programs that save water, save energy and reduce solid waste—while saving money—to help PROTECT OUR ONE AND ONLY EARTH! These hotels include any hotels, motels, and inns, but have to be certified green by an independent third-party or by the state they are located in.

"Green" Hotels Association is an organization that enjoys high reputation in the lodging industry, created by Patricia Griffin in 1993. The goal of this association is to reduce the amount of energy and water consumed by the lodging industry. GHA provides hotels around the world with easy access to environmentally friendly products and ideas. "Green" Hotels Association is also interested in reducing the amount of solid waste produced by the lodging industry. Managers can add their hotel to the growing list of "Green" Hotels Association's members by simply paying an annual membership fee of one dollar per room. Members receive a book consisting of over 85 pages listing different ways to save energy and cut back on waste. The eco-friendly products and ideas are always updated and informed by GHA. The hotel's name is also placed on GHA's website: www.greenhotels.com.

Two of the most popular products provided by GHA are the printed towel rack hanger and sheet-changing cards. The towel-rack hanger card encourages guests to use towels more than once, and says "Please decide for yourself. Towels on the rack mean 'I'll use it again.' Towels on the floor or in the tub mean 'please exchange'". The sheet-changing card says, "Sheets are customarily changed daily, but if you feel that this is unnecessary, leave this card on your pillow in the morning, and your sheets will not be changed that day".

Hotels can save significantly by utilizing these cards. GHA reports that hotels can save approximately $1.50 per day per occupied room by using these two products. Guests who decide to use these cards help reduce the amount of water, detergent, labor, and utilities used by a hotel in a given day. Many guests eagerly participate in their hotel's green program because they want to help protect the beautiful destination they are visiting. Very few people wash their linens and towels daily at home, and it is time that we recognize doing this in hotels is unnecessary and wasteful.

By using GHA's towel rack hangers and sheet-changing cards hoteliers are taking the first step toward keeping our earth green.

Notes to the text

1. detergent　清洁剂

2. chemicals that can be detrimental to our environment　对我们环境有害的化学品

3. eco-friendly　环保的

4. institute　建立，制定；着手，实行

5. solid waste　固体垃圾

6. but have to be certified green by an independent third-party　但是它们须经第三方认证才能成为绿色环保饭店

7. lodging industry　酒店业

8. annual membership fee　会员年费

9. towel rack hanger　毛巾架

10. sheets are customarily changed daily　按常规，床单每天都要换

11. occupied room　已入住之客房

Follow-up questions

1. What are "Green" hotels?
2. What is "Green" Hotels Association? And what does it contribute to the lodging industry?
3. Please read the following items, and decide what could be basic characteristics of a green hotel.

    a. Housekeeping uses any cleanser and laundry detergent

    b. 100% organic cotton sheets, towels and mattresses

    c. Non-smoking environment

    d. Individual packages organic soap and amenities

    e. Guest room and hotel lobby bins

    f. Energy-efficient lighting

    g. Car rental services

    h. Serve organic and local-grown food

    i. Non-disposable dishes

    j. Newspaper recycling program

 *Exercises*

__Words exercises__

I. Test your vocabulary for "Green" Hotels. Fill in the blanks with words from the box.

bulk	replace	unoccupied	GREEN HOTELS ASSOCIATION
sheets	turn off	glass	
recycling bins	minimize	low-flow	
towels	encourage	eco-friendly	2008 MEMBER
recycler baskets	lower	leftover	Committed to Help Save Our Planet! 713/789-8889, greenhotels.com

This passage lists sustainable practices that hotels can implement to keep hotels green:

♦ Start a linen (both 1._____ and 2._____) reuse program in all guest rooms.

♦ Install 3._____ showerheads that can save water.

♦ Whenever possible, buy food and guest amenities in 4._____ (i.e., use refillable hair and skin shampoo)

♦ Educate your staff to 5._____ lights and turn down heating/air conditioning when rooms are 6._____.

♦ Provide guestroom 7._____ for newspaper, white paper, glass, aluminum, cardboard, and plastic.

♦ Provide 8._____ both in public areas, in the kitchen, and in the back office to make recycling as easy as possible.

♦ Install window film to 9._____ heating and cooling loads and reduce glare in guestrooms.

♦ Use recycled paper products 10._____ the amount of paper used for each guest (i.e., reduce paper size of invoices, etc.).

♦ Provide 11._____ cups and ceramic mugs (instead of plastic) for in-room beverages.

♦ Create an incentive program to 12._____ your staff to participate in and improve upon 13._____ practices.

♦ Donate 14._____ guest amenities, old furniture and appliances to charities.

♦ 15._____ regular light bulbs with energy-efficient bulbs.

II. Choose the best answer.

1. If you've never been to this city, you should take a look at our _____.
   a. menu   b. brochures   c. front desk   d. inn

2. We do not have a _____ service. You'll have to park your car yourself.
   a. room   b. dinner   c. laundry   d. valet

3. The room has a pull _____ couch, so it will sleep an extra person.
   a. off   b. over   c. out   d. on

4. We don't have any vacancies. We are completely _____.
   a. vacant   b. booked   c. complimentary   d. closed

5. After your long conference you can relax in the _____.
   a. kitchenette   b. parking lot   c. hot tub   d. front desk

6. I'll call housekeeping and ask them to bring you some fresh _____.
   a. milk   b. dinner   c. linen   d. ice

7. If you need to do your workout we have a _____ on the third floor.
   a. weight room   b. restaurant   c. library   d. telephone

8. I'll let you voice your complaint about the rate to the _____.
   a. housekeeper   b. valet driver   c. hotel manager   d. chef

9. Please put your used _____ in the basket and leave unused ones hanging on the rack.
   a. dishes   b. towels   c. menus   d. keys

10. If you need a midnight snack there's a _____ machine full of potato chips on your floor.
    a. bellboy   b. kitchenette   c. cot   d. vending

Grammar exercises

Fill in each blank with the proper article: a, an, or the.

I went to (example) the airport at 6:00 AM yesterday. I had to catch 1._____ flight to Paris. The lines at 2._____ airport were very long, so I had to wait 3._____ long time.

Once 4._____ plane took off I tried to get some sleep but I couldn't. Then I ate 5._____ pretty good meal on airplanes! Later, I spoke to one of 6._____ flight attendants for 7._____ while. She was pretty. She told me that 8._____ pilot of the airplane was French. I managed to fall asleep for about 9._____ hour. After I woke up, I felt refreshed. I ordered 10._____ drink, then another. Generally, it was a pretty smooth flight.

___ Translation ___

1. 很高兴为您服务。有需要请随时通知我们。
2. 先生，时间充足，请慢慢来。
3. 先生，这完全不需要。但我依然要感谢你。
4. 对不起，我不能保证，但我一定会尽我全力去做。
5. 这是我的荣幸，我很高兴一切都能令您满意。
6. I'm sorry, I don't quite understand. Should I get the manager?
7. It's good value for the price.
8. Could you speak slowly, please?
9. We all look forward to serving you again. And have a safe trip home.
10. Please don't forget to say hello to the rest of the family for me.

Hotel Staff Training

As we know, it is very important that a hotel pays attention to the training of its staff, as there exist many weak parts in its various departments. Staff training must have a purpose, which is defined when a hotel considers its training needs, which are in turn based on job descriptions and job specifications.

A job description should give details of the performance that is required for a particular job, and job specification should give information about the behavior, knowledge and skills that are expected of an employee who works in it.

Unit 2

Room Reservation

 Learning Objectives

After this unit, you will be able to:
➤ take reservations through different means
➤ know well about procedures for room reservations
➤ make recommendation
➤ handle different requirements

 *Warming Up*

I. Look at the pictures below and identify each one. Use the words from the list.

connecting room	presidential suite	adjoining room
meeting room	standard suite	banquet hall
game room	standard single room	lake-view room

1_____

2_____

3_____

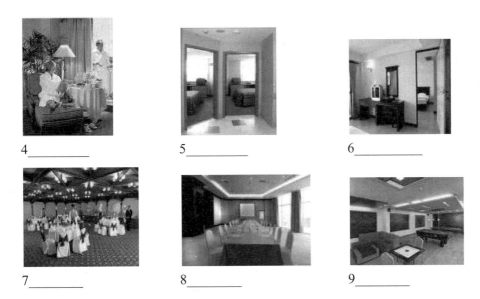

4_____   5_____   6_____

7_____   8_____   9_____

II. Suppose you are the reservationist of a hotel. Look at the hotel reservation form below. What information should you get from a guest when handling a reservation?

Hotel Reservation Form

Reservations information			
Last Name		First Name	
Address		Telephone	
Fax		E-mail	
Special request	( ) non-smoking	( ) king-size bed	( ) twin beds
ROOM TYPE	Room Rate	Arrival Date	Departure Date
Single Room			
Double			
Twin			
Deluxe Suite			
Superior Suite			

Situational Conversations

Pre-questions

Suppose you are a reservationist in a hotel.

1. What ways are available for people to reserve their rooms in a hotel?

2. What is the main duty of a reservationist?

3. If there is no room available in your hotel, what will you do for the guest?

4. How can you confirm the reservation details?

5. If you are a reservationist, how would you confirm a cancellation?

Conversation 1　Making a Reservation

(*R: Receptionist*　　*G: Guest*)

R: Good Morning, Hilton Hotel, Room Reservations. Can I help you?

G: Yes, I'd like to book a room.

R: Thank you, Sir. For which day and how many people will be there in your party?

G: Next Friday and Saturday night. Just my son and myself.

R: What kind of room would you like, Sir?

G: A suite, please. I'd appreciate it if you could give me a room with a view over the lake.

R: Hold on please. I'll check our room availability…Thank you for waiting, Sir. We do have a deluxe suite on the 8th floor with a really splendid view.

G: Fine. What's the room rate per night?

R: $100 per night, will that be all right?

G: Ok, I'll take it.

R: May I have your name and telephone number, please?

G: Sure, my name is Goldfield, Tony Goldfield, and my telephone number is 8363-5252.

R: Could you spell it, please?

G: G-O-L-D-F-I-E-L-D.

R: Thank you, Mr. Goldfield. May I know your arrival time, please?

G: At about 6 p.m. next Friday.

R: That's fine. Thank you, Mr. Goldfield. You'd like to have a deluxe suit next Friday and Saturday night. Is that right?

G: Yes it is. Thank you.

R: Thank you for choosing Hilton Hotel and we are looking forward to your arrival. Goodbye.

G: Goodbye.

Conversation 2　Desired Room Being Fully Booked

(*R: Receptionist*　　*C: Caller*)

R: Good afternoon, Sir. What can I do for you?

C: Good afternoon, I'd like to book a double room with a bath for this weekend.

R: Just a moment, please. Let me have a check… I'm sorry, Sir, all the double rooms are fully booked for the weekend and there is no vacancy.

C: Oh, that's too bad.

R: Is it possible to change another date?

C: Oh, I'm afraid not.

R: Would you like me to contact some nearby hotels to see if they have vacancies?

C: But my wife prefers to stay here and she always appreciates your service.

R: Oh, I see. Don't worry, Sir. We sometimes may have cancellations. Would you like us to put you on our waiting list and call you in case we have a cancellation?

C: Thank you. That's very kind of you. Could you let me know as soon as possible if you do have any cancellation?

R: Yes, of course. Besides, would you like to have a standard room? It is also nice and comfortable for a weekend.

R: That's fine. How about the rate per night for a standard room?

R: Well, there is a minimum price for off-season stay and a maximum price for peak-season stay. A standard room at the moment would run you $40.

C: That's fine and I will talk with my wife and call you later. Thank you for your kindness.

R: You are welcome and wish you a nice day.

C: Thank you so much for your help. Good-bye.

R: Good-bye and thank you for calling us.

Key Words & Expressions

available	[ə'veiləbl]	adj.	可用的
cancel	['kænsl]	vt.	取消
receptionist	[ri'sepʃənist]	n.	接待员
schedule	['ʃedju:l]	n.	日程安排表
minimum	['miniməm]	adj.	最低的
maximum	['mæksiməm]	adj.	最大值的
reservation	[rezə'veiʃn]	n.	预订
four star hotel		四星级酒店	
sauna bath		桑拿浴	
fully booked		定满	
off-season		淡季	
peak-season		旺季	

Additional Useful Expressions

1. Finding out what the client wants

a. Hello, would you like to make a reservation?

b. What kind of room would you like, Madam?

d. Who's the booking for, please, Madam?

e. How long will you be staying?

f. When for, Madam?

g. May I know how many persons are coming with you, Madam?

2. Accepting a booking

a. We can confirm a room for 7th and 9th.

b. We do have a single room available for those dates.

c. We have a special right now.

d. It's all right for 6th, but not 7th.

3. Asking name, address and telephone number

a. Could I have your name, please?

b. How do you spell it, please?

c. What is your address, please?

d. What about your telephone number?

e. Let me give you your confirmation number. It's: 7576385. I'll repeat that: 7576385. Thank you for choosing Holiday Hotel and have a nice day.

f. I need your name and a credit card number.

4. Introducing the room rates

a. The current rate is $50 per night.

b. Sixty-nine dollars for a single, which includes a continental breakfast.

c. A single room is 260 Yuan per night. There is also 19% tax and a 10% service charge.

d. It is 5 hundred Yuan a day including heating fee, but excluding service charge.

5. Desired room being fully booked

a. Which kind of room would you prefer?

b. I'm afraid we have no double rooms available, but we can offer you a twin room.

c. I'm sorry but we all booked for next week.

d. Is it possible for you to change your reservation date?

e. We don't have any single available.

f. Would you mind a double room instead?

6. Confirmation call

a. I'd like to confirm a reservation.

b. May I have the date of your reservation?

c. I'll check our reservation record. Your room is confirmed for that day.

d. In whose name was the reservation made?

7. Change or cancellation of reservation

a. We'll extend the reservation for you.

b. Will there be any change in your room type? Your reservation is for a twin room.

c. Is the reservation for yourself or for another party?

d. We hope we'll have another opportunity of serving you.

e. I'm glad that we'll be able to accept your extension request.

8. Advance information on payment

a. How will you be paying the bill? We accept American Express.

b. You'll have to send us a deposit of…

c. Who will be paying the bill?

d. Is the company willing to cover all the expenses?

Classroom Activities

__ *Listening Practice* __

I. Listen to the recording and complete the following conversation.

（*C = Clerk，   G = Guest*）

C: Room Reservations. May I help you?

G: Yes. I'd like to cancel a reservation, because 1._____ has been changed.

C: That's OK. Could you tell me 2._____ was the reservation made?

G: White. W-H-I-T-E.

C: And what was 3._____ of the reservation?

G: From 4._____ for 3 nights.

C: Excuse me, but is the reservation for yourself or for 5._____ ?

G: It's for 6._____ .

C: Well, may I have your name and phone number, please?

G: Yes, it's Ellen Green, and my number is 245-3971.

C: Thank you. I will 7._____ for September 15th for 3 nights. My name is Wang Ying and we look forward to 8._____ to serve you.

C: Thank you the same. Miss Wang.

G: It's my pleasure.

II. Listen to the recording and answer the questions.

1. What kind of Reservation has the client made?

2. How many days do the guests need?

3. What kind of room do they need?

4. Are the rooms available?

5. Is there a special rate for a group reservation?

6. Why does the reservationist want to know the flight number?

7. Does the client know the flight number at the moment?

8. On which day do the guests have the meeting according to the program?

9. Is a big conference hall available here?

 __ *Communicative Practice* __

Role Play

Work in pairs or groups and create conversations according to the given situations.

Situation 1: Room Reservation

Your name is Bruce. You'd like to book a single room with bath from the afternoon of October 4th to the morning of October 10th. A quiet room away from the street if that is possible. Hotel reservationist accepts the booking.

Situation 2: Confirmation call

Your name is Peter. You've booked a double room for July 1st under your own name. Now you'd like to confirm a reservation. Hotel reservationist checks your reservation record, and tells you it is confirmed for that day.

Situation 3: Making Group Reservation

Your name is Peter. You want to book 5 double rooms from October 16th to 19th and you want to know whether you are given any deductions for group reservations. The receptionist accepts the booking and gives special rate for group reservations.

 *Reading*

Pre-reading questions

1. Where does an advance reservationist work?

2. What is the job of the advance reservationist?

3. Do you want to be an advance reservationist? And why?

The Duties of Reservationists

Room reservation section belongs to the Front Office Department. The reservationist works at the Front Desk by the lobby. His/Her responsibility is: answering questions, concerning reservations, booking and assigning rooms for guests who request rooms in the hotel. He/She also takes reservations, cancellations and revisions and writes and sends out the hotel's letters of confirmation.

There are many ways of guests to make their reservations in hotels. Some people send reservation letters to the hotel. Others go directly to the hotel and make reservations in person or call the hotel and make reservations over the telephone. Still others telegraph the hotel for rooms. Sending fax is another way of reservation. With fax, the communication is instantaneous. The hotel can confirm a guest's booking immediately with a reply fax and incoming fax from the guest can be kept as the confirmation of the guest's booking.

Today, it becomes fashionable to make a booking through the internet, which is quick and convenient. But telephone is still the most popular way of making reservations.

When a reservationist receives a reservation request, he/she first checks the hotel's booking situation and see if the hotel has any vacancy during the specified period. If the hotel is able to accept the booking, the reservationist would fill out a reservation form and record the information in a reservation diary.

Hotels generally accept two types of reservations: non-guaranteed and guaranteed. A non-guaranteed reservation is a reservation that has no credit card or other form of payment attached to it as backup. It is held by the hotel until a certain cut-off hour which is set by hotel policy. Rooms reserved in this manner are returned to the room inventory after the cut-off hour has passed and can be sold to a walk-in guest. While a guaranteed reservation should be paid in advance. The payment is generally held until the arrival date or until check-out time the next day. The payment is usually made with a check or credit card. The payment is forfeited by the guest if the reservation is not cancelled in advance. In taking a guaranteed reservation, the reservationist must advise the guest of the room rates and the booking conditions.

When making a reservation, the reservationist must bear in mind what information should be contained in the reservation record, Such as, guest name, address, and telephone number; arrival date and time, and length of stay; type and number of rooms and number in the party; rate quoted; guaranteed method. Also information such as method of payment, special request (non-smoking room or handicapped) and the purpose of guest's visit is helpful in satisfying the guest's needs.

Once the information is gathered and recorded, the Reservations Department issues a reservation confirmation to the guest. This can be done by issuing a confirmation number over the telephone or by sending a letter of confirmation. Both methods verify the information on the reservation record and the guest's needs.

Notes to the text

1. Front Office Department   前厅部

2. lobby   大堂

3. in person   亲自，当面

4. takes reservations, cancellations and revisions   保留、取消和修改

5. The communication is instantaneous.   沟通非常快捷。

6. The hotel can confirm a guest's booking immediately with a reply fax and incoming fax from the guest can be kept as the confirmation of the guest's booking.   酒店可以通过回复电传确认客人的预订，客人发来的电传可以被保留作为客人的预订的确认。

7. When a reservationist receives a reservation request, he/she first checks the hotel's booking situation and see if the hotel has any vacancy during the specified period.   当预订员收到预订请求，他/她首先检查了酒店的预订情况，看看酒店是否在指定期间内有空房。

8. fill out a reservation form   填写预订表格

9. reservation diary   预订日志

10. non-guaranteed reservations and guaranteed reservations   无担保预订和担保预订

11. bear in mind   牢记在心

12. satisfy the guest's needs   满足客人的需求

Follow-up questions

1. What are the reservationist's duties?

2. How many ways are there to make room reservations? And which one do you prefer?

3. What kind of advance reservation do you think would be popular in the future? And why?

 *Exercises*

__Words exercises__

I. Test your vocabulary of hotel types, bed types and hotel facilities. Fill in the blanks with words from the box.

queen beds	Lounges	Hide-a-beds	Hostels
the front desk	Gift shops	Long boys	resorts hotels
Lobbies	Motels	youth hostels	Meeting rooms
Suites	Game rooms	rollaway	

Kinds of hotels in the United States:

Places to stay for a short time may be called hotels, hostels, motels or motor hotels, inns, lodges or resorts. 1._____, also referred to as 2._____, are often for students working away from home. 3._____ have plenty of parking space and are usually near a freeway or highway. Inns are usually like motels. Lodges and 4._____ are in the mountains, on the coast, or near lakes.

Kinds of beds:

Beds go by many different names. Starting with the smallest, there are single, twin, double, queen and king size ones. "5._____" are for exceptionally tall people. At some hotels, 6._____ are the smallest size used, so a double room has two of them. Some hotels even offer their guests waterbeds. A 7._____ can be moved into a room to sleep an extra person. 8._____ are sofas that fold out to make beds.

In hotels:

People go to 9._____ to check in or out, to turn in or pick up their keys or mail and messages, or complain about something in the hotel.

10._____ are big, open rooms near the front desk. Usually people go there meet their friends.

11._____ are comfortable bars. People go there to have drink and relax.

12._____ are sets of rooms— usually a bedroom and living room, sometimes with kitchen— that you can rent in a hotel.

13._____ are for meetings. People rent them to other people or talk about business when they don't want to do it in their rooms.

14._____ have games like pool, billiard, backgammon, chess, etc., in them. People go there to play games and relax.

15._____ have souvenirs, books and cards.

II. Match the room types and the definitions.

1. twin room	A. a room occupied by one person
2. suite	B. a room with two single beds for two people
3. connecting room	C. a two-story suite connected by a stairway
4. family room	D. a room used for entertaining
5. duplex room	E. a room with four or more beds, particular suitable for a family with children
6. lounge	F. two or more rooms with a door to allow across from one room to another
7. junior suite	G. a large room with a partition to separate the bedroom area from the sitting room area
8. hospitality room	H. a room with one large bed for two people
9. double room	I. a set of two or more rooms including a bedroom and a sitting room

10. single room   J. a room not used as a bedroom, where guests may read, watch TV, etc.

___Grammar exercises ___

By using the future continuous tense, the tone will be more tactful, polite, and sincere. Please finish the sentences with the future continuous tense.

Example: We ***will be expecting*** you next Monday.

1. How long _____you _____ (stay)?

2. What time _____you _____ (arrive)?

3. Our airport representative _____ (meet) you at the airport.

4. We_____ (leave) Sunday morning.

5. How _____you _____ (pay) the bill, Madam?

6. _____you _____ (come) by train?

7. One of my daughters _____ (bring) a friend.

8. When _____ you _____(see) Mr. White?

___Translation ___

1. We have rooms available then. You require two single rooms?

2. We look forward to seeing you next Tuesday.

3. Would you like to make a reservation?

4. I need your name and a credit card number.

5. Could you hold the line please? I will check our room availability.

6. Certainly, Sir. We will book you into a room with the queen size bed.

7. How many guests will be there in your party?

8. A single room is 80 US dollars per night with ten percent tax and ten percent service charge.

9. We offer special range for your company. For a single room there is 15% discount.

10. I'm sorry but we are fully booked those days as it is the peak season.

Guidelines for Avoiding the Errors in the Reservation Record

The reservations system or agent should verify the information entered on the reservation record by displaying or reciting the information back to the person creating the reservation record. In addition, displaying or quoting the hotel's cancellation policy is appropriate at this time to avoid any issue of no-show billing or non-return of deposits. Such communication can be especially important to hotels catering to international travelers. An error which prevents access to a reservation record can be disastrous to a hotel-guest relationship.

Unit 3

Bell Service

 Learning Objectives

After this unit, you will be able to:
➤ help the guests with their luggage
➤ show the guests to their rooms
➤ deliver the luggage or deposit some items
➤ introduce hotel services

 Warming Up

I. Look at the pictures below and identify each one. Use the words from the list.

bellman	bell	trolley/luggage cart	parcel	elevator
backpack	baggage receipt	Reception desk	luggage or baggage	

1_____

2_____

3_____

4_____   5_____   6_____

7_____   8_____   9_____

II. Working in a hotel, a doorman or a bellboy must have a good command of basic terms about special services and facilities. Now have a brainstorming to collect as many words or phrases as possible according to the following classification.

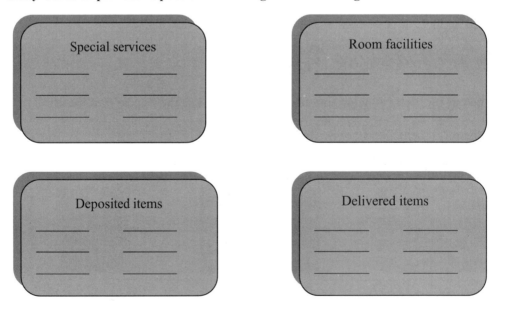

Special services

_____   _____

_____   _____

Room facilities

_____   _____

_____   _____

Deposited items

_____   _____

_____   _____

Delivered items

_____   _____

_____   _____

 *Situational Conversations*

Pre-questions

Suppose you are a doorman or a bellboy in a hotel.

1. What are the main duties of a hotel doorman?

2. What qualities should a good hotel doorman have?

3. When handling the luggage for group guests, what are the most important points you should always remember?

4. Which facilities should be introduced to the guest?

5. How can you anticipate the guest's need and offer your best service to him?

Conversation 1   Showing the Guests to Their Rooms

A car pulls up in front of a Star Hotel. A doorman goes forward to meet the guests, and opening the door of the car for them.

(*D: Doorman   G1: Guest1   G2: Guest2*)

D: Good evening, Sir and Madam. Welcome to West Lake State Hotel.

G1: Good evening.

D: May I help you with your luggage?

G2: Thank you.

D: (Opening the trunk, taking out the baggage and looking at the name on the baggage tags.)
     So, you have got altogether three pieces of baggage.

G1: Oh, no. Four pieces in all.

D: Four? Oh, sorry. Let me have a check again… But here just three pieces.

G2: Oh, no. Always poor memory! We've got only three.

G1: I see. (To the doorman) Sorry, boy. You're right. Three pieces.

D: Never mind, Sir. Now I will show you to the Front Desk. This way, please.

G1: Thank you.

(After checking in a few minutes…)

D: Now I will show you to your room. May I have your room number, please?

G2: Sure and thank you. My room number is 1820.

D: This way, please.

G1: Thank you.

D: Here we are. Room 1820. May I have your key card, please?

G2: Sure. Here you are.

(After entering the guestroom)

D: Sir and Madam, may I put your suitcases here?

G1 and G2: Sure. Just put them anywhere.

D: Is there anything else I can do for you?

G1: Yes, I'd like a wake–up call at 7 a.m. tomorrow morning.

D: Yes, I'll make sure you get one.

G2: Ok. Thank you very much indeed. By the way, could you tell me something about the hotel service?

D: Sure, our hotel is one of the first-class 5-star hotels in Beijing. There are all kinds of guestrooms here and we offer Chinese and Western cuisine in the two restaurants on the second floor. Also there is a 24-hour bar for you to have a chat with your friends.

G2: That sounds perfect. do you have a Directory of Services?

D: Yes, here it is. It contains various services and information of our hotel. Here is the remote control for TV and this is the channel selector.

G2: Good! That's very kind of you. Now I want to know if I can surf on internet in the room.

D: Sure you can.

G2: Ok. Have you got a swimming pool here?

D: It is on the top floor of the hotel with a beautiful view of the city, and there is also a beauty salon, a souvenir shop and a business center on the first floor which will provide all the necessary services for you.

G1 and G2: All right. Thank you very much, young man.

D: You are always welcome. Please call Front Desk if you need any further services.

Conversation 2   Depositing Some Items

A guest wants to deposit some valuable items and then go shopping and sightseeing with his family.

(*A: Attendant   G: Guest*)

A: Good morning, Sir. What can I do for you?

G: Yes, do you have anywhere I can keep my valuables safe?

A: Sure things. You can put them in the safe at reception or you can use the safe deposit box in your room.

G: Can you show me how to use the safe in my room?

A: Certainly Sir. If you want to use the safe, please go to the service center first and fill out a signature card, then the clerk there will give you an activation pin.

G: Activation pin? What's the use of it?

A: Once you get the pin, please plug in and open the door of the safe, insert the pin, then "open" will be indicated on the door.

G: How can I lock the safe?

A: You close the door of the safe, enter a code of your choice and it will lock. Just enter the code to open it again.

G: That's very easy. Can other people open it?

A: Unless they know the code. The safe will not unlock if you put in the wrong code, and it will show "ERROR".

G: Well, it's very safe.

A: I think so. But be sure not to forget the code you set. Otherwise, you have to contact the Service Center and ask the clerk to open it for you.

G: Oh, I see. Thank you very much.

A: It's my pleasure. One more thing, if you stop using the safe, please remove the activation pin and return it to the service center.

G: Sure. Thank you again. Good-bye.

A: Good-bye, Sir. Wish you a pleasant journey.

Key Words & Expressions

attractions	[ət'rækʃnz]	n. 景点	automatically	[ɔ:tə'mætikli]	adv. 自动地
castle	['ka:sl]	n. 城堡	deposit	[di'pɔzit]	v. /n. 储存,押金
electric	[i'lektrik]	adj. 电动的	elevator	['eliveitə(r)]	n. 电梯
keycard	['ki: ka:d]	n. 钥匙卡	landscapes	['lændskeips]	n. 景观
luggage	['lʌgidʒ]	n.行李	recommend	[rekə'mend]	v. 建议
transport	['trænspɔ:t]	n. 交通运输	valuables	['væljuəblz]	n. 贵重物品

Additional Useful Expressions

1. Offering help

a. Welcome to our hotel. May I help you with your luggage in the trunk?

b. Let me take your suitcases to the Front Desk for you, Sir.

c. I'm the bellboy. May I help you with your luggage and show you to your room?

d. We can take care of your luggage until you are back.

e. We'll send a bellboy up to your room right away.

2. Introducing hotel services and facilities

a. This is the Directory of Services.

b. And here is the remote control for TV and a clock radio with alarm. You can set it for the time you want to wake up.

c. The bathroom is over there with hot water supplied round the clock.

d. Here is the light switch and this is the temperature adjuster.

e. The wardrobe is here and the cotton bathrobes are inside of it. Beside the wardrobe is the minibar, and there is a mini-safe in the wardrobe.

f. You can find all you may need: soap, shampoo, toothpaste and toothbrush, shower cap, comb, razor and shaving cream.

3. Special courtesy English for bellboy

a. After you, Sir.

b. Follow me, please.

c. This way, please, Sir.

d. Please watch your steps, Madam.

e. Let me help you with your baggage, Sir.

4. Baggage Delivery

a. Let me put them on the trolley. I'll take your bags to your room as soon as it's ready, Sir.

b. I'm the doorman, Sir/Madam. So you have got altogether…pieces of baggage?

c. You are welcome. Where can I put your luggage?

d. Mr. Xxx. I'm the bellboy. I have brought up your luggage.

5. Taking the elevator

a. I'll hold the elevator for you, Sir.

b. Which floor would you like, Sir?

c. I can press the buttons for you, Madam.

d. The elevator is out of order now, so we have to go upstairs, Sir.

e. Mind the closing doors, Sir.

6. Escorting a guest to a room

a. Let me escorting you to your room.

b. Don't worry, it's not far.

c. The lights come on automatically when you put your key card here.

d. Your TV is here and this is the remote.

e. There is a deposit box in the wardrobe.

7. Depositing some Items

a. You can use the safe deposit box in your room.

b. I'll show you how it works.

c. Enter a code of your choice and it will lock, but don't forget your code.

d. Enter the code to open it again.

e. You can keep your passport, cash, traveller's cheques and jewellery safe in there.

_ Listening Practice _

I. Listen to the recording and complete the following conversation.

(*B: Bellman*   *G: Guest*)

B: Good afternoon, Sir! <u>1.   </u> the Lake View Garden Hotel.

G: Thank you.

B: <u>2.   </u> of luggage do you have?

G: Just two pieces.

B: <u>3.   </u>. Is that correct?

G: Yes. That's all.

B: I'll show you to <u>4.   </u>. This way, please.

G: I see. Thanks.

B: I will take care of your luggage when you do the <u>5.   </u>

G: OK.

… *On the Way to the Room.*

B: Let me see your <u>6.   </u>, Sir.

G: That's it. Room 1203.

B: Your room is on the 12th floor. Let's take the <u>7.   </u> over there.

G: OK. By the way, where is the bar?

B: It's on the third floor. It opens around the clock.

G: It's very kind of you. Thank you.

B: You are welcome. The elevators on the right are for the guests of the hotel. You can take it up to the 12th floor. The elevators on the left are for the staff and luggage. I will take the elevator on the left up to your floor with your luggage. Your elevator is right here. <u>8.   </u>, Sir.

G: Thank you.

B: See you later!

G: Sure.

II. Listen to the recording and answer the questions.

    1. Where is the old lady?

    2. What does the old lady suddenly remember?

3. What is she going to do?

4. What is she going to do with her luggage?

5. Is it possible for her to do so?

6. What will the Porter Section do?

7. When will the lady come back?

8. What does the bellboy ask the lady to do?

9. What did the bellboy give the lady?

10. What's it used for?

 __ *Communicative Practice* __

Role Play

Work in pairs or groups and create conversations according to the given situations.

Situation 1: Helping the guest with her/his luggage

Bellman: Greeting the guest at the door of the Lake View Garden Hotel. Make sure how many pieces of luggage the guest takes, and show the guest to the Front Desk.

Guest: Taking 2 suitcases, 1 shoulder bag with him and warning the bellboy something breakable in one of the suitcases.

Situation 2: Delivering the luggage to the lobby from the guest room

One morning, a guest is going to check out. She is calling to the Concierge or Porter Section to deliver her luggage to the lobby. And then she asks for arranging a taxi to send her to the airport.

Bellboy:

1. ask her name and room number

2. hope she enjoyed her stay

3. ask her where to go and when to leave

4. ask her when her plane leaves

5. arrange a taxi to wait at 2:45 at the entrance with two bellmen to help with her luggage

Guest:

1. call to the Concierge or Porter Section to deliver her luggage to lobby first

2. tell them Room Number 1102 and the name is Mary Brown.

3. leave at 3:00 this afternoon. The flight leaves at 5:30.

Situation 3: Help a guest to check the information of lost baggage card

Ken Puffer, a guest in Jin Nian Hotel, lost his Luggage claim check (宾客行李包存单).

Now he is asking for help at the Bell Captain's Desk. A bellman is checking the record of Puffer's luggage card. Use the information in the Luggage claim check to make a conversation between Ken Puffer and the bellman.

Luggage claim check
(Hotel Use Only)

Dear Guest,

Welcome to Jin Nian Hotel

Please note that we bear no responsibility for money and valuable contents. The Hotel will not be responsible for loss or damage due to fire, water or other caused beyond our control.

The Hotel is authorized to deliver the luggage to any person presenting this luggage claim check without identification.

If the articles are not claimed after three months, the Hotel is entitled to dispose of the articles without advice

Pieces of Luggage: _____2 suitcases_____

Signature: _ _Ken Puffer_____

Date: _____Dec 20th, 2022_____

Room: _____1314_____

Prepared by _____Wang Lei_____

Add: Beijing San Huan Yangqiao Shanxi   Building   **Tel:010-8789999**

Reading

Pre-reading questions

1. What are the hotel responsibilities?
2. What is bell service?
3. What kinds of Bell Services do you do as a bellboy?
4. Do you want to be a bellboy? And why?

The Duties of Doormen and Bellboys

Hotels should supervise bellman and doorman daily performance to ensure the smooth and normal operation of the section and the implementation of all bell service tasks. They are responsible for all the quests that stay there. Generally speaking, a bellboy captain arranges the bellboy and doorman to greet the group guest before they arrives.

Bell service includes such activities as luggage service upon guests' check-in and check-out, luggage storage, message service, and information service and other related tasks. Bell service also includes some assistance to guests and patrons alike. Check and record storage of guest luggage in the baggage storeroom on a daily basis and ensure that it is within the luggage storage guidelines.

Besides, bell service includes the daily posting and updating of the Events Board in the lobby in co-ordination with Catering and F&B Office. Bell service should monitor and help guests on the guest transportation bookings, especially promote hotel transportation. Bell service should help to arrange mail service, film development, or other duties requested by guests. Ensure the proper distribution of the daily newspapers to all in house guests, especially for VIPs and long staying guest.

Finally, bell service should ensure guests messages, faxes are passed to guests, or delivered to guest- room immediately and accurately.

As to the good doormen or the bellboys, they always keep the following know-hows in their minds:

● Assist with heavy packages, coats, suitcase, etc..
● Being alert to give assistance courteously and quickly, before having to be asked.
● Welcome guests at the main entrance, offering the greeting appropriate to the time of day.
● Assist arriving and departing guests by opening and closing car and taxi doors.
● Maintain a spotless porter cohere and drive way.
● Guide the guest to the front desk and wait behind the guest during the check-in. Keep eyes on the front desk clerk who provides the signal for you and escort the guests accordingly without delay.
● Be familiar with the layout of the hotel and memorize the preferred route for escorting guests.
● Be familiar with the lift workings and emergency stairs.
● Provide information to guests about the hotel facilities and services.
● Upon arrival of newspaper, prepare them and deliver them to guest rooms as assigned by the bell captain.
● Arrange transport and coordinate luggage.
● Never break into the guests' room without knocking at.
● Never ask guests for tip.
● Say sorry to the guests or apologize sincerely if you do something wrong.
● Listen attentively with concern and don't argue with the guest.

Notes to the text

1. layout of the hotel　酒店的布局

2. arrange transport　安排交通工具

3. assist with heavy packages, coats, suitcase　协助搬沉重包裹、大衣、箱包

4. being alert to give assistance courteously and quickly　要随时准备提供礼貌的、及时的帮助

5. ensure the proper distribution　确保正确分发送达

6. monitor and help guests on the guest transportation bookings　对交通预订的客人，要帮助

客人督办

7. posting and updating of the Events Board in the lobby in co-ordination with Catering and F&B Office　与餐饮部协调合作在大堂发布和更新活动板内容

8. supervise bellboys or doormen daily performance　监督行李员或门童日常表现

9. ensure the smooth and normal operation of the section and the implementation of all bell service tasks　确保部门的顺利和正常运作、所有行李服务任务的落实

10. promote hotel transportation to maximize transportation revenue　促进酒店运输服务使之利益最大化

Follow-up questions

1. The following items are the duties of a bellboy. Please find out the right procedure according to the text above.

   A. To assist other departments when necessary.

   B. Call a taxi for the guests and answer inquiries.

   C. Accompanied the guests into the room and explain the hotel and room facilities.

   D. Departure and arrival of guests for the loading, unloading luggage.

   E. Quickly delivered to guest's luggage room.

   F. For the guests luggage, the guidelines for arriving guests to check-in shops where registration.

   Right order: 1._____ 2._____ 3._____ 4._____ 5._____ 6._____

2. What can make guests get fed up with, and make complaints at the concierge or the bell captain' desk?

3. How does a bellboy deal with the guests' complaints?

 *Exercises*

__Words exercises__

I. Test your vocabulary of bell service. Fill in the blanks with words from the box.

Surf	bellhop	Bellman	
Luggage	concierge	luggage tag	
Bell	safe box	items	
Porter	Bellboy	remote control	
laundry	bathroom	wake up	

People Who Work at concierge:

Bellboy or 1.＿＿＿＿ is a hotel 2.＿＿＿＿ who helps guests with their 3.＿＿＿＿ while checking in and out. The job's name is derived from the fact that the hotel's Front Desk would ring a 4.＿＿＿＿ to summon an available employee to receive instructions. 5.＿＿＿＿ is also called bellhop, who refers to the employee that would "hop" (jump) to attention at the Front Desk in order to receive instructions. The term 6.＿＿＿＿ is much less gender specific than "bellman" or "bellboy."

Bell service--Depositing luggage:

Heavy luggage can be entrusted to deposit at 7.＿＿＿＿ or in the bell captain' desk, while cash, jewelry and other valuables must be deposited in a hotel 8.＿＿＿＿ . Otherwise the hotel will have no responsibility for it if they are lost. In almost every hotel, you can find the instructions below: Guests should keep the key or 9.＿＿＿＿ safe, otherwise both key and lock have to be replaced, which cost a lot, and you'll pay half of them for it.

When checking out, the guests fail to return the keys or luggage tag to the hotel, and then the hotel has rights to open the safe box and take the 10.＿＿＿＿ out without any responsibilities or legal effects for it.

Introducing some room service:

Here is a Directory of Services and here is the 11.＿＿＿＿ for TV and a clock radio with alarm. You can set it for the time you want to 12.＿＿＿＿ . There are some soft drinks, soda water, beer and juice in it. And this is the 13.＿＿＿＿, warm water is provided 24 hours.

There are 14.＿＿＿＿ bags in the closet, you can simply put your clothes in the bag and leave it at the floor service desk. You can 15.＿＿＿＿ on internet in the room, but you have to leave some deposit at the Front Desk.

II. Choose the best answer.

1. There is ＿＿＿＿ in the luggage.

   a. something breakable   b. breakable something

   c. anything breakable   d. breakable anything

2. I will ＿＿＿＿ your luggage up in a minute.

   a. lift   b. put   c. lay   d. send

3. May I help you with your luggage and ＿＿＿＿ you to your room?

   a. carry   b. lead   c. send   d. show

4. I'll ＿＿＿＿ the elevator for you, Sir.

   a. catch   b. call   c. press   d. hold

5. ＿＿＿＿, do you have room service and can I have a menu?

   a. On the way   b. By the way   c. In the way   d. In a way

6. Now I want to know whether I can ＿＿＿＿ on internet in the room.

   a. surfing   b. surf   c. to surf   d. surfed

7. This is the bathroom, warm water ＿＿＿＿ 24 hours.

a. is being provided   b. provides   c. was provided   d. is provided

8. We have a restaurant named Chuan Mei Restaurant specializing in Sichuan food. It's on the first floor,_____ the banquet hall.

a. close to   b. near to   c. next to   d. beside to

9. Thank you _____ so much about the hotel services.

a. for tell me   b. for telling me   c. tell me   d. to tell me

10. Here is the remote control for TV and a clock radio with alarm. You can _____ it for the time you want to wake up.

a. do   b. make   c. design   d. set

___Grammar exercises ___

Write responses to show conditions with these statements by using "If..., will/can..."

Example: you are ready. The bellboy take you to your room.

　　　If you are ready, the bellboy **will** take you to your room.

1. You like history. You have a day trip to the castle.

_____.

2. The traffic is good. It takes you about 25 minutes.

_____.

3. I get you a 10% discount. You like to have dinner.

_____

4. I order a taxi for you. You came to see me tomorrow.

_____.

5. Follow the signs to the museum. You get to the central business district.

_____.

6. We'd like tickets for the water park for tomorrow. We can have 15% off the face value.

_____

7. You learn a lot about our history. The tour guides are very knowledgeable.

_____.

8. You prefer a trip to the countryside. A tour guide shows you the local wildlife.

_____.

___Translation ___

1. Can you send up a bellboy?

2. The bellboy will take you to your room.

3. The bellboy will take your luggage to the bus.

4. Here are your keys. The bellboy will take your luggage upstairs.

5. Can you send a bellboy up for my luggage by then?

6. If you are ready, the bellboy will take you to your room.

7. When VIP guest arrives at the hotel, the bellboy and doorman should open the car door immediately, and with smile on the face, meanwhile call the guest's name.

8. Your luggage could be kept at the Bell Captain's Desk.

9. The bellboy captain arranges the bellboy and doorman greets the group guest before they arrives.

10. You could come down to the Bell Captain's Desk with your claim tag to pick up your bags.

 *Learning Tips*

Bellboy & Bellhop

Historically, bellboy or bellman was a boy or young male who may have been otherwise unskilled but able to carry luggage; hence the term *bellboy*. Today's bellman must be quick witted, very communicative, outgoing, and can understand the basics of each guest's psychology. Duties that are often included in this job are opening the front door, moving or delivering luggage, calling cabs and responding to any of the guests' needs.

This position can also be held by a woman today, with the progression of equality in the workplace. Bellboy is also called *bellhop*, which refers to the employee who would "hop" (jump) to attention at the Front Desk in order to receive instructions. The term "bellhop" is much less gender specific than "bellman" or "bellboy."

Unit 4

Reception

 Learning Objectives

After this unit, you will be able to:
➤ help the guest with reservation to check in
➤ help a walk-in guest to get a room
➤ extend a stay
➤ deal with complaints

 Warming Up

I. Look at the pictures below and identify each one. Use the words from the list.

lost property	passport	hotel lobby	assistant manager
key card	room service	registration form	receptionist
hotel directory			

1. _____   2. _____   3. _____

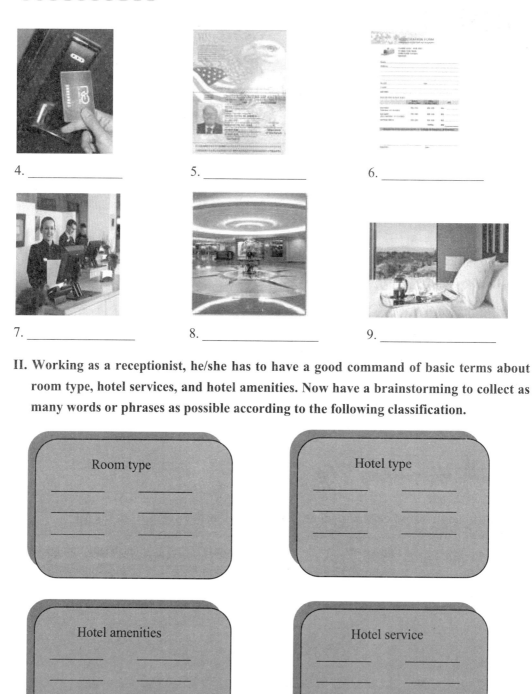

4. _____   5. _____   6. _____

7. _____   8. _____   9. _____

II. Working as a receptionist, he/she has to have a good command of basic terms about room type, hotel services, and hotel amenities. Now have a brainstorming to collect as many words or phrases as possible according to the following classification.

Room type
_____   _____
_____   _____
_____   _____

Hotel type
_____   _____
_____   _____
_____   _____

Hotel amenities
_____   _____
_____   _____
_____   _____

Hotel service
_____   _____
_____   _____
_____   _____

 *Situational Conversations*

Pre-questions

Suppose you are a receptionist in the reception desk in a hotel.

1. As a hotel receptionist, what personal qualities and skills should you possess?

2. What are the main points the receptionist has to tell group guests?

3. What should you do when the guests are checking in in-group?

4. If the guest wants to change the room, what will you do?

5. If walk–in guests check in, what should you do?

Conversation 1　Checking in Guest with a Reservation

Mr. Arthur Henry checks in at the Reception Desk in the afternoon.

(*A: Arthur Henry　R: Receptionist*)

R: Good afternoon, Sir. What can I do for you?

A: I booked a single room for 4 nights the day before yesterday and I would like to check in. I'm Mr. Arthur Henry.

R: Just a moment, please, Mr. Henry. I'll check the reservation list (after a while…). Sorry to have kept you waiting, Sir. Yes, we do have a reservation for you, Mr. Henry. Would you please show me your passport or some photo ID?

A: Here you are.

R: Thank you, Sir. One moment. You're saying for 4 nights, is that correct?

A: That's right.

R: How would you like to settle the deposit, in cash or by credit card?

A: By credit card.

R: OK, I'll need to swipe your credit card.

A: Here you are.

R: Please sign our guest book and fill out this form while I prepare your key card for you?

A: Well, what should I fill in under room number?

R: You can skip that. I'll put in the room number for you later on.

A: (After he completed the form) Here you are.

R: Let me see…name, address, and nationality, forwarding address, passport number, signature and date of departure. Now everything is OK. Mr. Henry, your room number is 1820. Here is your key card. Would you like someone to take your bags to your room?

A: No, thank you, I can manage.

R: Very well, enjoy your stay.

A: That's for sure.

Conversation 2   Helping a Walk-in Guest

(*G: Guest   R: Receptionist*)

R: Good afternoon, Sir. Welcome to Marriott Hotel.
    What can I do for you?

G: Yes, I'd like to check in, please.

R: Do you have a reservation?

G: I'm afraid not. Is there a vacant room here?

R: Just a moment please… Let me see if there is a room available. What kind of room do you
    want?

G: I'd like a double, non-smoking room.

R: You're lucky, we have one free. It's high season at the moment so we're very busy.

G: How much do you charge for the room?

R: It's $60 per night for a double room.

G: Would you give me some discount?

R: Certainly, Sir. We give 5% discount for one week, 10% for two weeks and over. How long
    do you intend to stay?

G: For a week.

R: Then we can give you 5% discount.

G: All right.

R: May I have your name, please?

G: I'm Tony Green.

R: Could you fill out the registration form, please?

G: Fine.

R: How will you be paying, Mr. Green?

G: By Visa Card.

R: May I take a print of your card?

G: Sure, here you are.

R: Thank you, Mr. Green. Your room number is 1622. A bellboy will show you to your room.
    Enjoy your stay here, please.

G: Thank you.

Key Words & Expressions

departure   [di'pɑːtʃə(r)]   *n.*   离境

nationality	[ˌnæʃə'næliti]	n.	国籍
passport	['pɑːspɔːt]	n.	护照
receptionist	[ri'sepʃənist]	n.	接待员
signature	['signətʃə(r)]]	n.	签名
forwarding address		转发地址	
pick-up service		接机服务	
be solid booked		订满了	
in case		万一	

Additional Useful Expressions

1. Special courtesy English for receptionist

a. Good morning. Can I help you?

b. What can I do for you?

c. Are you being attended to, Sir?

d. Is there anything I can do for you, Madam?

2. Extending a stay

a. You want to stay two more days, is that right, Sir?

b. You have to change your room if you want to extend your stay.

3. Checking in guest with a reservation or without a reservation

a. What name is the reservation under?

b. I'm afraid you can't check in until 4:00 pm.

c. Please show me your passport or some photo ID, Sir.

d. Would you please fill out this registration form?

e. Here is your key card. Your room number is…. It's on the …floor.

f. A bellboy will come and take you up to your room.

g. Please fill in your name and address here and then put your signature here.

h. Let me see if I can fit you in. What kind of room do you want?

i. I'll see what we have. You're in luck.

j. It's high season at the moment so we are very busy.

4. Introducing hotel services and facilities

a. We have 380 rooms, three restaurants, two big banquet halls, a bar, a tea house, a beauty salon.

b. We have a restaurant named ××× Restaurant specializing in Sichuan food. It's on the first floor, next to the banquet hall.

c. We have fitness services. We have a big Fitness Center with a lot of appliances. And we have an indoor swimming pool, an outdoor tennis court, a billiard room, a bowling room and a Recreation Center.

d. Here is the Hotel Service Information Booklet. There is detailed information about our services in it.

e. We have computers equipped in the meeting room with the internet access and there is a screen for you to display your PPT documents. If you have laptop we also have free wireless internet access.

f. We can provide you with a car and a driver and have it charged to your bill.

g. The coffee shop serves snacks and light food all day.

h. The pay-per-view channel will be charged to your room.

i. Just call the front desk to order food. The florist's is in the lobby.

5. Dealing with complaints

a. I'm terribly sorry for that. That shouldn't have happened.

b. We shouldn't have made such mistakes. I promise that it will not happen later.

c. We'll manage it, but we don't have any spare room today.

d. Very sorry, it's hotel policy. If you want to extend your stay in our hotel, you'll have to pay half of the rate more if you check out after 12:00. And if you leave after 6:00 pm, you'll have to pay the full day rate.

e. I'll speak to the person in charge and ask him to take care of the problem.

f. We'll look into the matter immediately. Thank you for telling us.

Classroom Activities

__ *Listening Practice* __

I. Listen to the recording and complete the following conversation.

（*A: Receptionist*　　*B: Guest*）

A: Good morning! Can I help you?

B: I want a double room with 1._____ . How much a day do you charge?

A: It is a hundred Yuan a day including breakfast but excluding service charge.

B: It's quite reasonable.

A: How long do you intend to stay in this hotel?

B: I shall leave in a 2._____ .

A: Have you got through with the 3._____ procedure?

B: Oh, yes, I'm going to fill in the form of registration right now. By the way, I'd like check in a suite room for my friend tomorrow morning.

A: Sorry, we have no 4._____ room for your friend tomorrow morning. But tomorrow afternoon is OK.

B: That sounds very good! Can I book the air ticket here?

A: Please go to the CAAC office to book your air ticket. If you want to book train ticket or ship ticket, you'd better go to the Shanghai International Travel Service.

  (*Next afternoon*)

B: Can I check in a suite room for my friend beforehand as he will arrive in Shanghai this evening?

A: Sure. Here is the form for you, Sir. Would you mind filling in this 5._____ and pay 6._____ in advance for him.

B: All right. This is five hundred Yuan to pay.

A: Thank you. This is 7._____ for paying in advance. Please keep it.

B: Could you tell me how many kinds of rooms do you have?

A: There are single rooms, double rooms, suites and 8._____ in our hotel. Every room is equipped with a telephone and a TV set.

B: Oh, I see. Thanks.

A: You are welcome.

II. Listen to the recording and answer the questions.

1. Are they checking out late?

2. What complaint have the kids made about hotel service?

3. Does the hotel they stay in charge them for a late checkout?

4. How does the guest feel about everything?

5. Did they swim well last night?

6. How will the guest pay for swimming in cash or by credit card?

7. How much did they think they should pay?

 *__ Communicative Practice __*

Role Play

Work in pairs or groups and create conversations according to the given situations.

Situation 1: Checking in guest without a reservation

Guest: You don't have reservation. You are hoping to get a single room facing the sea with a bath for two nights. You name is John Bradley. Pay in cash.

Reservationist: Tell him he is lucky. There is only one free. Then tell him to fill in a form including his name, address, nationality, forwarding address, passport number, place of issue，signature and date of departure. His room number is 1520. It is on the 15th floor and the daily rate is RMB 450 Yuan. Tell him you take debit cards, credit cards and cash. Finally hand the key card to him.

Situation2: Extending the stay

Guest: You booked a room in the Hilton hotel only for 2 nights. But when you do the registration, you realize the business trip can not be completed in 2 days. So you tell the receptionist to extend the stay in the hotel for 2 more nights.

Receptionist: Help the guest to do the registration, and help him check if there will be a room available 2 days later. You tell the guest there is a room available. But the guest has to move to a new one.

Situation3: Filling in the Registration form

Suppose you are a receptionist. Please help a foreign guest to fill in the reservation form below.

宾客入住登记单

Registration card

姓 SURNAME		名 FIRST NAME		生日 BIRTHDAY	
国籍 NATIONALITY	中国 CHINESE	地址 ADDRESS	省	市	县
	其他国家 OTHERS				
	身份证 ID CARD	号码 NUMBER			
证件 IDENTIFICATION CARD	护照 PASSPORT	号码 NUMBER 有效期 VALID DATE 入境口岸			
	其他 OTHERS	名称 NAME 号码 NUMBER			
房间类型 ROOM TYPE		房价 ROOM RATE	服务费 SERVICE CHARGE		
到达时间 ARRIVAL DATE			离开日期 DEPARTURE DATE		
付款方式 PAYMENT METHOD	现金 CASH 银行卡 BANK CARD 支票 CHECK 合同单位　CONTRACTED UNIT 预付 PAYMENT ADVANCE		押金 DEPOSIT	人民币 RMB 其他 OTHERS	

备注 REMARK	贵重物品寄存 LUGGAGE INFORMATION		
	其他 OTHERS		
顾客签名 GUEST SIGNATURE			
		接待员签名 RECEPTIONIST	

Reading

Pre-reading questions

1. Where does a receptionist, reservation clerk or a cashier work?
2. What do they do when they are on duty?
3. Do you want to be a receptionist, reservation clerk or a cashier? And why?

The Duties of Receptionists and Reservations Clerks

Hotel Receptionist

A receptionist is the first person that hotel guests see or talk to when they arrive or ring to make a booking. A hotel receptionist needs to be welcoming, friendly and helpful, efficient and professional, well-organized and able to handle several tasks at once. In the larger hotels, the front office job is often split into three — that of receptionist, cashier and reservations clerk. In smaller hotels, however, the receptionist could be performing the duties of all three. So the front desk receptionist has to play a very important role in a hotel. Besides, the receptionist even has to deal with some complaints from the angry guests. The receptionist should listen to them, apologize for the trouble, clarify what the exact problem is and let them know you understand.

When checking in guests, you should perform these tasks:

- welcoming guests as they arrive;
- assign rooms, introduce services for the guests and issue room keys;
- check with the housekeeping departments that rooms are ready for occupation;
- liaise with the bell desk to deliver luggage to the rooms;
- note requests for wake-up calls, transport arrangements and other general enquiries;

- settle guests' complaints with tack and diplomacy;
- put together the guest's bill, take payment and help guests with any special requests;
- communicate with other departments regarding group and VIP check-ins;
- order taxis for guests and book excursions on request.

Reservations Clerk

The reservations clerk has to handle and process reservation requests and maintain reservation records.

Main duties:

- keep a record of guests' arrivals, day and time of check-in, length of stay, and their special needs and preferences;
- liaise with other departments such as housekeeping, restaurants and security, regarding VIP and group check-ins;
- Manage the booking of rooms.

Notes to the text

1. enquiries   问询
2. excursions   短途旅行
3. making people feel welcome   让人有宾至如归的感觉
4. order taxis for guests and book excursions on request   为客人安排出行
5. to be welcoming, friendly and helpful, efficient and professional, well-organized and able to handle several tasks at once   热情，友善，热心，高效，专业，有条理，勤快麻利，一心多用
6. assign rooms and issue room keys   分配房间和房间钥匙
7. liaise with the bell desk to deliver luggage to the rooms   与行李台联络，把行李送到房间
8. transport arrangements and other general enquiries   交通安排和其他一般咨询

Follow-up questions

1. The following items are the duties of a receptionist. Please find out the right procedure according to the text above.

   A. check with the housekeeping departments that rooms are ready for occupation;

   B. liaise with the bell desk to deliver luggage to the rooms;

   C. keep a record of guests' arrivals, day and time of check-in, length of stay, and their special needs and preferences;

   D. settle bill payments and expenses quickly and accurately for guests who are checking out;

   E. greet the guests when they arrive or ring to make a booking;

   F. check and accept a reservation in the reception desk;

   G. introducing Hotel Services and facilities after getting to the room;

H. looking forward to serving the guests again.

2. What can make guests get fed up with, and make complaints in a reception desk?

3. How does a receptionist deal with the customers' complaints?

 *Exercises*

__Words exercises__

I. Test your vocabulary of hotel reception. Fill in the blanks with words from the box.

payment	signature	receptionists
occupancy	passport	the other hotel
checks	destination	registration card
obligation	cashiers	prior reservation

Reception

The reception in a hotel is the desk or office that arranges to stay in a hotel or 1._____ in for people and answers their questions. Hotel 2._____ are often found in or near hotel entrance halls, close to the centre of activity. 3._____ have to maintain accurate account balances for hotel expenses and collect payment from guests. When performing reservation and cashier duties, they may be working in the back office.

Registration

It is important for the hotel receptionist to make sure that guests are registered correctly. A 4._____ is used to record the full name, nationality, home address, and 5._____ of each guest. Foreign visitors must provide additional information such as 6._____ number and its place of issue, and their next 7._____. Many hotels use the registration card to find out more about their customers and ask questions about occupation, method of 8._____, and purpose of visit.

Walk-in guest

In hospitality sector, a walk-in guest refers to that person who has come to hotel without any 9._____. Hotels do not have any sorts of 10._____ to provide proper accommodation to walk-in guests if there is no available room. On the other hand, accommodating walk-in guest can enhance sales and daily 11._____ if it is managed properly. If the agent cannot accommodate a guest then he should refer him to 12._____ of that hotel group or any nearby hotel. By this way, if hotels of a locality maintain good relationship with each other then high percentage of such guests can be accommodated.

II. Choose the best answer.

1. The room at that hotel cost $300 a night, and that is a little _____ for me. There's no way I could pay for that.

   a. reasonable   b. expensive   c. cheap   d. realistic

2. Do you have any rooms with a _____ where I can prepare basic meals?

   a. kitchenette   b. cooking   c. suite   d. pool

3. Let me _____ to see if we have any rooms available.

   a. view   b. check   c. test   d. look

4. This hotel is one of the best in the city, and the employees try to roll out the _____ carpet for special guests.

   a. blue   b. green   c. red   d. black

5. I'd like to _____ an executive room for April 21st.

   a. check in   b. schedule   c. make   d. order

6. The _____ at the place I always go does a great job at perming your hair.

   a. hair salon   b. barber shop   c. hairstylist   d. barber's

7. It's a must to _____ in the pool.

   a. wear caps   b. wear sports shoes

   c. take a shower before swimming   d. wear swimming glasses

8. The _____ is the place where a woman can have her hair done.

   a. barber's   b. hairdresser's   c. front desk   d. lobby

9. If you want to _____ your straight hair, why not try a long wave style?

   a. charge   b. dye   c. wash   d. change

10. I want to _____ my hair cut and dyed.

    a. take   b. need   c. had   d. have

___ Grammar exercises ___

Make some sentences with attributive clauses by using who, which, that, where.

Example: Reception desk is a counter _**where**_ guests are received.

   A single room is a room _**that /which**_ has only one single bed.

   Cashiers are those _**who**_ have to maintain accurate account balances for hotel expenses and collect payment from guests.

1. Reservation desk is a counter _____ guests can book rooms.

2. Registration desk is a counter _____ guests can check in a hotel.

3. Adjoining room is a hotel room _____ shares a wall with an adjoining room but is not connected by a door.

4. Connecting room is a hotel room _____ shares a wall with an adjoining room and is connected by a private door.

5. Those _____ have heart disease or high blood pressure are not allowed to take sauna, for

their health' sake.

6. The hotel relies on the clerks, _____ are responsible for the reception and reservation performance.

7. There will be half-day charge for clients _____ are checking out after 12:00 but before 6:00 pm.

8. A receptionist is the first person _____ hotel guests see or talk to when they arrive or ring to make a booking.

___Translation ___

1. Please keep all valuables with you.
2. Please let me know if you have any special requests.
3. We highly appreciate your cooperation and understanding.
4. You could come down to the Bell Captain's Desk with your claim tag to pick up your bags.
5. We will arrive thirty minutes behind the schedule.
6. Please fill in your name and address here and then put your signature here.
7. We can give you some discount for group check-in.
8. You are a guest in the hotel, so the left-luggage room will be free for you.
9. You booked a suite at our hotel and now you want to extend your stay for two more days, is that right, Sir?
10. Here is the Hotel Service Information Booklet. There is detailed information about our services in it.

 *Learning Tips*

How to Deal with Walk-in Guests

If you are a front desk agent then follow this guideline to deal with walk-in guests:

Treat the guest warmly with ready smile as like as registered guest.

Create such situation so that the guest does not feel hesitated.

Ask his desire length of stay and room preference.

Check whether such room is available or not in those days.

If not then offer other room.

Quote the room rate and room facilities.

If the guest agrees then proceed for reservation. Otherwise, if the guest wants then send him to another hotel.

Unit 5

Switchboard

 Learning Objectives

After this unit, you will be able to:
- ➤ receive all incoming calls
- ➤ deal with the outgoing calls
- ➤ make wake-up calls
- ➤ ask for leaving a message
- ➤ deal with complaints

 *Warming Up*

I. Look at the pictures below and identify each one. Use the words from the list.

wake-up call	long distance call	hotel directory
sign of phone service	leaving a message	information desk
message form	operator	switchboard

1_____ 2_____ 3_____

4 _____

5 _____

6 _____

7 _____

8 _____

9 _____

II. Working as an operator, she/he has to have a good command of figures. Now read the figures out as quickly as possible.

Time:	Room number:
10:50	2735
7:45	1522
6:20	917

Mobile phone:	Telephone number:
13974582115	001-212-5557878
13015430678	010-65948896
13538152908	415-469-2130

Situational Conversations

Pre-questions

Suppose you are an operator in a hotel.

1. What information should an operator learn if someone calls and asks him to pass a message to a registered guest in the hotel?

2. What kinds of rule shall you bear in mind when doing your job as an operator?

3. What kind of telephone services offered in a hotel?

4. How do you help guests to make an IDD call?

5. Should the operator check with the caller after he learns all the information?

Conversation 1   Receiving a Phone Call

(*O: Operator   G: Guest*)

O: Hello, International Hotel. How can I help you?

G: Hello, I'd like to be put through to Mr. Smith and his room number is 1208.

O: I'll put you through, Madam…I'm sorry the number is engaged. Would you care to hold on please?

G: Of course.

O: Sorry, there is no reply from Mr. Smith. No one is picking up. Would you like to leave a message?

G: Could you try again?

O: Certainly, Madam. Just a moment, please…Thank you for waiting. I'm afraid there is still no reply. Maybe he is not in the room at the moment.

G: May I leave a message?

O: Of course, Madam.

G: Please tell him that the meeting will be at 4 p.m..

O: Ok, the message is — the meeting will be at 4 p.m..

G: That's correct.

O: Can I take you name, please?

G: Yes, it's Mary Banks.

O: Ok, I'll make sure he gets the message.

G: Thank you, Good-bye.

O: You are welcome. Good-bye!

Conversation 2   Explaining the Way to Make Phone Calls

(*O: Operator   G: Guest*)

O: Good evening, Holiday Inn. What can I do for you?

G: Good evening. I'd like to know how to make a call?

O: For room to room calls, dial room number directly please. For local calls, first dial 9, then the number you want.

G: Thank you. I'd like to make an international call to New York. What can I do then?

O: You may call directly from your room. Dial 9 first, then the country code and area code and last the number you want.

G: I see. Thanks a lot.

O: The call charges will be added to your bill.

G: I see. By the way, what time is it in New York now?

O: There is a time difference of 13 hours. It's 8 o'clock in the morning.

G: I'd like to make a call now. You are so helpful.

O: You are welcome, Sir. I'm always at your service.

Conversation 3   Placing a Morning Call

(*O: Operator   G: Guest*)

O: Good evening. Operator speaking. May I help you?

G: Good evening. I'm leaving for New York tomorrow and I have to wake up early to catch a plane.

O: We can give you a morning call to wake you up.

G: That's great! I need a morning call for 5 a.m..

O: Ok. We will give you a wake-up call at 5 a.m..

G: Oh, yes. I'd like to inform my girl-friend in New York of my return. May I use the phone in my room?

O: Certainly, Sir. Just dial the country code, the area code and the number you want.

G: Thank you for your information. Please don't forget. It's very important that I don't miss my plane.

O: Don't worry. We won't forget.

G: Thanks, Goodnight.

O: Goodnight.

Key Words & Expressions

appointment	[ə'pɔintmənt]	*n.* 约会，约见
charge	[tʃɑ:dʒ]	*v.* 索（价）；收（费）
dial	[daiəl]	*v.* 拨号
press	[prɛs]	*v.* 按
reply	[ri'plai]	回答，答复
area code	地区号	
banquet hall	宴会厅	
country code	国家代码	
leave a message	留言	

local call	市内电话
put through	接通电话
wake-up call	叫醒电话

Additional Useful Expressions

1. **Receiving a phone call**

   a. Hello, this is Information Desk.

   b. Hello, International Hotel. May I help you?

   c. Operator. May I help you?

2. **Finding out what phone call the caller wants to make and explaining how to make a long distance call**

   a. Which country are you calling, please?

   b. Could you tell me the party's full name and telephone number, please?

   c. What's your name and room number, please?

   d. Would you like a pay call or collect call?

   e. How would you like to make the call?

   f. Would you like me to place the call for you?

   g. May I remind you there is still a handling charge?

   h. Please dial "1" before the country code and then the area code and then the number.

   i. The country codes are listed in the Services Directory in your room. You can make a call directly.

   j. I'm afraid all calls to…must go through the operator.

   k. We've got DDD system and IDD system in our hotel.

3. **Receiving the incoming calls**

   a. One moment, please.

   b. I'll switch you to Room1103.

   c. Just wait a moment and I'll connect you.

   d. I'll transfer your call to Information Desk, you should check the room number first.

   e. I'm afraid you have the wrong numbers.

   f. I am afraid this is a direct line. We cannot transfer your call to the Chinese Restaurant. Please call 2234-1156.

   g. Sorry, there is no one by the title of Johnson here.

4. **Making calls inside the hotel**

   a. For calls inside the hotel, you can simply dial the room number, please.

   b. There is no charge for house calls.

   c. I'll transfer your call. Could you hold the line, please?

5. No reply or unable to put the call through

   a. I'm sorry, there's no reply from the room 1111.

   b. They aren't answering, would you like to leave a message?

   c. Sorry, he has moved to another room.

   d. Sorry, Mr. Lee is not in right now. Would you call back?

   e. Sorry, the receiver in his room is not on the right place.

   f. The line is busy; please call again after a while.

6. The wake-up call/morning call

   a. At what time shall we call you?

   b. Don't worry. I'll wake-up you on time tomorrow morning.

   c. The computer will record the time and the room number automatically.

   d. Ms. Wang is in Room 725. We'll ring you up at half past six tomorrow.

   e. What kind of morning call would you like to have, by phone or by knocking at the door?

   f. You may dial five to place a morning call with the operator.

   g. Anyone who stays in our hotel can ask for the morning call service.

7. Asking for leaving a message

   a. Would you like to leave a message?

   b. May I read back the message to see if it's correct, please?

   c. Would you please tell me the spelling of your name?

   d. Sorry, I can't hear you. Could you please speak a little louder?

   e. Sorry, I can't follow you. Could you speak slowly?

Classroom Activities

__ Listening Practice __

I. Listen to the recording and complete the following conversation.

```
                        Sunshine HOTEL
       Message for  [                  ]
       Room No.     [              ]
       Caller's name: [                ]
       Telephone No: [                 ]
            She is going to meet him_____ . In the _____
       _____around _____ .
```

II. Listen to the recording and answer the questions.

1. What complaint has the guest made about the phone?

2. What is the room number of the caller?

3. Who did he try to ring?

4. How many times was he cut off ?

5. How long has he spoken for before the connection was broken?

6. What's the guest's boss number?

7. What did the operator say about it?

8. Is the operator sure the faults is in their equipment?

 __ *Communicative Practice* __

Role Play

Work in pairs or groups and create conversations according to the given situations.

Situation 1: Dealing with the telephone problem

A guest called his family in New York, but he was cut off. So he calls the operator. The operator says she'll try to dial again to see if the fault is theirs.

Situation 2: Asking for a morning call

You are the guest in room 925. You tell the operator you need a wake-up call at 5:30 tomorrow morning so as to go to the airport to meet your wife. You'd like to use the computer wake-up system.

Situation 3: Leaving message

The caller, Mrs. Green wants to speak to Miss Richard in room 1221. The operator calls the number, but there is no answer. Mrs. Green leaves a message that she will meet Miss Richard in the hotel tomorrow afternoon. The operator writes down the message and promise to pass the message.

 *Reading*

Pre-reading questions

1. Where does an operator work?
2. What does an operator do, when he or she is on duty?
3. Do you want to be an operator? And why?

The Duties of Switchboard Operators

In every hotel, regardless of its size and situation, there will be a telephone. The larger the establishment, the greater will be the need for more outgoing lines and internal extensions, thus necessitation a telephone switchboard. In a hotel, a switchboard would be placed in a room where one or more telephone switchboard operators would be employed to deal with the numerous incoming and outgoing calls.

If guests need telephone services, they can call the switchboard operator. Their duties will include the receiving of all incoming calls, connecting them with the required extension and dealing with outgoing calls. As soon as the incoming call is answered by the operator, the calls commences to be charged, therefore prompt attention and a speedy connection are imperative. If the required extension is engaged, the caller should be invited to "hold the line" "ring back" or "leave a message".

There are many types of calls a guest may place during a hotel stay, such as local calls, long-distance calls, international calls, collect calls and so on. Most hotels provide in-room local and long-distance telephone service 24 hours a day. Some of these calls require operator assistance while others are completed by the guest independent of an operator. All employees answering calls should be courteous and helpful. Front office staff should time-stamp telephone message the record and place them in the guest's mail and message rack slot. When guests want to make a long distance call, DDD or IDD, the operator will put them through after she makes sure that there is enough advance payment in the guest's account through the computer system.

If a guest wishes to send a telegram over the telephone, this will have to be done via the hotel operator so that she or he can record the charges as this cannot be done by the meter. In most hotels using this type of switchboard, guests, by direct dialing, are able to telephone each other's room without going through the hotel operator. Likewise, hotel services (reception, housekeeper, floor service, etc.) can be dialed directly.

Telephone operators should show courtesy, patience and cheerfulness. It is important for operators to acquire the art of using the telephone. The art is based on two everyday qualities, common sense and courtesy. The telephone should be treated, not as an inanimate object, but as a real live being. After all, there is a real live person at the other end of the line, who must be communicated with. Therefore, if a telephone conversation is treated in the same way as a conversation being conducted face to face, it is easier to remember to fulfill all the usual courtesies.

In addition, the switchboard offers the services such as reserving for the room, table, conference, making a morning call, paging a guest, answering service, leaving a message, etc.. And if you have problems call the switchboard operator.

Notes to the text

1. regardless of   不顾，不管

2. necessitation   必然性

3. telephone switchboard   总机，电话交换台，电话交换机

4. incoming and outgoing calls   接听和拨打电话

5. as soon as   一……就……

6. If the required extension is engage...   如果所要电话占线……

7. Some of these calls require operator assistance while others are completed by the guest independent of an operator.   一些电话要有总机接线员提供帮助，而其他的电话客人是不需要总机接线员帮助的。

8. be courteous and helpful   彬彬有礼，乐于助人

9. advance payment   预付款

10. send a telegram   发电报

11. be based on   以……为基础

12. Therefore, if a telephone conversation is treated in the same way as a conversation being conducted face to face, it is easier to remember to fulfill all the usual courtesies.   因此，如果对待一个电话交谈就如同与人面对面谈话，那么履行所有常见的礼遇将会更容易些。

13. in addition   另外，除此之外

Follow-up questions

1. If the required extension is engaged, what should the operator do?

2. What are the switchboard operator's duties?

3. Why dose a telegram over the telephone have to be done via the hotel operator?

Exercises

__Words exercises__

I. Test your vocabulary of telephone service. *Fill in the blanks with words from the box.*

International prefix	Country code	DDD
Person-to-person call	Pay call	External call
Station-to-station call	Area code	Switchboard
Telephone directory	IDD	Collect call

1. _____ is long-distance operator-assisted call whereby the caller specifies the name of the person being called. The caller does not need to pay for the call if the specified person is not available.

2. _____ is used within many nations to route calls to a particular city, region or special service.

3. _____ is a telephone call that the receiving party is asked to pay for.

4. _____ is a telephone that requires immediate payment for operation, as by a coin or credit card. Also called pay station.

5. _____ is a panel equipped with apparatus for controlling the operation of a system of electric circuits, as in a telephone exchange.

6. _____ is a telephone switching system that is available to process an outgoing call.

7. _____ is an international telephone call dialed by the caller rather than going via an operator. These calls are made by dialing the international call prefix for the country one is in, followed by the country calling code for the country one wishes to call, then the phone number within that country.

8. _____ is a kind of telephone call in which callers, without operator assistance, call any other user outside the local calling area.

9. _____ is a book which lists alphabetically the names of persons, businesses, etc. having telephones in a specified area, along with their addresses and telephone numbers.

10. _____ is a long-distance telephone call in which the caller is charged upon reaching anyone at the receiving number.

11. _____ is the code dialed prior to an international number (country code, area code if any, then subscriber number). In most nations, this will be 00. In some nations in Asia, this

is 001 (in some cases, alternate codes are available to select the particular international carrier). In North America, this is 011 (or 01 for special call processing—collect, person-to-person, calling card, etc.).

12. _____ is used to reach the particular telephone system for each nation or special service.

II. Choose the best answer.

1. I'm sorry, Sir, he's unavailable right now. Would you like me to _____ you to his voicemail?

    A. put   B. connect   C. transfer

2. No, thank you. I'll _____ again later.

    A. be   B. try   C. attempt

3. One _____, please.

    A. instant   B. flash   C. moment

4. I'm busy right now. Can you _____ later?

    A. hang up   B. telephone   C. call back

5. Could you _____ to the Chinese Restaurant, please?

    A. put me through   B. put me on   C. put me out

6. Thank you for calling Holiday Inn! _____ can I help you today?

    A. Who   B. What   C. How

7. For outside call, Madam, please _____ "0" first.

    A. dial   B. hang up   C. answer

8. When you pick up the phone to call someone you hear a _____.

    A. ringer   B. dial tone   C. receiver

9. The computer will _____ the time and the room number automatically.

    A. record   B. answer   C. make

10. Could you _____ the line, please?

    A. take   B. hold   C. hang

Grammar exercises

Fill in the blankets by using the following modal verbs.

> **A modal changes the meaning of the verb that follows.**
>
> **_Can_** has different meanings, including ability, possibility and request.
>
> **_Cannot_ or _can't_** is the negative form.
>
> **_Could_** is used to indicate tentativeness or politeness.
>
> **_May_** can be used to ask for permission.
>
> **_Must_** means necessity / obligation or prohibition.
>
> **_Shall_** is used in questions with _I_ and _we_ for making offers of suggestions or asking advice.

> *Would* is used to make a polite request.
>
> Example: I'm afraid you <u>can't</u> see her right now. She is at the hair dresser's.
>
>   <u>Would</u> you like a pay call or collect call?
>
>   <u>Could</u> you get me extension 1623, please?

1. I have a message from Kathy on my answering machine. She leaves a home number, but I _____ get all the numbers.
2. _____ I speak to Mrs. White? Her room number is 1011.
3. _____ we say 6 o'clock sharp?
4. _____ you hear the last number?
5. We _____ say Good-bye now.
6. _____ you like to leave him a message or to call it again?
7. Sorry, I _____ wait. Please cancel the call.
8. _____ you hold the line, please?

___ *Translation* ___

1. Our hotel telephone system has IDD service.
2. I'm afraid I can not tell you the guest's room number. This is our hotel policy.
3. While making IDD call, first, please dial the hotel long distance call code 0, then dial the international prefix, followed by the country code, next, dial the area code, and finally, dial the expected telephone number.
4. I would like to make a local call from my room.
5. Would you please hold the line? I can transfer you to his room.
6. This is Room Reservations. I'll transfer your call to Restaurant Reservations.
7. I am afraid this is a direct line. We cannot transfer your call to the Chinese Restaurant. Please call 2234-1156.
8. I am afraid you have the wrong number.
9. Don't worry. I'll wake-up you on time tomorrow morning.
10. May I have your name and phone number, please?

 *Learning Tips*

Always Possessing a Pleasant Manner

    A well-run hotel with a charming and efficient Front Office staff will not appear so to the outside world, if the switchboard operator is not equally well trained and polite. Very often the first and sometimes only contact a person with a hotel is by telephone and the speed and manner with which the call is handled can leave a lasting impression, either good or bad.

The attitude of the operator is so often reflected quickly in the person with whom he is dealing. Telephone operators therefore need a clear, friendly voice, the tone of which indicates courtesy, patience and cheerfulness.

Unit 6

Information Service

 Learning Objectives

After this unit, you will be able to:
➤ ask the way
➤ arrange a city tour
➤ take a message
➤ ask the time
➤ introduce restaurants

 *Warming Up*

I. Look at the pictures below and identify each one. Use the words from the list.

taxi	tourists attractions	tour bus	sign of Information
tour guide	sign of airport	weather report	brochure direction

1_____   2_____   3_____

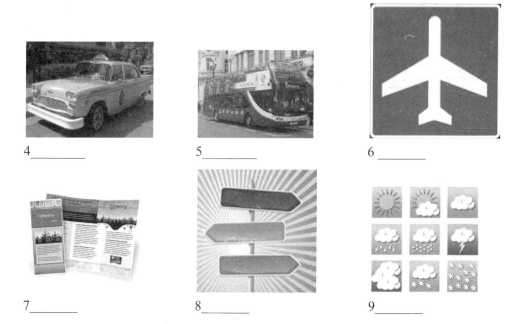

4 _____   5 _____   6 _____

7 _____   8 _____   9 _____

II. Working in a hotel, a desk clerk has to have a good command of basic words to express weather, direction, temperature and transportation. Now have a brainstorming to collect as many words or phrases as possible according to the following classification.

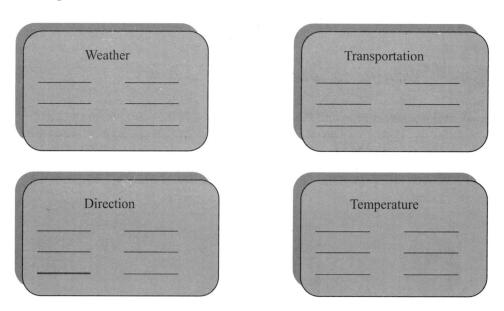

Weather

_____ _____

_____ _____

_____ _____

Transportation

_____ _____

_____ _____

_____

Direction

_____ _____

_____ _____

_____

Temperature

_____ _____

_____ _____

_____

 *Situational Conversations*

Pre-questions

Suppose you are a clerk of the information desk in a hotel.

1. What are the main duties of a clerk of the information desk?

2. How can you be a qualified clerk of the information desk?

3. What information would you provide to the guest who wants to book tickets?

4. How do you give directions to the hotel?

5. What information would you provide to the guest who needs one day tour service?

Conversation 1   Information for Shopping & Sightseeing

(*G: Guest   C: Clerk*)

G: Excuse me, I'd like to ask you a few questions about the city.

C: OK, go ahead.

G: My wife wants to take the children shopping, where is the best place to go?

C: I would recommend the mall, it's about 15 minutes south in a taxi. It has a wide range of shops and restaurants.

G: Thank you. Also, we'd like to do some sightseeing while we're in town. Can you recommend some local attractions?

C: How old are your children?

G: I have a 7-year-old boy and a girl who is 9.

C: I would recommend a day at the zoo. It's fun for all the family. There is also a water park just outside the city if you would like a day trip.

G: That sounds great.

C: Have a look in the rack by the entrance. We have a selection of leaflets about local tourist attractions. If you find something you like I can help you get discounted tickets and I can arrange transport for you.

G: That's great. Thank you for your help.

C: You're welcome.

Conversation 2   Giving Directions to Hotel

(*C: Clerk   T: Taxi Driver*)

C: Hello, Hotel International. How can I help you ?

T: Hi. I have two of your guests in my cab but I don't know where to find you. How do I get there?

C: Where are you now?

T: I'm at the airport.

C: Take the highway from the airport to the city center.

T: OK.

C: Follow the signs to the museum until you get to the central business district.

T: OK, I know where that is.

C: Take the first left after the Microsoft building and then take the third right.

T: Got it.

C: We're just on the right after the park.

T: OK, thanks for that.

C: That's OK. It should take you about 20 minutes if the traffic is good.

T: Thanks, bye.

Conversation 3   Taking a Message

(*R: Receptionist   G: Guest*)

R: Good evening! This is the Information Desk. What can I do for you?

G: Good evening. I tried to contact Mr. Black in Room 1602, but I failed. I'd like to be put through to him.

R: Hold on, please…

G: OK.

R: There is no reply form Mr. Black. No one is picking up. I'm afraid he is not in. Would you like to leave a message?

G: Yes, thank you. When he gets back, please let him know that Jane had called and I need him to call me back.

R: Does he have your number?

G: He does. But I'll give it to you again, 5-2-6-4-4-5-3-6.

R: That was 5-2-6-4-4-5-3-6, right.

G: Yes. Thank you very much.

R: You are welcome.

Key Words & Expressions

complete	[kəm'pli:t]	*a.* 全部的
complicated	['kɔmplikeitid]	*a.* 复杂的
contact	['kɔntækt]	*v.* 联系

locate	[ləuˈkeit]	v.	找出（位置）		
prosperous	[ˈprɔspərəs]	a.	繁荣的		
receipt	[riˈsiːt]	n.	收据		
transportation	[trænspɔːˈteiʃn]	n.	交通		
Bell Drum Towers		钟鼓楼		The Forbidden City	故宫
scenic spot		景点		The Summer Palace	颐和园
traveler's cheque		旅行支票		The Temple of Heaven	天坛

Additional Useful Expressions

1. Asking the way

a. You may go there by train. Here is the timetable.

b. Could you give me some information about transportation?

c. You can take the Line 13 subway.

d. It is not very convenient to go there. The best way is to take a taxi.

e. Can you please write down the address in Chinese?

f. Go straight along this street to the traffic lights. Then turn right. A short way along the right, you'll see it.

g. Where is the washroom (elevator)?

h. It's in the lobby near the main entrance.

i. It's in the basement at the end of the corridor.

2. City tour

a. Can I have sightseeing pamphlet?

b. Please tell me some places to visit.

c. Are there any city sightseeing buses?

d. Could you tell me what there is to see here?

e. Can you tell me the best sightseeing route to take?

f. There are many tours to Tianjin offered by the travel agent in the hotel.

3. Introducing restaurant

a. I'm wondering if you could recommend to me a good local restaurant where I can find Beijing Roast Duck.

b. The restaurant serves very good local dishes.

c. If spicy local dishes are what you are looking for, there is no other place in the whole city that will please your appetite better than the Dragon Palace.

4. Leaving a message

a. I tried to contact Mr. Lee in Room 1223, but he was out.

b. Would you like to leave a message?

c. I'll tell him as soon as he comes back to the hotel.

d. Is that the complete message?

e. The message is for Mr. Lee in Room 1223 from Mr. White.

5. Searching for guests

a. I'm looking for a friend, Mr. Black. Could you tell me if he is in the hotel?

b. I'll see if he is registered.

c. Black, Mr. Black? There are a lot of Blacks here today.

6. Arranging a tour bus

a. For the scenic spots, I would recommend…

b. Our bus can pick up your group at the gate.

c. Do you want an air-conditioned bus?

d. Do you want me to arrange a proper lunch or just packed lunches?

7. Describing location

a. Excuse me, what floor is the business center on?

b. It's next to the restaurant, on B1.

c. The vending machine is on the first floor of the hotel.

d. Go straight across the lobby and the coffee shop is next to the lift on the left.

e. Turn left out of the lift and it's at the end of the corridor.

f. Just take the elevator up to the top floor.

8. Asking the time

a. I don't know what time it is in Beijing now.

b. The time difference between Beijing and New York is 13 hours.

c. Is New York time earlier or later than Beijing time?

Classroom Activities

__ Listening Practice __

I. Listen to the recording and complete the following conversation.

1. Introducing restaurants

(*C: Clerk   G: Guest*)

C: Good morning. What can I do for you?

G: Good morning. I'm planning to take a friend of mine to dinner. You see, we both love Beijing Roast Duck. I'm wondering _____ where I can taste Beijing Roast Duck.

C: I'd love to, if Beijing Roast Duck is what you are looking for, there is no other place in the whole city that will please your appetite better than Qian Men Roast Duck Restaurant. _____. You might want to try there.

G: How far is it from here?

C: It is on Qian Men Street, near Tian'anmen Square. _____.

G: Thank you very much. One more thing, could you write down the name of the restaurant on this piece of paper so that I can show it to the taxi-driver?

C: Yes, here you are.

G: By the way, do you know _____?

C: Perhaps 50 Yuan is OK.

G: Thank you for your information. Good bye.

C: You are welcome. Bye-bye.

2. Searching for guests

(*C: clerk   G: guest*)

C: Good afternoon. What can I do for you?

G: Good afternoon. I'm looking for a friend, Mr. Black. Could you tell me_____?

C: Mr. Black? Just a minute, please. I'll see if he is registered.

G: Ok, thank you.

C: Black, Mr. Black? _____... Mr. David Black, Mr. Charles Black...

G: Mr. David Black from Canada. Isn't he staying at this hotel?

C: Oh, yes, here's his name Mr. and Mrs. David Black and family. They are in Room 203. _____, let me phone him... Mr. Black said he's waiting for you in his room.

G: OK. _____, please. Here it is.

C: Thank you.

G: It's my pleasure.

II. Listen to the recording and answer the questions.

1. Where does the guest want to call?

2. How many hours is the time difference between Beijing and New York?

3. Is the guest's call an urgent one?

4. When is it suitable for the guest to make this call?

5. Suppose it is 11:00 a.m. on July 6 in Beijing, then what time is it in New York?

_ *Communicative Practice* _

Role Play

Work in pairs or groups and create conversations according to the given situations.

Situation 1: Leaving a message

Mr. White goes to the hotel to meet his friend Mr. Green from Canada. Unfortunately, Mr.

Green is out. Because Mr. White has a meeting in two hours, he asks the clerk to take a message for him and tells Mr. Green to phone him at 01012345678 in the evening.

Situation 2: Asking the weather

Linda is living in a hotel. Today she will go out early in the morning, but she doesn't know the weather, so she asks the information clerk. The clerk tells her it is cloudy in the morning but rainy in the afternoon, and the high degree is 13℃. Linda is not used to centigrade. Then the clerk tells her how to transfer to Fahrenheit.

Situation 3: Asking time

You are a clerk at information desk in Beijing International Hotel. The guests in your hotel are from all over the world. They come to ask the time in different cities. Suppose now it is Friday 13:30 Beijing time. Please tell them the exact time of different cities and the time differences between Beijing and other cities.   (You can use the given list to help you)

Amsterdam	Fri	06:30
Athens	Fri	07:30
Bangkok	Fri	12:30
Beijing	Fri	13:30
Chicago	Thu	23:30
Denver	Thu	22:30
Geneva	Fri	06:30
Guatemala	Thu	23:30
Hanoi	Fri	12:30
London	Fri	05:30
Moscow	Fri	08:30
New Delhi	Fri	11:30
New York	Fri	00:30
Paris	Fri	06:30
Seattle	Thu	21:30
Seoul	Fri	14:30
Tea		$1.25
Soft Drinks - Coke, Sprite, Root Beer, etc.		$1.75

*Reading*

Pre-reading questions

1. Do you know hotel desk clerks?

2. What does a hotel desk clerk do when he or she is on duty?

3. Do you want to be a hotel desk clerk? And why?

The Duties of Hotel Desk Clerks

Hotel desk clerks serve as the front line in the effort to ensure that hotel guests have an enjoyable experience. They are usually the first people that guests interact with when they first arrive at a hotel. On the one hand, they must make sure the hotel makes as much money arrive as possible. But on the other hand, they must make sure that all guests are happy with their stay.

When new guests arrive, desk clerks:

◆ Welcome and register them

◆ Assign rooms and rates, and issue room keys or cards

◆ Provide information about services available in the hotel and in the community

◆ Verify customers' credit and establish how the customer will pay for the accommodation

◆ Promote and sell guest rooms

◆ Respond to special requests

When guests check out, desk clerks:

◆ Review accounts with them

◆ Inquire about satisfaction with their stay

◆ Receive payment for accounts

◆ Balance cash accounts

◆ Advise housekeeping which rooms have been vacated and are ready for cleaning

Desk clerks also may:

◆ Keep an inventory of room reservations

◆ Respond to reservation inquiries

◆ Answer telephones and take messages

◆ Handle guest mail

◆ Record guest comments

◆ Deal with customer complaints or refer dissatisfied customers to a manager

In large hotels, hotel desk clerks usually specialize in a particular area such as keys, reservations, or information. Hotel desk clerks who work in small hotels are responsible for more general operations. They usually process mail, collect payments, record accounts, handle reservations, operate the telephone switchboard, and do bookkeeping. All hotel desk clerks must be familiar with the floor plan of the hotel, the hotel's fire escape routes, and the hotel's various mechanical systems. Hotel desk clerks often direct guests to local stores, restaurants, and tourist attractions.

Those interested in becoming hotel desk clerks should have a pleasant and courteous personality. They should be skilled at dealing with the public. They should be dependable, responsible, and mature.

Notes to the text

1. in the effort to　为了
2. ensure　确保
3. interact with　与相互影响
4. register　登记，注册
5. issue　分配，发给
6. verify customers' credit　核实顾客的信誉
7. balance cash accounts　结现金账
8. keep an inventory of room reservations　详细记录房间的预订情况
9. specialize in　专攻
10. All hotel desk clerks must be familiar with the floor plan of the hotel, the hotel's fire escape routes, and the hotel's various mechanical systems.　酒店的所有前台人员必须熟悉酒店的建筑平面图、防火通道和各种机械设备。
11. Those interested in becoming hotel desk clerks should have a pleasant and courteous personality.　对从事酒店前台工作感兴趣者必须很和气、彬彬有礼。
12. They should be skilled at dealing with the public.　他们必须善于与公众打交道。
13. mature　成熟的

Follow-up questions

1. The following items are the duties of a hotel desk clerk. Please classify them into groups according to the text above.

   A. Receive about satisfaction with their stay

   B. Promote and sell guest rooms

   C. Respond to special requests

   D. Inquire about satisfaction with their stay

   E. Provide information about services available in the hotel and in the community

   F. Assign rooms and rates, and issue room keys or cards

   G. Receive payment for accounts

   H. Verify customers' credit and establish how the customer will pay for the accommodation

   I. Balance cash accounts

   J. Review accounts with them

   When guests check in: _____

   When guests check out: _____

2. What may hotel desk clerks do in addition to what is mentioned in exercise 1?

3. What is the difference of clerks' duties between large hotel and small hotel?

 *Exercises*

__Words exercises__

Choose the best answer for responding.

1. Can you call me a taxi?

   a. Certainly. Your name, please?

   b. Your name. I need to know your name.

   c. Name?

2. Where is the entrance to the restaurant?

   a. Turn to the right.

   b. Under the sign that says "restaurant".

   c. It's right there to your right.

3. How can I get to the train station from here?

   a. You should really walk.

   b. It's really close, so walking is your best bet.

   c. Walk. It's close.

4. Is there a shuttle bus leaving for the railway station soon?

   a. Yes. It's written on that board, as you can see.

   b. Check the board behind you.

   c. There is a complete list of departures on the board behind you.

5. Could you please show me where I am on the map?

   a. Please find it yourself.

   b. Of course, let me show you.

   c. Since you asked me I will.

6. Can you get someone to bring my luggage to my room?

   a. OK, if you need help with your bags, I'll ask someone.

   b. Are they too heavy for you?

   c. OK, I'll have it brought up.

7. Where can I park my car?

   a. In the parking lot, of course.

   b. In the parking lot to the right.

   c. In the parking lot, where else?

8. Did someone leave a package for me?

a. No, Madam. There's no package for you.

b. No, Lady. There's no package for you.

c. No, Madam. I would have told you if you had mail.

9. I think we need some extra blankets.

a. I'm a little busy now. Come back later.

b. It's not so cold, is it?

c. I'll get someone sent up to your room.

10. My microwave oven is not working.

a. Is it? It was fine yesterday.

b. I'll have someone look at it as soon as possible.

c. Did you break if, Sir?

___ *Grammar exercises* ___

For or Since quiz. Please fill in the blanks by using *For* or *Since*.

Example: I have been waiting for Mr. White in Room 223 *for* half an hour.

It has been raining **_since_** last night.

1. It is convenient to go there. You need to walk just _____ twenty minutes.

2. This scenic spot is open to the public _____ 1993.

3. The restaurant serves very good local dishes. It has been there _____ 89 years.

4. I have tried to contact him _____ he settled down in this hotel.

5. I'll see if he is registered. Please sit here _____ a minute.

6. It is sunny _____ the whole day.

7. The time difference is fifteen hours, so you haven't spent a night _____ you departed from Shanghai.

8. Our bus will pick up your group at the gate, so you needn't wait _____ a long time.

___ *Translation* ___

1. Could you give me some information about transportation?

2. There are many tours to Tianjin offered by the travel agent in the hotel.

3. I'm wondering if you could recommend to me a good local restaurant where I can find Beijing Roast Duck.

4. The message is for Mr. Lee in Room 1223 from Mr. White.

5. I'm looking for a friend, Mr. Black. Could you tell me if he is in the hotel?

6. Do you want an air-conditioned bus?

7. The time difference between Beijing and New York is 13 hours.

8. Turn left out of the lift and it's at the end of the corridor.

9. I tried to contact Mr. Lee in Room 1223, but he was out.

10. Go straight across the lobby and the coffee shop is next to the lift on the left.

 *Learning Tips*

The Right Attitude

In a conversation or discussion it is bad manners to take more than your share of the time in talking when others wish to talk also. It is bad manners to interrupt anyone else when he is talking. It is bad manners to be dogmatic and sure of your own point of view, suggesting by your speech or action that no one else's is of any value. It is bad manners to get cross in a conversation or discussion. If you are thinking as much of others as of yourself, you will not make any of these mistakes, and your conversation with others can go on smoothly.

Unit 7

Foreign Exchange and Cashier's

 Learning Objectives

After this unit, you will be able to:
➤ exchange the foreign currency
➤ change coins
➤ check out
➤ know the cashier's work procedure

 *Warming Up*

I. Look at the pictures below and identify each one. Use the words from the list.

credit card	cashier	cash	ATM	cheque
coins	credit card swiper	foreign currencies		bill

1_____   2_____   3_____

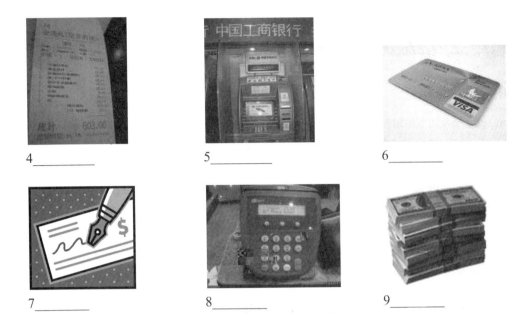

4_____ 5_____ 6_____

7_____ 8_____ 9_____

II. **Working at a hotel, a cashier has to know the kinds of foreign currencies, credit cards, cheques and coins. Now have a brainstorming to collect as many kinds as possible according to the following classification.**

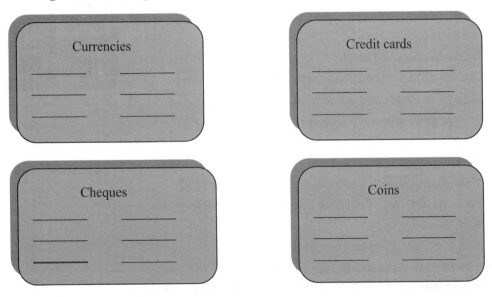

Currencies
_____ _____
_____ _____

Credit cards
_____ _____
_____ _____
_____

Cheques
_____ _____
_____ _____

Coins
_____ _____
_____ _____

Situational Conversations

Pre-questions

Suppose you are a cashier or a clerk of the front office in a hotel, think about the following questions and give your answers.

1. What is your usual job?

2. When guests come to exchange foreign currency, what do you think you should know?

3. If a guest wants to exchange more money than the change limit, what should you do?

4. How do you deal with the cheque when a guest pays his or her bill by cheque?

5. What do you take into consideration when guests check out?

6. Do you know the differences among different credit cards?

Conversation 1   Exchanging Money

(*C: Clerk   G: Guest*)

C: Good morning, Sir. What can I do for you?

G: Good morning. I'd like to change some money. Can you do that for me?

C: Of course, Sir. How much?

G: 200 US dollars, please. What's the exchange rate today?

C: Today's exchange rate is 6.37 Yuan to the dollar.

G: Is it the same rate as the bank gives?

C: Exactly the same. Could you give me your name, room number and show me your passport, Sir?

G: Here is my passport. I'm Mark Sheridan in Room 1130.

C: Fine. Mr. Sheridan, would you please sign your name on this memo?

G: Sure. Is it all right?

C: That's all right. Here are your RMB and passport.

G: Thanks a lot. What should I do with the RMB left with me?

C: You have to go to the Bank of China or the airport exchange office.

G: Thank you very much.

C: It's my pleasure.

Conversation 2   Changing Coins

(*C: Clerk   G: Guest*)

C: Good morning. Can I help you?

G: Good morning. I'm leaving this night, but I still have some RMB here. Could you please help me to change them back into US dollars?

C: I'm sorry I can't exchange your RMB for US dollars. You can only do it at the Bank of China or the Foreign Exchange Bank at the airport.

G: In that case I'll change my money at the airport.

C: What else could I do for you then?

G: Could you change some coins for me, please? I'm a coin collector.

C: Certainly. How many coins do you want?

G: Can I have 40 Yuan coins?

C: All right. How would you like them?

G: 10 Yuan for 1-Yuan coins, 10 Yuan for 50-cent coins and 20 Yuan for 10-cent, 5-cent, 2-cent and 1-cent coins. Will that be all right?

C: Yes, of course. Here you are.

G: Thank you very much.

Conversation 3   Checking Out

(*C: Clerk   G: Guest*)

C: Good morning, Sir. May I help you?

G: I'm Tom Chan, in Room 123. I'd like to check out. Can I have my bill now?

C: Of course, Sir. Just a moment, please.

G: Thank you.

C: Did you have breakfast this morning at the hotel or have you used any hotel services since breakfast?

G: Yes, I had breakfast, but I paid cash, and I haven't used any services.

C: Fine. The total including service charge for two days is one thousand five hundred and thirty dollars. Please check it.

G: Okay. I can't find any miscalculations.

C: Thank you, Sir. How would you like to pay, by cash or by credit card?

G: By credit card. Here you are.

C: Thank you. Could you sign your name here, please?

G: Fine.

C: Thank you and here is your receipt. Please drop in again. Good-bye.

G: Bye-bye.

Key Words & Expressions

bill	[bil]	n.	账单
change	[tʃeindʒ]	n.	零钱
charge	[tʃɑ:dʒ]	n.	费用
coin	[kɔin]	n.	硬币
coin collector		n.	硬币收集者
credit card			信用卡
drop in			拜访
exchange office			外币兑换处
exchange rate			兑换率
Foreign Exchange Bank			外汇银行
service charge			服务费

Additional Useful Expressions

1. Foreign Exchange

a. How much would you like to change?

b. How would you like to change?

c. Which kind of currency do you want to change?

d. We change foreign currencies according to today's exchange rate.

e. Would you like to change some money?

f. What denominations would you like?

g. The traveler's checks cost one percent of total amount of purchase.

h. If you want to cash the check, please sign again on the bottom line.

i. How much in foreign exchange certificates can I get for a fifty pound note?

2. Change limit

a. I'm sorry, but you cannot change that much here at night.

b. We restrict the amount of cash kept at night for safety's sake.

c. I'm afraid we have a change limit of 500 dollars between 9 p.m. and 8 a.m..

d. If we change large amounts, our cash supply runs out and we are unable to oblige our other guest.

3. Changing coins

a. Could you change some coins for me please?

b. How many coins do you want?

c. 10 Yuan for 1-Yuan coins, 10 Yuan for 50-cent coins and 20 Yuan for 10-cent, 5-cent, 2-cent and 1-cent coins.

4. Checking out

   a. I'm Tom Chan, in room 123. I'd like to check out.

   b. The total including service charge for two days is one thousand five hundred and thirty dollars.

   c. The total cost would be $ 120.

   d. Have you used any hotel service?

   e. I'd like to settle my bill now.

   f. Can I pay by American Express?

   g. How about the charge for the days you shared the room with your friends?

   h. Here is your change, please check it.

   i. Have you used any hotel service this morning?

   j. Hope you enjoyed your stay with us here and have a pleasant trip home.

   k. What's your way of payment, Sir, please?

   l. I'd like to pay by credit card instead of in cash, would that be all right?

5. A miscalculation

   a. I found out that there might be something wrong with the bill.

   b. That is exactly seven days. But I paid for eight days.

   c. I do apologize for my overcharge.

   d. We made a mistake in your bill and overcharge you $ 50.

Classroom Activities

__ *Listening Practice* __

I. Listen to the recording and complete the following conversation.

(C: Clerk   G: Guest)

C: Good evening, Madam. May I help you?

G: Yes, _____.

C: How much would you like to change?

G: Let me see. I'll need about 700 dollars.

C: I'm afraid _____ between 9 p.m. and 8 a.m..

G: Well, I'll be leaving at 7:00 a.m. on an all day tour tomorrow and I'll need at least that money. _____?

C: I'm afraid that we have to place a limit on exchange for the benefit of all our guests. If we change large amounts, _____ and we are unable to oblige our other guest.

G: _____?

C: We restrict the amount of cash kept at night for security reasons.

G: Well, I suppose it can't be helped.

II. Listen to the recording and answer the questions.

1. Which room does Peter Lee live?

2. When will his flight leave?

3. What does Peter want to do?

4. How much does Peter need to pay if he leaves after twelve?

5. Where can he leave his luggage?

 *__ Communicative Practice __*

Role Play

Work in pairs or groups and create conversations according to the given situations.

Situation 1: Checking out

Mr. Green is in Room 1220 and he would like to check out. His bill is $890. He asks the cashier to explain what charge of $34 is for. The cashier tells Mr. Green it is for the laundry charge. Mr. Green likes to pay his bill with credit card. It is American Express and the hotel accepts American Express.

Situation 2: A miscalculation

Miss Lee has stayed in the hotel for six days and she is checking out now. The cashier draws up the bill for her. Miss Lee checks the bill and finds that the hotel overcharges her $28. It is for the breakfast of last Wednesday. But on last Wednesday morning, Miss Lee went out and didn't have breakfast at the hotel. The cashier corrects the bill and Miss Lee pays her bill by cheque.

Situation 3: Foreign exchange

You are a clerk at the currency exchange desk. The guests in your hotel are from all over the world. They come to the desk and change different currencies into US Dollars. Please tell them the exchange rates and how much they can change. (You can use the given list to help you)

Exchange Rates Table for American Dollar	
	1USD
Australian Dollar	1.40907
Canadian Dollar	1.3341
British Pound	0.65854
Chinese Yuan	6.3747
Euro	0.93791
Hong Kong Dollar	7.75072
Indian Rupee	65.94744
Japanese Yen	123.38449
Mexican Peso	16.7791
Russian Ruble	65.28949
Singapore Dollar	1.4226
South African Rand	14.34505
South Korean Won	1168.75
Swedish Krona	8.7367
Swiss Franc	1.01065

 Reading

Pre-reading questions

1. What is the major work of a front cashier at a hotel?

2. What should a front cashier pay attention to when preparing a guest's bill?

3. How many ways of payment do you know? What are they?

4. Do you think what the procedures a front cashier should follow when a guest pays his bill by credit card?

5. What skills should a front cashier have?

What Does a Cashier Pay Attention to?

Cashiers who work for hotels generally keep track of charges to guests for room services, telephone calls, dealing with foreign currency exchange, and valet service. Some sophisticated cash registers are linked to computer systems that can do all these things automatically. Sometimes cashiers assign and take care of safe-deposit boxes in which guests store jewelry and other valuables. They may also have front desk duties such as notifying hotel desk clerks when guests check out.

When preparing a guest's bill, the cashier should pay special attention to the following things:

◆Check if the guest has paid a reservation deposit. If he has, take the amount of his deposit out of the bill.

◆Check with the guest if he is entitled to any kind of discount or complimentary rate. If he is, make the necessary deduction.

◆Remind the guest to return his room key to the reception before he leaves the hotel.

◆If the guest settles his account in traveler's check, make sure that he countersigns the check in front of you. Do not accept checks that have already been countersigned. Then compare the two signatures carefully. When a traveler's check is suspected to be a counterfeit, one first look at the check closely and see if the portraits and patterns are clearly printed. Then feel the check with your hand. With some traveler's checks, the cashier can look for watermarks by holding the check against the light or look for the special ink color by putting the check under an ultraviolet light.

◆In cases when the guest wants to pay his bill by credit card, the cashier should always follow the procedures below:

1. Check and see if the card is still valid. The expiration date can be found at the front bottom of the card.

2. If your hotel has received a warning notice, check and see if the guest's card number is listed on the latest copy. If it is, the card is no good.

3. Imprint the card onto a sales voucher and then write out on it the amount of transaction and date.

4. Make sure that the amount of sales does not go beyond the authorized credit limit.

5. Ask the cardholder to sign in the designated space and then compare the signature with the signature panel on the back of the card.

6. Give the cardholder's copy to the guest and keep the establishment copy in your files for one year.

Cashiers must be pleasant and agreeable and dress neatly. Above all they must be honest and trustworthy, since they often handle large sums of money.

Notes to the text

1. keep track of　记录
2. valet service　洗烫衣服务
3. sophisticated　老练的，在行的

4. safe-deposit boxes　保险箱

5. Check with the guest if he is entitled to any kind of discount or complimentary rate.　查看客人是否有条件享受折扣或优惠价格。

6. When a traveler's check is suspected to be a counterfeit, one first look at the check closely and see if the portraits and patterns are clearly printed.　如果怀疑旅行支票是假的，首先仔细察看支票上的图像和图案是否清晰。

7. If the guest settles his account in traveler's check, make sure that he countersigns the check in front of you. Do not accept checks that have already been countersigned.　如果客人用旅行支票结账，要确保客人当面在支票上签字。不要接受事先签好了的支票。

8. ultraviolet light　紫外线

9. expiration date　过期日期

10. Imprint the card onto a sales voucher and then write out on it the amount of transaction and date.　将信用卡印记在销售凭证上，然后写下交易金额和日期。

11. trustworthy　可靠的

Follow-up questions

1. The following items are the procedures that a front cashier should follow when a guest pays his or her bill by credit card. Please find out the right order according to the text above.

    A. If your hotel has received a warning notice, check and see if the guest's card number is listed on the latest copy. If it is, the card is no good.

    B. Make sure that the amount of sales does not go beyond the authorized credit limit.

    C. Check and see if the card is still valid. The expiration date can be found at the front bottom of the card.

    D. Ask the cardholder to sign in the designated space and then compare the signature with the signature panel on the back of the card.

    E. Imprint the card onto a sales voucher and then write out on it the amount of transaction and date.

    F. Give the cardholder's copy to the guest and keep the establishment copy in your files for one year.

    Right order: 1._____　　2._____　　3._____
　　　　　　　4._____　　5._____　　6._____.

2. What preparing the guest's bill, what should a cashier pay attention to?

3. If a guest pays by cheque, what should the cashier pay attention to?

 *Exercises*

__Words exercises__

I. Test your vocabulary of cashier's. Choose the corresponding words from the box according to the English explanations.

coins	clerk	change
currency	bill	discount
bank card	cash	checkout
charge		

1. Paper or coin money that the customer gives for payment _____

2. A piece of paper that records the place, time, and price of items or services purchased

_____

3. The money you give back to a customer _____

4. Type of money used in each country (eg. Dollar, yen) _____

5. Small amounts of money; circular shape _____

6. Person who serves customers; usually stands behind a desk _____

7. A price reduction _____

8. A card that allows customers to purchase an item using money from their bank account

_____

9. To request a certain payment _____

10. The place where customers go to pay for purchases _____

___Grammar exercises___

Rewrite the following sentences after the given models.

Example: Where is the toilet?

Could you tell me where the toilet is?

1. How can I get to the post office?

Could you tell me _____?

2. Which kind of currency do you want to change?

Could you tell me _____?

3. How many coins do you want?

Could you tell me _____?

4. What's your way of payment, Sir, please?

Could you tell me _____?

5. How much do you want to change?

Could you tell me _____?

6. Where is the best place for guests to wait?

Could you tell me _____?

7. What is your room number?

Could you tell me _____?

8. How much is total cost?

Could you tell me _____?

___ Translation ___

1. May I know your name and room number?

2. I'm afraid we don't accept non-convertible currency, Sir. Could you change it at a Foreign Exchange Bank?

3. Here is your change and receipt.

4. I'm sorry, Sir. This is indeed a mistake. We'll deduct this amount from your bill right away.

5. Shall I send you a porter to carry the baggage for you?

6. Would you like to settle the difference in cash?

7. We restrict the amount of cash kept at night for safety's sake.

8. Could you change some coins for me please?

9. We change foreign currencies according to today's exchange rate.

10. Excuse me. We're leaving today. I'd like to pay our bills now.

 *Learning Tips*

Tips for Cashiers

Here are some tips to remember for those who want to get into being a cashier in the future:

Be kind and courteous to all your customers.

Wear comfortable shoes!

As a cashier, you will be doing repetitious work.

Be sure you know how to identify fake bills.

When you don't have any customers on your counter and don't want it that way, you shouldn't look away or talk with other cashiers.

Don't hurry when you count your money, even if there are ten other people waiting in line behind your current customer.

Unit 8

Housekeeping (I)

 Learning Objectives

After this unit, you will be able to:
➤ get the rooms clean and in good order
➤ introduce the room facilities
➤ communicate with guests in English
➤ deal with complaints

 Warming Up

I. Look at the pictures below and identify each one. Use the words from the list.

bathroom	coffeemaker	towel	safe	remote
bathtub	mini-bar	lamp	pillow	

1_____   2_____   3_____

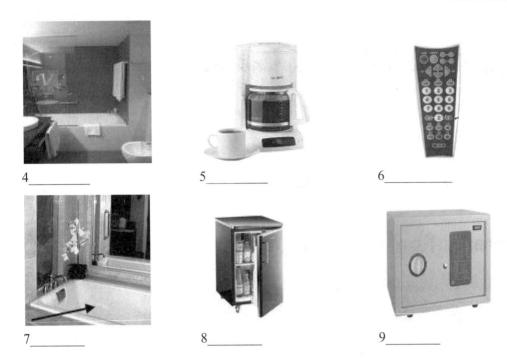

4 _____   5 _____   6 _____

7 _____   8 _____   9 _____

II. Working in a hotel, a room attendant has to have a good command of basic names about furnishings. Now have a brainstorming to collect as many words or phrases as possible according to the following classification.

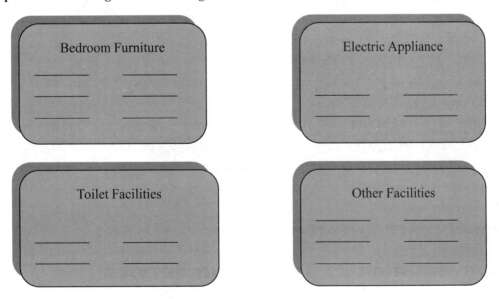

Bedroom Furniture

Electric Appliance

Toilet Facilities

Other Facilities

Pre-questions

Suppose you are a room attendant in a hotel.

1. What does a room attendant usually do in a hotel?

2. What are the main duties of the Housekeeping Department? Name some of them.

3. What does "turn-down service" mean?

Conversation 1   Cleaning the Room

(A: Housekeeping Attendant   B: Guest)

A: Housekeeping. May I come in?

B: Yes, please.

A: Good morning. I'm sorry to disturb you, Sir.

B: It doesn't matter.

A: We'd like to clean the room. Can we do it now?

B: Well, I'm busy typing my report. Could you come back later?

A: Certainly, Sir. What time would it be convenient?

B: Let me see. Could you come around 11:30 a.m.?

A: Sorry, I'm afraid no cleaning can be done from 11:30 a.m. to 1:30 p.m., May I come between 1:30 p.m. and 2:30 p.m.?

B: I think so. I'll be out then.

A: Let me press the "Do Not Disturb" button for you. If you want me to make up your room, please turn off the "DND" sign or dial 8 to the floor service desk. I'll be back to your service right away.

B: Thank you very much.

A: You're welcome. I'm always at your service.

Conversation 2   Turn-down Service

(A: Housekeeping Attendant   B: Guest)

A: Turn-down service. May I come in?

B: Come on in, please.

A: Good evening, Sir. May I do the turn-down service for you now?

B: Turn-down service? What do you mean by that?

A: It's a kind of chamber service done by the Housekeeping Department in the afternoon. It includes taking away bedspread, tidying up quilt and blanket, drawing curtain, switching on some lights, cleaning bathroom, emptying dustbin, adding or changing boiled water, etc..

B: I see. Well, would you please tidy up the bathroom? I've just taken a bath and it is quite a mess now.

A: Certainly, Sir. I'll clean the bathroom, and then make up the bed.

B: That's fine. Could you change the bath towels for me? They are a little bit dirty.

A: Right away. I'll place some fresh towels there.

B: Yes, that would be nice.

（*Having done all on request*）

A: It's getting dark. Would you like me to draw the curtains for you, Sir?

B: Why not? That would be so cozy.

A: May I turn on the lights for you?

B: Yes, please. I'd like to do some reading.

A: Is there anything I can do for you, Sir?

B: No more. Thank you very much.

A: Pleased to be at your service. Have a very pleasant evening.

Key Words & Expressions

attendant	[ə'tendənt]	*n.*	服务员
bathroom	['bɑ:θru:m]	*n.*	浴室，盥洗室
cozy	['kəuzi]	*adj.*	舒适的，安逸的
curtain	['kə:tn]	*n.*	窗帘
disturb	[di'stə:b]	*v.*	打扰
empty	['empti]	*v.*	倒空，腾空
housekeeping	['hauski:piŋ]	*n.*	客房服务
quilt	[kwilt]	*n.*	被子
towel	['tauəl]	*n.*	手巾，毛巾
bed sheet			床单
draw up			拉上
in a mess			糟糕，混乱
make up			整理
right away			立即，马上
switch on			打开
tidy up			打扫，整理
turn-down service			做晚床

Additional Useful Expressions

1. Asking for the Guest's Permission

    a. May I do the turn-down service for you?

    b. May I clean the room now?

    c. May I tidy up your desk?

    d. May I vacuum your room now?

    e. May I move the things on your desk so that I can dust it?

2. Doing the room

    a. Would you like me to clean up your room now?

    b. When would you like me to make the bed?

    c. When would you like me to do the room?

    d. What time would you like me to come back, Sir?

    e. I'll come and clean your room immediately.

3. Promising to take actions

    a. I'll change the bed sheet for you at once.

    b. I'm sorry. I'll bring you another one.

    c. I'll try and see if I can do anything for you.

    d. I'm not sure but I'll try my best for you.

4. Offering help

    a. May I be of any help?

    b. Please call 8 to the Housekeeping Department if you want to tidy up your room.

    c. Anything you need, please call me over the phone?

    d. I'm always at your service.

    e. It's getting dark. Let me switch on the lights.

5. Polite expressions when disturbing the guest

    a. I'm sorry to disturb you.

    b. I hope I haven't disturbed you

    c. Please excuse my disturbing you.

Classroom Activities

__ *Listening Practice* __

I. Listen to the recording and complete the following conversation.

(*A: Clerk   B: Guest*)

A: Good afternoon. Welcome to the tenth floor.

B: Good afternoon, I have just checked in. My room number is 1016.

A: Let me show you to your room…. Here we are.

B: Thank you very much.

A: Now, Sir. May I introduce the 1._____ to you? Here is the light switch and this is the 2._____. The wardrobe is here and the cotton 3._____ are inside of it. Beside the wardrobe is the 4._____, and there is a mini safe in the wardrobe.

B: Great. Now can you tell me something about the TV programs?

A: Well, the television provides satellite channels plus pay movies, with TV channels in Chinese and English. You can watch news from CNN and BBC. By the way the panel on the 5._____ between the beds controls the facilities.

B: It's amazing. Oh, by the way, I need a shower after such a long flight.

A: The 6._____ is over there with hot water supplied round the clock. You can find all you may need: soap, 7._____, toothpaste and toothbrush, 8._____, comb, razor and shaving cream. If you have any laundry, just put it in the laundry bag. It will be picked up every morning.

B: Thank you very much. You have made me feel welcome.

II. Listen to the recording and answer the questions.

1. What complaint did the guest make?

2. What was wrong with the room?

3. How did the clerk deal with the complaint?

4. Did the guest accept the clerk's offer?

5. Was the guest satisfied with the solution?

_ *Communicative Practice* _

I. Role Play

Work in pairs or groups and create conversations according to the given situations.

Situation 1: Cleaning the room

Ms. Jones is on the phone when a room attendant knocks at the door to ask if she would like to have room cleaned. Ms. Jones does not want her room cleaned. She needs some coffee. The room attendant promises to bring it at once.

Situation 2: Handling complaints

Mr. Moore in Room 9015 complaints to the Housekeeping Department that his room is not cleaned and it is in a mess. The clerk apologizes to him and finds a best way to cope with the complaints.

Situation 3: Turn-down service

Mr. Smith is holding a meeting of his team while a room attendant knocks at the door.

She identifies herself and asks if Mr. Smith needs a turn-down service. Mr. Smith does not need a turn-down service at the moment, but he needs some hot water and green tea. The room attendant promises to take them back soon.

II. Suppose a guest wants some information from you. Choose the most natural-sounding response.

1. I don't want my sheets changed every day.

    a. There's a card you can put on your door handle to let the cleaning staff know.

    b. Yes, it's part of room service.

    c. The cleaning staff does that every day.

2. Can you get someone to clean my room?

    a. Yes, I'll get someone to do that right away.

    b. Yes, it was cleaned this morning.

    c. Yes, all of our rooms are always clean.

3. We need some clean towels.

    a. There is a shower in every room.

    b. The cleaning staff will pick up the dirty towels when they clean the room.

    c. I'll ask the cleaning staff to bring you some.

4. I'd like to file a complaint with the manager.

    a. There's a conference in the hotel this weekend.

    b. He's not around right now, but I'll have him call you as soon as possible.

    c. The manager likes to complain, but he's a good person.

5. One of my lamps isn't working.

a. I'll get someone to take a look at it.

b. What would you like me to do about it?

c. What do you want me to do about it?

6. I always stay at your hotel when I'm in town.

a. Oh, I see.

b. Thank you. We appreciate your business.

c. You realize that this is a good hotel.

7. This room is pretty small!

a. Yes, they're like that.

b. Too small for you? Too bad, we don't have any other rooms available, Sir.

c. Unfortunately, we don't have anything bigger right now.

8. I think we need some extra blankets.

a. It's not cold, is it?

b. I'm a little busy now. Come back later.

c. I'll get some sent up to your room.

9. Can you help me, please?

a. One second. I'll be right with you.

b. Wait. I'm on the phone, Sir.

c. Wait a little bit.

SAVE OUR PLANET

Dear Guest,
Every day millions of gallons of water are used to wash towels that have only been used once.

You Make The Choice:

A towel on the rack means "I will use again."

A towel on the floor means "Please replace."

Thank you for helping us conserve the Earth's vital resources.

Reading

Pre-reading questions

1. What is the Housekeeping Department responsible for?

2. Besides room maids, who might also perform housekeeping duties?

3. What is the job title for the person leading the Housekeeping Department?

Housekeeping Department

The Front Office receptionist's prime duty is to sell accommodation, but without the Housekeeping staff, there would be no accommodation fit to sell. Without the Housekeeping Department, a hotel cannot operate. To see to the cleanliness and good order of all rooms in the hotel is the main function of the Housekeeping staff.

In order to allocate and supervise the work of the staff, a head housekeeper is appointed and is entirely responsible for the administration of this department, who ranks as one of the executive staff on a par with the head chef of the Food and Beverage Department.

Room maids have to be informed of which rooms are due to be vacated or relet. This information is obtained from the Housekeeper's copy of the arrival and departure list compiled by the Front Office receptionist.

It is generally the supervisors who check rooms to see if they are let or vacant and if they are properly cleaned and ready for letting and at the same time check that all furniture and furnishings are in good order and repair. As he/she checks the rooms the supervisor compiles a report called a bed occupancy list, sleeper's list or room status report. Once this list is completed, it is sent to the Front Office Reception Desk to be checked against the room board. Such a list is compiled two or three times each day. In this way, the receptionist is able to verify that the room board is accurate and agrees with the actual occupancy state of the rooms.

There is a linen-room under the control of a linen keeper, who is directly responsible to the head housekeeper. It is in the linen- room that all the linens and staff uniforms are stored, sorted, checked, issued and repaired. Needless to say, the laundry service is a must of the Housekeeping Department.

In all hotels room maids are employed to do the actual cleaning of the guest rooms. With regard to the cleaning of public areas, it is the PA cleaner's job, which includes the cleaning of all public rooms, lounges, corridors, halls, public toilets and the various offices of the hotel. But the cleaning of the restaurants, banqueting rooms and bars is often the responsibility of the staff working in those areas and not the cleaners.

Since the Housekeeping Department is a predominantly female department, it is necessary to hire some housemen to deal with the heavy work, such as the moving of the furniture or heavy linen baskets and trolleys.

Notes to the text

1. on a par with　和……处于平等的地位

2. head housekeeper　客房部主管

3. room maid　客房女清洁员

4. vacate　腾出，空出

5. let　出租（房屋、房间等）

6. compile　编写（列表、报告等）

7. sleeper　是指前厅部客房状态显示为走客房或空房，而客房部客房状态显示为住客房。

8. room status report　房态报告

9. verify　核实；查对；核准

10. linen-room　布草房　酒店房间里的布制品、如床单、被单、浴巾、毛巾只类的客房用品通常被称为布草。

11. Needless to say　不必说；不用说

12. With regard to 　至于……

13. PA (Public area)　公共区域

14. To see to the cleanliness and good order of all rooms in the hotel is the main function of the Housekeeping staff.　负责酒店所有房间的清洁与井然有序是客房工作人员的主要职能。

15. Room maids have to be informed of which rooms are due to be vacated or relet.　客房清洁员必须被告知哪个房间要到期腾出或要再租售。

16. It is generally the supervisors who check rooms to see if they are let or vacant and if they are properly cleaned and ready for letting and at the same time check that all furniture and furnishings are in good order and repair.　通常由主管检查客房看是否有客人住宿以及房间是否清洁以备出租，同时查看所有家具及室内陈设品是否完好无损。

17. Once this list is completed, it is sent to the Front Office Reception Desk to be checked against the room board.　一旦写完房态报告，就要送到前厅的总服务台来核对客房布告牌。

18. There is a linen-room under the control of a linen keeper, who is directly responsible to the head housekeeper.　布草保管员掌管布草，并直接对客房部主管负责。

Follow-up questions

1. Which of the following statement are not the duties of the Housekeeping Department?

a. keeping the cleanliness and good order of all rooms in the hotel

b. coordinating the work closely with the Front Office

c. compiling a bed occupancy list, room status report two or three times a day

d. constructing guest history file for future references

e. storing, sorting, checking, issuing and repairing all the linens

f. providing services such as handling mails, telegrams and messages for guests

g. providing laundry service

i. providing room service

j. selling the guest rooms

2. What are room maids, housemen, linen-room keepers, housekeepers respectively responsible for?

3. Talk about the importance of the Housekeeping Department for a hotel.

 *Exercises*

__*Words exercises*__

I. Match each word or phrase in the column at the left with its meaning in the column on the right.

1. cozy   a . a woman who cleans and tidies the bedrooms in a hotel

2. receptionist   b. comfortable and warm

3. laundry   c. interrupt

4. tidy up   d. untidy and dirty

5. disturb   e. a hotel employee whose job is to clean the clothes of hotel guests

6. in a mess   f. clothes need to be washed

7. valet   g. a person whose job is to book rooms for people and answer their questions.

8. chambermaid   h. make a place clean and in order

II. Choose the best answer.

1. Turn-down service is a kind of service done by the _____ Department.

    a. Tourism   b. Housekeeping   c. Hospitality   d. Laundry

2. The housekeeping is responsible for _____ of all guestrooms in a hotel.

    a. accommodating   b. neatness and cleanliness

    c. management   d. serve

3. In hotels the "DND" sign stands for _____.

    a. Do Not Drop   b. Do Not Diffuse   c. Do Not Delay   d. Do Not Disturb

4. I'm sorry, we don't have any rooms_____ that weekend.

    a. available   b. rentable   c. service   d. servant

5. Everything is in _____.

    a. good   b. order   c. right   d. place

6. Hotels and restaurants are also known as the _____ industry.

    a. tourism   b. banquet   c. hospitality   d. food service

7. Let me know if I can be of further _____.

    a. service   b. assess   c. assistance   d. assistant

8. The concierge will _____ you to your room.

    a. get   b. take   c. carry   d. show

9. This service is _____ as part of your room rate.

    a. given   b. provided   c. seen   d. regarded

10. The room being "out of order" means the following EXCEPT the room_____.

    a. is occupied   b. is very dirty   c. is untidy   d. needs repairing

___Grammar exercises ___

Rewrite the following sentences according to the model using the emphatic structure "It is/was… that…".

Example: All the linens and staff uniforms are stored, sorted, checked, issued and repaired <u>in the linen- room</u>.

→ *It is **in the linen-room** that all the linens and staff uniforms are stored, sorted, checked, issued and repaired.*

1. I want to show you <u>this picture</u>.

_____

2. The weather began to cool down <u>by the end of September.</u>

_____

3. <u>Mike and Mary</u> helped the old man several days ago.

_____

4. He realized it was not so important <u>after he got what he had desired.</u>

_____

5. <u>Our being late </u>caused him to serve dinner an hour later than usual.

_____

6. He <u>didn't</u> go to bed <u>until his wife came back.</u>

_____

7. I met <u>Li Ming </u>at the railway station yesterday.

_____

8. He was captured by the enemy<u> in the World War I.</u>

_____

___Translation ___

1. A towel on the rack means "I will use it again".
2. The room's ready. Is there anything else I can do for you?
3. Would it be convenient for you if I come again at 11?
4. When would you like me to clean up your room?
5. You can call the front desk when you want your room done.
6. We are sure that we will make further improvement in our service.
7. Certainly, Madam. I'll let the overnight staff know.
8. May I move the things on your desk so that I can dust it?
9. Here is the guide book with all the information on your room and the hotel services.
10. We have many articles on loan to guests. Just refer to your "Welcome booklet".

 *Learning Tips*

Floor Attendant

Receiving guests is one of the major duties of a floor attendant. He or she should greet guests as soon as they walk out of the lift and into the corridor. Then the floor attendant should lead them into their rooms and introduce facilities and services. Meanwhile, the floor attendant should make sure whether or not guests have some requirements, and respond to them according to the hotel rules and regulations.

Unit 9

Housekeeping (II)

 Learning Objectives

After this unit, you will be able to:
- describe the guest services terms
- provide laundry service
- provide room service
- master working procedures

 Warming Up

I. Look at the pictures below and identify each one. Use the words from the list.

electric iron	wardrobe	bedside table	bed spread	blanket
toilet roll	clothes hanger	dressing table	hair dryer	

1_____   2_____   3_____

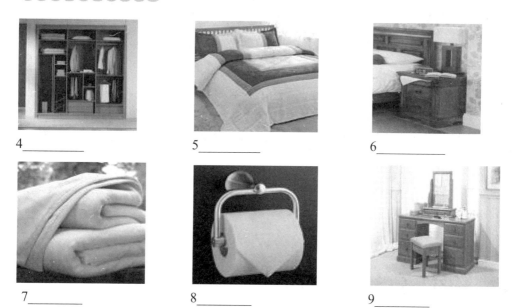

4 _____   5 _____   6 _____

7 _____   8 _____   9 _____

II. **Working in a hotel, an employee has to have a good command of basic names about hotel facilities and services provided for the guest. Now have a brainstorming to collect as many words or phrases as possible according to the following classification.**

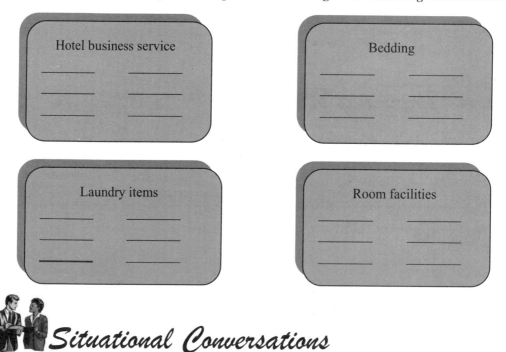

Hotel business service

_____ _____
_____ _____
_____ _____

Bedding

_____ _____
_____ _____
_____ _____

Laundry items

_____ _____
_____ _____
_____ _____

Room facilities

_____ _____
_____ _____
_____ _____

Situational Conversations

Pre-questions:

Suppose you are a room attendant in a hotel.

1. Do you know what the room service is?

2. How do you provide a morning call service?

3. How do you introduce the laundry service?

Conversation 1　Laundry

(A: Laundry clerk　　B: Mrs. Bell)

A: What can I do for you?

B: Could you send someone up for my laundry, please? Room 908, Bell.

A: Certainly, Mrs. Bell. A valet will be up in a few minutes.

B: Good. I also have a silk dress which I don't think is color-fast. Will the color run in the wash?

A: We'll dry-clean the dress. Then the color won't run.

B: You're sure? Good! And the lining of my husband's jacket has come unstitched. It might tear over further while washing.

A: Don't worry, Madam. We'll stitch it before washing.

B: That's fine. Now, when can I have my laundry back?

A: Usually it takes about two days to have laundry done. But would you like express service or same-day?

B: What is the difference in price?

A: We charge 50% more for express, but it only takes 5 hours.

B: And for same-day. Will I get the dress and skirt back this evening?

A: Yes, Madam.

B: I'll have same-day service then.

Conversation 2　Room Service

(A: Waiter　　B: John Smith)

A: Good evening, Room Service. This is Peter speaking. How may I assist you?

B: I want to order dinner for two. We will start with soup. What is the soup of the day?

A: The soup of the day is cream of corn.

B: OK. Two soup of the day. For main course, we'd like two fried noodles.

A: And for dessert?

B: Two apple pies with ice cream.

A: What would you like to drink?

B: A bottle of red wine, please.

A: Would you like French or American?

B: No. The local Dynasty wine is fine.

A: All right. Let me repeat your order, two cream of corn, two fried noodles, two apple pies with ice cream and one bottle of Dynasty red wine. Am I correct?

B: Right. When will it be served?

A: In about 25 minutes.

B: Very good. Thank you.

A: May I have your name and room number, Sir?

B: This is John Smith, room 1806.

A: Ok, Mr. Smith, your order will be ready soon. Good-bye.

Conversation 3   Morning Call

(A: Room attendant   B: Mr. Jackson)

B: Good evening! This is Mr. Jackson in Room 815.

A: Good evening, Mr. Jackson. What can I do for you?

B: This is my first visit to China. I wonder if your hotel has the morning call service.

A: Yes, Sir. Anyone who stays in our hotel can ask for the service. Would you like a morning call?

B: Yes, I must get up earlier tomorrow. I want to go to the Bund to enjoy the morning scenery there. You know this is my first visit to Shanghai. People say there is a marvelous view of a poetic yet bustling life at the Bund just at dawn.

A: That's true. At what time do you want me to call you up, Sir?

B: At 6:00 sharp tomorrow morning, please.

A: What kind of call would you like, by phone or by knocking at the door?

B: By phone. I don't want to disturb my neighbors.

A: Yes, Sir. I'll tell the operator to call you up at 6:00 tomorrow morning. Anything else I can do for you?

B: No. Thanks. Good night.

A: Good night, Sir. Sleep well and have a pleasant dream.

Key Words & Expressions

bustling	[ˈbʌsliŋ]	*adj.*	热闹的
colorfast	[ˈkʌləfɑːst]	*adj.*	不褪色的
laundry	[ˈlɔːndri]	*n.*	洗衣，要洗的衣服
lining	[ˈlainiŋ]	*n.*	衬里，内衬
poetic	[pəʊˈetik]	*adj.*	诗意的
stitch	[stitʃ]	*v.*	缝，缝合
valet	[ˈvælet]	*n.*	洗烫工
cream of corn			奶油玉米汤

dry-clean	干洗
express service	快洗服务
morning call service	叫醒服务
room service	送餐服务
the Bund	上海外滩

Additional Useful Expressions

1. Explaining hotel services

a. We have a computer wake-up service.

b. Room service is available 24 hours.

c. Anyone who stays in our hotel can ask for the service.

d. If your want baby-sitting service, please call the information desk.

2. Asking about services

a. I wonder if your hotel has the morning call service.

b. Do you have room service?

c. Can I have my shoes polished here?

d. Do you bring food to room?

3. Laundry service

a. Excuse me, Madam. Do you have any laundry?

b. Would you like express service?

c. Well, just put your stuff in the laundry bag and put it outside your room.

d. Would you like your clothes pressed, washed or dry clean, please?

e. The room maid will pick it up early tomorrow morning.

f. Your laundry will be returned to you at ___ (time).

4. Room service

a. How many orders of ××× would you like?

b. Will there be anything else, Sir?

c. Let me repeat your order.

d. At what time do you want your breakfast to be served?

e. Your order will be there in about 20 minutes.

f. May I ask how many of you will be sharing the food?

5. Morning call

a. Would you like a morning call?

b. At what time do you want me to call you up, Sir?

c. OK. So we will wake you up at 7:00 tomorrow morning.

d. I'll tell the operator to call you up at 6:00 tomorrow morning.

6. Extra charge information

a. We charge forty percent extra for express.

b. We charge 50% more for express, but it only takes 5 hours.

 *Classroom Activities*

 __ *Listening Practice* __

I. Listen to the recording and complete the following conversation.

(F: Floor attendant   G: Guest)

G: Good morning. Would you please do me a favor?

F: Yes, Sir. 1._____.

G: My friend is coming here tonight for two days. Could I have 2._____?

F: Please contact 3._____first. I'll get you the extra bed with their permission.

G: Have you any idea how much an extra bed costs?

F: It's $30 for one night.

G: By the way, could you get us a few more 4._____? I have so many clothes. I am long-staying guest, as you know.

F: Yes, Sir. We are happy to have you. We do hope you are 5._____.

G: Thanks. Could you change 6._____ for me? This one is too thin, and with 7._____ on it.

F: Certainly, Sir. I'll 8._____ right away. I do wish we had known earlier.

G: How nice of you to say so!

F: It's my pleasure. I'll be back in a minute, Sir.

II. Listen to the recording and answer the questions.

1. What complaint did the guest make?

2. How did the clerk deal with the guest's complaint?

3. Was the guest satisfied with the solution?

Communicative Practice __

I. Role Play

Work in pairs or groups and create conversations according to the given situations.

Situation 1: Baby-sitting service

    Mr. & Mrs. Black are going to attend a press conference this afternoon. Now Mrs. Black asks the housemaid if she could look after her baby for her. The housemaid says that it's against their hotel regulations. But the housemaid tells Mrs. Black that the housekeeping department has a very good baby-sitting service. Mr. & Mrs. Black thank the housemaid.

Situation 2: Arranging a conference room

Mr. Smith is going to have a business meeting tomorrow morning. He needs a conference room for twelve people. Now Mr. Smith asks the clerk if he could arrange it for him. The clerk tells Mr. Smith that they have a conference room which can seat up to 20 people and he'll arrange all the things for Mr. Smith.

Situation 3: Complaining about service

Mrs. Green sent a silk shirt to the laundry and asked for dry cleaning, but it has come back badly shrunk, and worse still, the color has run. She makes complaints to the clerk of the hotel. The clerk apologizes for that and agrees to refund the cost of the laundry and the shirt.

II. Suppose a guest wants some information from you. Choose the most natural-sounding response.

1. Can someone bring my bags up to my room?

    a. I'll get someone to do that right away.

    b. I'll get the bags into your room.

    c. Are you going to take the bags yourself?

2. Can you give me a different room? This one is too small.

    a. I'm sorry it's so small.

    b. Yes, would you like to pay for the extra room by credit card?

    c. I'm sorry but it's the biggest room we have available right now.

3. Can my guests stay in my room overnight?

    a. Yes, but they have to register at the reception desk.

    b. We have many international guests staying at our hotel.

    c. Would you like to reserve a room for your guests?

4. I reserved a room for Friday. I'd like to change that to Saturday.

    a. OK, you will be leaving on Saturday?

    b. I see that you've already made a reservation.

    c. OK, let me check your reservation.

5. Please have the valet get my car for me.

    a. Yes, we provide valet parking free-of-charge for our guests.

    b. Is there a problem with your car?

    c. Certainly.

Pre-reading questions

1. What does a room attendant or housekeeper do, when she or he is on duty?
2. In addition to keeping the rooms clean, what are the other responsibilities of the room attendants?
3. Do you want to be a room attendant? Why or why not?

The Duties of Room Attendants

The actual work of cleaning and caring for the guest room is performed by the room attendants. Their duties include recognizing the guests, introducing room facilities and service, making or changing beds, dusting furniture, sweeping or cleaning floors and carpets, washing bathrooms, replacing towels and washing clothes, making up room and doing turn-down service. They should also supply any personal service to satisfy the guests' reasonable demands, such as wake-up service, room service, laundry service, shoeshine service and baby-sitting service. Whenever and wherever possible, the staff should offer to do extra things for the guests. In addition, they are expected to check up rooms and report any signs of damage or wear and tear that may make repairs and maintenance necessary. Finally, to be competent hotel staffs, they should be capable of handling with unexpected emergency and try to minimize the damage or negative influence.

Room attendants have an intimate contact with the guests. A guest may ask the attendants to make up his room at a certain time, or he may indicate he does not want to be disturbed at all, or he would like to have meals in his room. Almost all hotels provide signs that the guest can hang on the doorknob in either of these cases. In addition, guests frequently ask room attendant for items that are supplied by the housekeeping department, such as irons, transformers, special pillows, extra hangers, cribs for infants and hair dryers. In some hotels, the room attendants pick up and deliver clothing for the laundry and valet service.

Heavier chores are performed by men who are usually called housemen. Their work involves window-washing, shampooing carpets, polishing metals, removing and cleaning draperies, cleaning the public areas of the hotels, and many other tasks that might be beyond the physical capacities of women. The housemen also run errands for the housekeeping department, such as providing guests with extra things on request.

Notes to the text

1. personal service　个性化服务

2. baby-sitting service　照看婴儿服务

3. wear and tear　磨损

4. cribs for infants　婴儿床

5. hair dryers　吹风机

6. transformer　变压器

7. houseman　男勤杂工

8. drapery　大窗帘

9. run errands for　为……跑腿；供……差遣

10. The actual work of cleaning and caring for the guest room is performed by the room attendants.　客房服务员承担清洁和整理客房的实际工作。

11. In addition, they are expected to check up rooms and report any signs of damage or wear and tear that may make repairs and maintenance necessary.　此外，他们应检查房间，报告任何损坏的迹象或磨损，以便做出必要的维修和保养。

12. Finally, to be competent hotel staffs, they should be capable of handling with unexpected emergency and try to minimize the damage or negative influence.　最后，作为称职的酒店工作人员，他们应该有能力处理突发的紧急情况，尽量减少酒店的损失或负面影响。

13. Almost all hotels provide signs that the guest can hang on the doorknob in either of these cases.　几乎所有的饭店都提供这类标牌，让客人可以挂在房门的把手上。

14. In some hotels, the room attendants pick up and deliver clothing for the laundry and valet service.　在一些宾馆，客房服务员负责收取顾客的衣物送到洗衣房和洗烫服务部门。

15. Their work involves window-washing, shampooing carpets, polishing metals, removing and cleaning draperies, cleaning the public areas of the hotels, and many other tasks that might be beyond the physical capacities of women.　他们的工作包括清洗窗子，用清洁剂洗地毯，抛光金属，换窗帘和清洁窗帘，清洗酒店的公共区域，以及完成女人无法胜任的体力活。

Follow-up questions

I. Decide whether the statement is true or false. Tick T for True and F for False.

1. (T/F) The room attendants are responsible for neatness and cleanliness of all guest rooms and most public areas.

2. (T/F) Heavy chores are performed by room attendants.

3. (T/F) From this passage we can know that room attendants' work are very important.

4. (T/F) The room attendants have nothing to do with handling with unexpected emergency and minimizing the damage or negative influence.

5. (T/F) The room attendants clean the room and contact the housekeeping department back about the latest status and condition of the room.

II. Choose the correct answer.

1. The word "intimate" in the first line of the second paragraph means _____.

A. close and familiar   B. clear   C. internal   D. interesting

2. The word "crib" in the phrase "cribs for infants" means _____ .

    A. copy   B. bone   C. foods   D. a bed for new baby

3. Housemen do the following chores except _____ .

    A. washing window

    B. serving foods

    C. running errands for the housekeeping department

    D. cleaning draperies

4. Room attendants do the following work except_____ .

    A. making up room   B. dusting furniture

    C. polishing metals   D. doing turn-down service

5. Which of the following statement is NOT true?

    A. Room attendant cleans the room and contacts the housekeeping department back about the latest status and condition of the room.

    B. Housemen deal with the heavy work, such as the moving of the furniture.

    C. Room attendants have an intimate contact with the guests.

    D. Window-washing is one of the duties of a room attendant.

Exercises

__Words exercises__

I. Test your vocabulary of hotel and services. Fill in the blanks with words from the box.

bellboy	complimentary	rate
amenities	damage charge	pillow case
cot	front desk	concierge
housekeeping	linen	valet service
lobby	room service	towels

1. In hotels laundry service includes washing and_____ includes dry cleaning and pressing.

2. You can get your swimming pool _____at the front desk.

3. _____ means delivery of food or other services requested by guests.

4. Our _____ change depending on the season.

5. Room 201 doesn't need their sheets changed, but they requested one new _____ .

6. You can stand in the _____ and wait for your bus.

7. The "reception desk" is often referred to as the _____ .

8. We will have to add a _____ for the hole you put in the wall.

9. If you need an extra bed, we have _____ available.

10. All of our rooms have _____ soap, shampoo, and coffee.

11. The word "_____" refers to "comforts" or conveniences. These may include a pool, a sauna, a restaurant, etc..

12. The _____ will take your bags to your room for you.

13. We will come in and change the _____ while you are out of your room.

14. Put a sign on the door if you want _____ to come in and change the sheets on the bed.

15. The _____ will show you to your room.

II. Choose the best answer.

1. I'll call housekeeping and ask them to bring you some fresh_____.
   a. milk   b. dinner   c. linen   d. ice

2. I'll let you voice your complaint about the rate to the _____.
   a. housekeeper   b. valet driver   c. hotel manager   d. chef

3. We don't have any vacancies. We are completely _____.
   a. vacant   b. booked   c. complimentary   d. closed

4. Special requirements for laundry mean the following EXCEPT _____.
   a. not using bleach b. using soft soap c. dry-cleaned   d. repairing

5. If you need a midnight snack there's a _____ machine full of potato chips on your floor.
   a. bellboy   b. kitchenette   c. cot   d. vending

6. Please put your used _____ in the basket and leave unused ones hanging on the rack.
   a. dishes   b. towels   c. menus   d. keys

7. If you've never been to this city, you should take a look at our _____.
   a. menu   b. brochures   c. front desk   d. inn

8. A laundry bag is provided for the guest to put their _____ in.
   a. clothes   b. pants   c. clothes to be washed   d. socks

9. We also have a gym which you can use at your _____.
   a. dispersal   b. disposal   c. control   d. use

10. I'm sorry, we don't have any rooms _____ that weekend.
    a. available   b. rentable   c. empty   d. clean

___Grammar exercises ___

Subject-verb Agreement: Choose the correct verbal form in the brackets to complete each of the following sentences.

Example: The actual work of cleaning and caring for the guest room **is** (is, are) performed by the room attendants.

1. Walking _____ (is, are) good exercise.

2. Several of the students _____ (was, were) absent.

3. One of my friends _____ (needs, need) some help.

4. Mike, rather than his brothers, _____ (is, are) responsible for the loss.

5. Most of the book _____ (was, were) interesting.

6. The writer and poet_____ (is, are) here.

7. That I shall work with you _____ (is, are) a great pleasure.

8. What he says _____ (does, do) not agree with what he does.

9. This is one of the rooms that _____ (was, were) damaged in the war.

10. We went to two restaurants. Neither of them _____ (was, were) expensive.

___ *Translation* ___

1. What will be, if there is any laundry damage?

2. I will tell the maintenance and housekeeping departments immediately.

3. I will ask our manager to take care of your request.

4. It is a courtesy to our guests.

5. The hotel provides free shoe shining service for its guests.

6. We have express service at a 50% extra charge.

7. If you have any problems or requests, please don't hesitate to let us know.

8. The indemnity shall not exceed ten times of the laundry charge.

9. Do you have different styles of breakfast for room service?

10. The rate chart is contained in the stationery folder in your dresser drawer.

Learning Tips

Guidelines for Laundry Service

There may be situations when you are not sure how to handle or clean a particular item of clothing, or when you are not sure if the service can be done in the hotel.

- If you are unsure of how to deal with a guest request, tell the guest that you will find out from your supervisor or housekeeper, and that you will get back to the guest. Make sure that you contact your supervisor immediately, and ensure that the guest is informed of what action is being taken.

- If you are not sure how to clean, iron, press, fold or package an item of clothing, it is better to check with the supervisor. Using the wrong methods may cause damage to the item of clothing, which will then have to be paid for by the hotel.

Unit 10

Maintenance and Safety

 Learning Objectives

After this unit, you will be able to:
➤ know the FAQ of room facilities
➤ deal with the complaints about facilities
➤ tell the work procedure of maintenance
➤ handle some kinds of emergence in hotel
➤ know the hotel's fire safety

 *Warming Up*

I. Look at the pictures below and identify each one. Use the words from the list.

repairman	hair shampoo & conditioner	wash basin	showerhead
shower curtain	soap	toilet	Fire safety sign	faucet

1_____ 2_____ 3_____

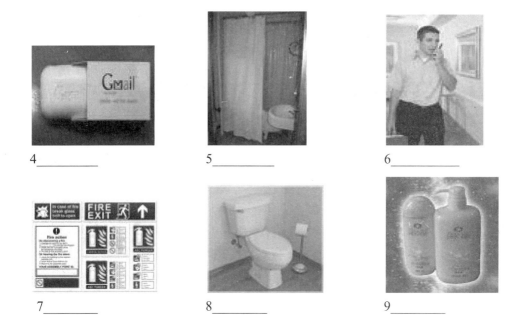

4_____   5_____   6_____

7_____   8_____   9_____

II. Working in the housekeeping department, you have to have a good command of basic terms about problems and maintenance. Now have a brainstorming to collect as many words or phrases as possible according to the following classification.

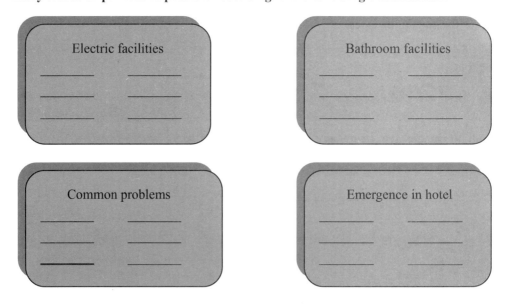

Situational Conversations

Pre-questions

Suppose you are a repairman or housekeeper in a hotel.

1. What do you usually do when you are on duty?

2. What do you say when you check out there is something wrong with the facility?

3. What are the frequently asked questions about room facilities?

Conversation 1   The TV Doesn't Work

(*A: Housekeeper   B: Maintenance man   C: Guest*)

A: Housekeeping. Can I help you?

C: Yes. The TV doesn't work in my room. Could you send someone to fix it?

A: I'm sorry to hear that. What's your room number, please?

C: 808.

A: Ok. Just a moment, I'll send the maintenance man to your room at once.

B: (after knocking at the door) Maintenance, may I come in?

C: (open the door)

B: Good afternoon, I've come to fix your TV set.

C: Oh, great. Come in.

B: What's wrong with the TV set?

C: The picture is blinking and the sound is not clear.

B: (After examining the TV) Don't worry. There is nothing wrong with the TV set. The cable
TV is under examination and repair today. It probably will be fine this evening.

C: Ok, I see. By the way, is there an internet connection in my room?

B: Yes, there is. You can find it right behind the dressing table. It's RMB 100 for 24 hours and
2 RMB per minute.

C: Oh, that is expensive.

B: We also have wireless internet access. It is free of charge.

C: That's terrific. Shall I input the pin number or password?

B: Not necessary. It's user-friendly.

C: Great. Thank you very much.

B: It's my pleasure.

Conversation 2 Changing a Noisy Room

(*A: Housekeeper   B: Guest*)

A: Good morning, Sir. Is there anything I can do for you?

B: I'm Louis Palmer. I'm in Room 1046. Can you change the room for me? It's too noisy. My wife was woken up several times last night by the noise from elevator. She said it was too much for her.

A: I'm awfully sorry, Sir. I do apologize. Room 1046 is at the end of the corridor and close to the elevator. It's possible that the noise is heard early in the morning when all is quiet.

B: Anyhow, I'd like to change our room.

A: No problem, sir. We'll manage it, but we don't have any room available today. Could you wait till tomorrow? One group will be leaving tomorrow morning. There'll be some rooms for you to choose from.

B: All right. I hope we'll be able to enjoy our stay in a quiet room tomorrow evening and have a sound sleep.

A: Be sure. I'll make a note of that. Everything will be taken care of. And if there is anything more you need, please let us know.

Conversation 3 Asking for a Duplicate Key

(*A: Room attendant   B: Electrician   C: Mrs. Green*)

A: Hello, Mrs. Green. What can I do for you?

C: I've locked myself out of the room. May I borrow a duplicate key?

A: Don't worry. I'll open the door for you.

C: Thank you very much. Sometimes I'm quite absent-minded.

A: It doesn't matter, Mrs. Green. What else can I do for you?

C: Ah, I'm afraid there's something wrong with the light bulb. One of the light bulbs is burnt out.

A: I'm sorry. I'll send for an electrician from the Maintenance Department. We can have it repaired. Please wait just a few minutes, Mrs. Green.

(She leaves the room. Ten minutes later, there is a knock on the door.)

B: May I come in?

C: (Opening the door) How do you do?

B: How do you do? The light bulb is out of order, isn't it, Mrs. Green?

C: Yes, it is.

B: Would you show me which one?

C: Yes, the one in the bathroom.

B: I'll change it immediately. (He finishes the repairing and checks other electric facilities in the room.) Mrs. Green, everything is OK now.

C: Thank you, young man. You are very helpful.

B: You are welcome. Enjoy your stay, Mrs. Green.

Key Words & Expressions

blink	[blaind]	*v.*	闪烁
corridor	['kɒridɔ:(r)]	*n.*	走廊
duplicate	['dju:plikət]	*adj.*	复制的
electrician	[i‚lek'triʃn]	*n.*	电工
burn out			烧坏
cable TV			有线电视
dressing table			梳妆台
electric facilities			电力设施
internet connection			网络连接
light bulb			电灯泡
maintenance man			维修人员
password			密码
pin number			密码
user-friendly			方便使用
wireless internet access			无线上网

Additional Useful Expressions

1. Asking for help

    a. There is something wrong with…

    b. The air conditioner in my room doesn't work.

    c. Please send someone to my room and check it out.

    d. I'm not sure what the matter with TV is, but I can see it's broken.

    e. Could you send someone to fix it?

2. Asking about the problem

    a. What's wrong with…?

    b. Please tell me what happened?

    c. What seems to be the problem?

    d. What's the trouble?

3. Giving the detail about the problem

    a. The toilet doesn't flush.

    b. The water tap is dripping.

c. The electricity is off in my room.

d. The light in this room is too dim.

e. One of the light bulbs is burnt out.

4. Offering maintenance service

a. I will send someone to your room to check it right away.

b. I will have the repairman come in and have a look at it.

c. Don't worry. I will let the overnight staff know. He'll do it for you.

d. I'm sorry to disturb you. I'm here to check the smoke detector in your room.

Classroom Activities

__ *Listening Practice* __

I. Listen to the recording and complete the following conversation.

(*H: Housekeeper   G: Guest   E: Electrician*)

G: I have 1._____ myself out of my room? May I borrow a 2._____ key?

H: Don't worry, Madam. I'll open the door for you.

G: Thank you very much indeed. Sometimes I'm quite absent-minded.

H: 3._____ Madam. What else can I do for you?

G: Well, I'm afraid there's something wrong with the TV. The 4._____ is not clear.

H: I'm sorry. May I have a look at it?

G: Sure. Come on in.

(*The housekeeper tried to fix it but in vain*)

H: I'll send for an 5._____ from the maintenance department. Please wait just a few minutes, Madam.

G: That's very kind of you.

E: (Knocking at the door.) 6._____. May I come in?

G: Come in, please.

E: Thanks, Madam. I'm here to check and fix your TV.

G: 7._____.

E: Let me have a look....Madam, everything is OK. Please have a try. Here is the 8._____ .

G: What efficiency! Thanks a lot. (*Taking out some money*) This is for you.

E: Oh, no. We won't accept 9._____ but thank you anyway. We wish you a 10._____
with us, Madam.

II. Listen to the recordings and then fill in the form.

	What's the trouble?	Solution
Conversation 1		
Conversation 2		
Conversation 3		
Conversation 4		

 *__ Communicative Practice __*

Role Play

A guest of a hotel finds out there are something wrong with the room facilities. He/She writes it down on the Room Maintenance card. The technician goes to see the guest to check the problem and offer maintenance service. Student A acts the guest, and student B will be the technician.

Room Maintenance

Won't you please help us maintain
our rooms in the best possible condition?
Is there anything in this room that
needs the attention of our
Engineering or Housekeeping Departments?

Room No. _____

Date _____   Time _____

Please leave at front desk for prompt action.
Thank you for your time.

Reading

Pre-reading questions

1. Do you think staying in hotels is safe?
2. What could be the potential risk when you stay in hotels?
3. Do you know any precautions to protect yourself in hotels?
4. Do you think hotels need to remind of travelers to be aware of the importance of their stay in hotel safely?

Hotel Safety Regulations Abroad

The more people travel, the less they tend to think about their safety. With an increasing number of terrorist attacks on hotels and the typical bad guys there, it is important to follow the hotel safety regulations abroad so that you do not become a victim of any possible holiday accidents while vacationing:

- ♦ Do not answer the hotel or motel room door without asking who is there at the door. If the person says that he or she is an employee or a staff member, it is wise to call the reception and ask whether a person has been sent to your room and what the purpose of his or her coming is.
- ♦ If you are returning to the hotel late in the night, it is always better to use the hotel's main entrance only.
- ♦ Before entering into the hotel parking spaces, you must be observant and watch around for any possible thieves or burglars.
- ♦ When you are inside your hotel room, always close the room door securely and use all the locking devices that are provided to you.
- ♦ Always keep your room keys safe and never leave them carelessly on the restaurant tables, swimming pool or any other place from where it can be stolen. In case you misplace it anyhow, immediately inform the front desk of the hotel.
- ♦ Do not display your expensive jewelry or cash in public as it may draw attention of any possible bad guys in the hotel.
- ♦ Avoid inviting any strangers into your hotel room.
- ♦ Always keep all your valuables in the safe deposit box of the hotel.
- ♦ Report any kind of suspicious activities to the management of the hotel.
- ♦ No matter how friendly and safe the hotel staff seems, never let anyone become too friendly with your children.
- ♦ Hotel rooms with an electronic key is much more safer than a standard key, as in an

electronic key, the combination gets changes with every new guest, unlike a standard key which remains the same with the room numbers.

It is acceptable that it you might ignore the safety precautions and Hotel Safety Regulations abroad in all the excitement and joy of the holiday, but some caution and a little care will avoid any possible holiday accidents and will definitely make your trip a trouble free and safe one.

Notes to the text

1. safety regulations　安全规则

2. abroad　广泛流传的

3. The more people travel, the less they tend to think about their safety.　人们出外旅行越多，他们对于自身安全的考虑就越少。

4. terrorist attacks　恐怖袭击

5. a victim of any possible holiday accidents　任何假期事故中的一名受害者

6. vacationing　度假中

7. observant　善于观察的

8. burglars　夜贼，破门盗窃者

9. anyhow　随便地；杂乱无章地

10. Do not display your expensive jewelry or cash in public　不要当众展示你的贵重珠宝或现金

11. safe deposit box of the hotel　饭店的保险箱

12. suspicious activities　可疑的活动

13. …as in an electronic key, the combination gets changes with every new guest, unlike a standard key which remains the same with the room numbers.　因为电子钥匙的数码组合总是随着新来的客人而改变，不像标准钥匙同一房间，同一钥匙。

14. …but some caution and a little care will avoid any possible holiday accidents　但是，稍加警觉和小心行事会避免任何可能发生的假期事故

15. trouble free　轻松自如

Follow-up questions

If you are the clerk in a hotel, what will you suggest your guest to do, when he or she is in the following situations?

1. If the guest hears someone knocking on the door, the guest should

_____.

2. If the guest finds his room key is missing, the guest should

_____.

3. If the guest takes something valuable checking in a hotel, the guest should

_____.

4. If the guest returns the hotel late in the night, the guest should

_____.

5. If the guest wants to take a shower or go to bed, the guest should

_____.

6. If the guest feels very sick in his or her room, the guest should

_____.

7. If the guest wants to meet some strangers, the guest should

_____.

8. If there is any indication or even a suspicion of a fire, the guest should

_____.

9. If the guest needs to use a big sum of money, the guest should

_____.

10. If the guest wants to smoke, the guest should

_____.

 *Exercises*

__*Words exercises*__

I. Test your vocabulary of maintenance. Fill in the blanks with words from the box, and change form where necessary.

toilet seat	meeting rooms	dripping
hazard	take place	make a note
instructions	check	fixtures
lower		

Guest Room Preventive maintenance

Emergencies will be reduced significantly if preventive room and equipment maintenance is 1._____.

The maintenance person likes to fix lamps and light 2._____ so he/she starts there and checks all the fixtures in the room by tightening switches, adjusting heating pipes, 3._____ the security of the plugs and making notes of any that need new shades. Next the maintenance person might cheek for 4._____ in the bathroom and replace or clean faucet aerators, and tighten knobs. While in the bathroom, tighten the 5._____ and shower rod. Look for grouting that needs repair and 6._____ so that several rooms can have their grouting and tile worked on at once. The key to guest room preventive maintenance is in actually getting some things in the room fixed or adjusted, not in making big lists and certainly not in undertaking on a big project.

Equipment and Public Space Maintenance

Equipment and public space preventive maintenance is a little different than the guest room program. Most pieces of equipment come with maintenance 7._____. Start with simple but important things, like keeping the machinery and equipment clean followed by servicing anything with moving parts.

Public spaces such as lobbies, halls, stairwells, restaurants and 8._____ need continuous attention. Chairs, tables, doors, carpet and wall coverings all get heavy use and abuse. Without regular attention these items can cause a hotel to start looking shabby. More importantly, some items become a safety 9._____.

In summary, preventive maintenance is going to 10._____ maintenance costs in the long run, enhance the guest experience and improve the hotel as an attractive and safe place to work.

II. Choose the best answer.

1. Which of the following is not used for washing floors?

    a. mop   b. broom   c. dustpan   d. washing machine

2. Deodorizer is used to _____.

    a. remove stain   b. remove smell   c. wash windows   d. tidy rooms

3. The process of keeping it in good condition by regularly checking it and repairing it when necessary. It is called _____ service in hotel.

    a. room   b. chamber   c. maintenance   d. safety

4. The opposite of messy is _____.

    a. dirty   b. tidy   c. damped   d. soapy

5. If the toilet water won't go down the drain, it is _____.

    a. clogged   b. plagued   c. bagged   d. soaped

6. A _____ is a man who mends broken machines such as televisions and telephones.

    a. clerk   b. waiter   c. housekeeper   d. technician

7. _____ is fixed to the ceiling of a guestroom, which can make a loud noise if there is smoke in the air, to warn people.

a. Air conditioner   b. Floor lamp   c. Smoke detector   d. Electrical kettle

8. _____ and grab rails can help to prevent slipping accidents especially where showers are located over baths.

   a. Slippers   b. Slip mats   c. Sticks   d. Towels

9. In hotel rooms, portable electrical appliances such as _____ and televisions require assessments. Regular inspection and testing is important as these items are subject to much wear and tear.

   a. hairdryers   b. kettles   c. irons   d. hairdryers, kettles, irons

10. Should you lose your key card please notify the front desk immediately so that your lock may be _____.

   a. replaced   b. repaired   c. re-coded   d. reused

___ Grammar exercises ___

Complete the Conditional Sentences with the correct form.

Example: If you <u>want</u>, I will take a message for you.

        If I <u>were</u> you, I would inform the front desk immediately.

        If you <u>had switched</u> on the lights, you would not have fallen over the chair.

1. If we _____ (meet) him tomorrow, we'll say hello.

2. He would have repaired the TV set himself if he _____ (have) the tools.

3. If I _____ (be) stronger, I'd help you carry the luggage.

4. If you _____ (drop) the vase, it will break.

5. We'd be stupid if we _____ (tell) him about our secret.

6. I wouldn't go to school by bus if I _____ (have) a driving license.

7. If we _____ (see) you, we would have stopped.

8. We try to do our best, but occasionally things don't always go as planned. Please let us know if we _____ (be) of service to you.

___ Translation ___

1. 请问出了什么问题？

2. 您的电视遥控器的电池没电了。我给您换一块电池。

3. 您房间的抽水马桶修好了。您可以用了。

4. 有个零件要换了。我片刻就来。

5. 如果您需要其他什么东西，请随时与我们联系。

6. If you're not satisfied with our accommodations or service, please let the front desk know without delay so we can make it right.

7. Wired or wireless access to the web brings you more comforts from home as you travel. The high-speed internet connection is free to guests at our hotel.

8. The hotel is equipped with up to date fire prevention devices and alarm systems.

9. This hotel is committed to providing accessible facilities for travelers with disabilities. If you encounter barriers during your stay, please contact the Manager on duty.

10. For cool air, press either the High Cool or the Low Cool button. In addition, turn the temperature knob to the left to adjust the desired temperature.

Fire Safety Procedures

The hotel is protected by the most up-to-date fire protection devices and alarm systems. Please make yourself aware of the emergency procedures listed here to further enhance your safety and security.

YOUR BEST DEFENSE AGAINST FIRE IS TO PLAN AHEAD.

- Locate two exits nearest your room. be sure they are unlocked and unblocked. Then count the doors between your room and exits so you'll have a reference point if it is smoky or dark.
- When you hear an alarm, ACT don't simply investigate.
- If the fire is in your room, leave if you can. First, feel the door. If it is cool, open.
- it slowly and go to the nearest exit. Crawl if there is smoke. Fresher air will be at the floor. Take your keys so you can go back to your room if you can't use the exits.
- **NEVER USE ELEVATORS DURING A FIRE.** They could stop at the fire floor.
- If your door is hot, don't open it. Your room may be the safest place to be. Seal all cracks with wet towels. Shut off fans and air conditioners. Signal from your window. Call the fire department and wait to be rescued.

Unit 11

Restaurant Service

Learning Objectives

After this unit, you will be able to:
➤ receive diners with and without reservation
➤ take orders and make recommendation
➤ serve food
➤ deal with complaints

Warming Up

I. Look at the pictures below and identify each one. Use the words from the list.

pizza	a cup and saucer	bacon and eggs	a bowl	a plate
salad	cheeseburger	a napkin	a knife, fork and spoon	

1_____   2_____   3_____

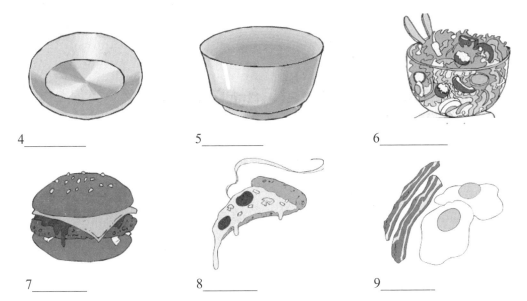

4 _____   5 _____   6 _____

7 _____   8 _____   9 _____

II. Working in a restaurant, a waiter or waitress has to have a good command of basic names about food, beverage and tableware. Now have a brainstorming to collect as many words or phrases as possible according to the following classification.

Meat

_____   _____
_____   _____
_____   _____

Vegetable

_____   _____
_____   _____
_____   _____

Drinks

_____   _____
_____   _____
_____   _____

Tableware

_____   _____
_____   _____
_____   _____

Situational Conversations

Pre-questions

Suppose you are a waiter / waitress of the restaurant in a hotel.

1. What do you usually do when the guest comes into the restaurant?

2. How do you give suggestions to your guests?

3. How do you take orders?

4. If you serve a wrong dish, what would you say?

Conversation 1   Receiving Guests

(*A: Receptionist   B: Guest*)

(A couple waiting to be seated in a crowded restaurant)

A: Good evening, Sir and Madam. Welcome to our restaurant.

B: Good evening. Do you have a table for two?

A: Do you have a reservation, Sir?

B: I'm afraid not. I've just arrived with my wife.

A: Are you staying at our hotel?

B: Yes. We're in room 312.

A: I'm sorry, Sir. The restaurant is full now. You have to wait for about half an hour. Would you like to have a drink in the lounge while you are waiting? We'll call you as soon as we have a table.

B: No，thanks. We'll come back later. May I reserve a table for two now?

A: Yes, of course. May I have your name, please?

B: Victor Johnson. By the way, can we have a table by the window?

A: We'll try to arrange it but I can't guarantee, Mr. Johnson.

B: That's fine.

A: Do you prefer smoking or non-smoking area?

B: Non-smoking. Thank you.

  (Half an hour later, the couple comes back.)

A: Your table is ready, Mr. Johnson. Please step this way.

B: Okay.

A: Would you like to take your seat, Sir? Here's the menu. The waiter will come in a few minutes to take your order.

Conversation 2   At the Western Restaurant

(*A: Waitress   B: Mr. Smith   C: Mrs. Smith*)

A: Good evening, Mr. and Mrs. Smith. How are you today?

B: Oh, very nice. Today we visited Nanshan. We're starving now, and we decided to end our day with a nice and quiet dinner.

A: I will be at your service this evening.

B: Thank you.

A: Then, may I suggest starting with a nice glass of wine? We have a very nice Californian wine as our specialty of month.

B: That's a good idea. Let's have a nice bottle of wine with dinner.

A: Do you prefer red or white wine?

B: We both prefer red wine.

A: All right, a bottle of red Californian red wine. And have you made a choice for the main course yet?

B: Yes. We have. I'd like the sirloin steak served with roast potatoes.

A: Which sauce do you prefer, black pepper, mushroom or Bearnaise?

B: For me the black pepper sauce, please.

A: And for you, Mrs. Smith?

C: I'd like the tenderloin with mushroom sauce, please.

A: How would you like your steak done?

C: Well done, please.

A: And while you are waiting for your main course may I suggest a soup? Our seafood chowder is very good.

B: Well, I'd like to try the soup.

C: No, not for me. Thank you.

A: Would you like to order dessert now or later?

B: Later.

A: May I repeat your order? A bottle of Californian red wine. Furthermore for Mr. Smith, one seafood chowder and the sirloin steak served with roast potatoes and black pepper sauce. For Mrs. Smith the tenderloin steak with mushroom sauce.

B: That's right. Thank you very much.

Conversation 3   At the Chinese Restaurant

(*A: Waiter   B: Guest*)

A: Are you ready to order now?

B: Yes. I'd like to try some local specialties. What do you recommend?

A: I recommend poached chicken. It is very famous in Hainan.

B: Good. What pork dishes do you have?

A: Do you like sweet and sour food? Many Guests like the sweet and sour pork.

B: Well, I do, but my wife doesn't. So I think it is better to order something else.

A: Maybe pan fried lamb. It is the local specialty in Hainan.

B: Yes. We will try that one.

A: Would you care for a soup too?

B: Where are the soups listed?

A: On the next page.

B: Oh here, I see. Yes, we'll take the bean curd soup with seasonal vegetable.

A: Certainly. Do you want some vegetable?

B: No, thank you.

A: And noodles?

B: No. rice is OK.

Key Words & Expressions

guarantee	[gærən'ti:]	v. 保证
lounge	[laʊndʒ]	n. 休息厅
starving	['stɑ:vɪŋ]	adj. 饥饿的
specialty	['speʃəlti]	n. 特色，特色菜
tenderloin	['tendələɪn]	n. 牛柳
bean curd soup		豆腐汤
Bearnaise		蛋黄酱
black pepper		黑胡椒
main course		主菜
pan fried lamb		干煸东山羊
poached chicken		白切鸡
seafood chowder		海鲜浓汤
sirloin steak		西冷牛排
sweet and sour pork		咕噜肉
well done		全熟

Additional Useful Expressions

1. Making a reservation

a. How many people is it for?

b. When would you like your table?

c. What time should we expect you, Sir?

d. In Whose name, please?

e. Let me just confirm. That's a table for 5 at 6:30 tomorrow night under the name of Bill.

2. Receiving guests

a. Good Evening, Sir and Madam. Welcome to this (our) restaurant.

b. Have you got a reservation?

c. May I have your name, please?

d. Would you come with me, please? Here is your table.

e. Will this table be all right?

f. Here's the menu. The waiter will attend to you in a minute.

3. Taking orders

a. Excuse me, Sir. Would you like to order now?

b. Are you ready to order, Sir?

4. Recommending dishes

a. Today's special is …

b. Perhaps I could recommend …

c. Why don't you try …? It's good indeed.

d. What would you like to go with your steak?

e. What vegetable would you like?

f. Any drinks?

5. Asking for special instruction on food

a. How would you like your steak cooked? Rare, Medium or well done?

b. Are you a vegetarian?

c. What kind of dressing would you like?

d. Shall I bring you some ketchup to go with your French fries?

e. If you need anything else, just feel free to tell me.

6. Serving dishes

a. Here's the breakfast you've ordered, Sir.

b. Sir, this is the salmon you've ordered.

c. May I serve you the birthday cake now?

7. Taking the bill

a. Sir, this is your bill.

b. Would you like to sign your bill here, Sir?

c. How would you like to pay for it? You can pay in cash, check and credit cards.

d. Sorry, we don't accept foreign currency. We accept cards.

8. Dealing with complaints

a. I'm very sorry to have kept you waiting.

b. I'm terribly sorry. There must have been some mistake.

c. We sincerely apologize for the inconvenience.

d. There's obviously been a misunderstanding between us.

e. We'll attend to it as soon as possible.

f. I assure you it won't happen again.

g. Sorry, this is the policy of our restaurant.

Listening Practice

I. Listen to the recording and complete the following conversation.

(*W: Waiter   G: Guest*)

W: Good afternoon, 1._____ can I help you today?

G: I'd like 2._____, please.

W: Right this way. Here you are.

G: Thank you. Can I have a menu?

W: Here you are. My name's Alan and I'm your waiter today. Would you like to hear 3._____?

G: Certainly.

W: Well, we have a wonderful 4._____ to start off with. Today's main course is fish and chips.

G: Fish and chips? Is the fish fresh?

W: Certainly, Madam. Fresh off the docks this morning.

G: Alright, I'd like the 5._____.

W: Would you like to have a 6._____ ?

G: Hmmm, I'm not sure.

W: Our salads are excellent, Madam.

G: I'd like a 7._____.

W: Very good. Would you like something to drink?

G: Oh, I'd like some 8._____, please.

W: OK. So that's a green salad, fish and chips and mineral water.

G: Yes, that's right.

W: Thank you and enjoy your lunch.

G: Thank you.

II. Listen to the recording and answer the questions.

1. What complaint has the guest made about her coffee?

2. Does the waiter get her another one?

3. What is wrong with fish?

4. How does the guest feel about it?

5. What does the waiter promise to do?

6. What does the waiter offer to give to the guest?

7. Has she accepted it? Why not?

8. What does the waiter persuade the guest to do?

9. Will she come again?

 ___ *Communicative Practice* ___

Role Play

Work in pairs or groups and create conversations according to the given situations.

Situation 1: Booking a table

Mr. White is going to have a birthday part for his 5 years daughter Jean. Now he calls the Four Seasons Restaurant to reserve a table for 3 at 6:30 this Friday evening. But the hostess says no tables are available until 7:30. Mr. White has to accept it.

Situation 2: Making complaints

Mr. Lee waits at his table for half an hour for being served in a restaurant. Finally, he can't help making complaints with the waitress and head waiter. The waitress and the head waiter ask the customer what happened, say "sorry", and find a best way to cope with the complaints.

Situation 3: Taking orders

Mr. and Mrs. Green come to a newly-opened restaurant to have their diner. The waitress receives the couple, gives them a menu, tells them the special of the day, takes and confirms the order as well as checks their bill. (using the given menu to help you)

Starters	
Chicken Soup	$2.50
Salad	$3.25
Sandwiches - Main Course	
Ham and cheese	$3.50
Tuna	$3.00
Vegetarian	$4.00
Grilled Cheese	$2.50
Piece of Pizza	$2.50
Cheeseburger	$4.50
Hamburger deluxe	$5.00
Spaghetti	$5.50
Drinks	
Coffee	$1.25
Tea	$1.25
Soft Drinks - Coke, Sprite, Root Beer, etc.	$1.75

 *Reading*

Pre-reading questions

1. Where does a waiter or waitress work?
2. What does a waiter or a waitress do when he or she is on duty?
3. Do you want to be a waiter or waitress? And why?

The Duties of Waiters and Waitress

Food and beverage serving and related workers are the front line of customer service in a lot of places besides restaurants. They could work in hotel or motel dining rooms, coffee shops, diners, or other places where food and drinks are served. These workers greet customers, show them to seats and hand them menus, take food and drink orders, and serve food and beverages. They also answer questions, explain menu items and specials, and keep tables and dining areas clean and set for new diners.

Waiters and waitresses, the largest group of these workers, take customers' orders, serve food and beverages, prepare itemized checks, and sometimes accept payment. Their specific duties vary considerably. In coffee shops serving routine, straightforward fare, such as salads, soups, and sandwiches, servers are expected to provide fast, efficient, and courteous service. In fine dining restaurants, where more complicated meals are prepared and often served over several courses, waiters and waitresses provide more formal service emphasizing personal, attentive treatment and a more leisurely pace. They may recommend certain dishes and identify ingredients or explain how various items on the menu are prepared. Some prepare salads, desserts, or other menu items tableside. Additionally, servers may meet with managers and chefs, before each shift to discuss the menu and any new items or specials, review ingredients for any potential food allergies, or talk about any food safety concerns, coordination between the kitchen and the dining room, and any customer service issues from the previous day or shift.

However, no matter where they work for, good waiters and waitress always keep the following know-hows in their minds:

- Always greet your guests with a smile. People sense when someone is bored or upset with their job and automatically feel uncomfortable with that person and the way they act around them.
- Make sure to check the table constantly and keep an eye out for drinks that need refilled or someone staring in your direction. A lot of customers will use eye contact as a way of notifying you if they want they want something.

- If the food is taking a while to cook, make sure to reassure your customer's that it's being cooked and it's just taking a little while longer than expected. You'll notify them when it's on its way out as well.
- Be patient and tactical when dealing with demanding customers. Do not exchange words with them. If you do something wrong indeed, you have to say "sorry" to your customers, explain why and tell them what you can do to remedy.
- Remember to bring and take the check quickly, because customers hate waiting on a check.

Notes to the text

1. diners　小餐馆，小餐厅
2. set for new diners　为新来的就餐者准备（餐桌）
3. prepare itemized checks　准备明细账单
4. serving routine, straightforward fare　提供常规，简单的食品
5. courteous　有礼貌的；客气的
6. served over several courses　上几道菜
7. emphasizing personal, attentive treatment and a more leisurely pace　特别注重个性化，周到的接待服务，同时又表现得从容不迫
8. chefs　主厨；厨师长
9. review ingredients for any potential food allergies　检查食物成分以免发生潜在的食物过敏反应
10. People sense when someone is bored or upset with their job　人们会感觉到某些人对工作的倦怠和厌烦
11. keep an eye out for drinks that need refilled or someone staring in your direction.　注意观察客人的酒是否需要斟上或客人是否在盯着你看
12. Be patient and tactical when dealing with demanding customers.　对待那些劳神的客人要耐心，要有策略。

Follow-up questions

1. The following items are the duties of a waiter or waitress. Please find out the right procedure according to the text above.

   A. collecting meals from the kitchen and drinks from the bar and carrying them either on a tray or on their arms to the correct tables

   B. accepting payments by cash, check or card, perhaps using the bill

   C. greeting customers and showing them to a table or asking them to wait

   D. writing down the orders for food and drinks, or entering the order details into an electronic point of sale and passing them to kitchen or bar staff

   E. adding up bills (but most restaurants use an automated bill)

   F. performing silver service at the table

G. cleaning each table and resetting it ready for the next customer

H. clearing away the empty plates of each course before bringing the next

I. taking telephone reservations

Right order: 1. _____ 2. _____ 3. _____ 4. _____ 5. _____

6. _____ 7. _____ 8. _____ 9. _____

2. What can make guests get fed up with, and make complaints in a restaurant?

3. How does a waiter or waitress deal with the customers' complaints?

Exercises

__*Words exercises*__

I. Test your vocabulary of Restaurant and Food. Fill in the blanks with words from the box.

appetizer	chef	fancy	
bar	cook	fast-food	
breakfast	dessert	lunch	
brunch	dinner	non-smoking	
buffet	dishwasher	salad	
smoking	tip	waiter	
soup			

People Who Work in a Restaurant:

The person who serves your food is called a 1._____. The person who cooks your food is called a 2._____ if it is a cheap restaurant or a 3._____ if it is an expensive restaurant. A 4._____ is somebody who washes dishes. If the food and service is good, people usually leave a 5._____.

Meals and the Time of Day:

Most people eat 6._____ after they wake up. Around noon people have their midday meal, or 7._____. And 8._____ is the meal that people eat in the evening. However, sometimes, especially on Sunday, people like to sleep in, so instead of having breakfast, they eat a meal between breakfast and lunch called 9._____.

Parts of a Meal:

At lunch or dinner sometimes people order a snack before the meal called an 10._____. A 11._____ or a 12._____ is often served alongside the main meal. After dinner, people sometimes treat themselves to 13._____.

Types of Restaurants:

It's nice to eat at a 14._____ restaurant, but that can be expensive. Sometimes, if you are short on time or short on money, you might go to a 15._____ restaurant because the food is cheaper and served faster. Some restaurants have a 16._____ which means you take a plate up to a table loaded with food and you can put as much food as you want on your plate. Other restaurants have a 17._____ where you can get an alcoholic drink while you are waiting for your table. Most restaurants these days have a 18._____ and a 19._____ section.

II. Choose the best answer.

1. Lemons taste _____.
   a. salty   b. sour   c. bitter   d. bland

2. Potato chips are not _____.
   a. crisp   b. salty   c. junk food   d. juicy

3. Smooth foods don't include _____.
   a. crackers   b. ice cream   c. pudding   d. whipped cream

4. In a restaurant, we normally eat an appetizer _____.
   a. after the entrée   b. just before dessert   c. first   d. last

5. Light food is the opposite of _____.
   a. heavy food   b. rich food   c. bland food   d. junk food

6. If something is tasty, you _____.
   a. don't really enjoy eating it   b. think it tastes good
   c. only eat it for breakfast   d. think it is unappetizing

7. Spicy food includes _____.
   a. milk   b. lemons   c. chili peppers   d. bananas

8. If milk is sour it is _____.
   a. delicious   b. too old   c. too fresh   d. from a goat

9. A beverage is _____.
   a. Beverley's birthday   b. something red
   c. an alcoholic drink   d. any drink

10. Appetizing means _____.
    a. you would like to eat it   b. the first course at a restaurant
    c. yucky   d. tangy

___Grammar exercises ___

Write response to show agreement with these statements by using *So* or *Neither*.

Example: I'm crazy about dessert.   *So am I.*

        I don't like greasy food.   *Neither do I.*

1. I'm crazy about Korean food.   _____

2. I think French food is delicious.　　_____

3. I can't stand greasy food.　　_____

4. I don't like salty food.　　_____

5. I have had Mexican food before.　　_____

6. I won't eat any rich food.　　_____

7. I'm in the mood for something spicy.　　_____

8. I haven't had any Indian food before.　　_____

___ *Translation* ___

1. I'm afraid all our tables are occupied now, Sir.

2. Do you mind sharing a table with others?

3. Do you like your tea strong or weak?

4. May I introduce our House Specialty?

5. That's all for your order. Please take your time and enjoy!

6. Do you have vegetarian dishes?

7. Our restaurant mainly serves Cantonese cuisine.

8. This dish sounds rather fascinating. How do you prepare it?

9. Chinese cuisine places great emphasis on three elements: color, aroma and flavor.

10. According to Chinese customs, we serve the food first and then the soup. But we'll bring you the soup first if you like.

 *Learning Tips*

Guidelines for Identifying the Complaints

People who make complaints and criticism can be friendly and reasonable, while they can also be rude and abusive. No matter how the person behaves, the restaurant staff should always try and be nice to them. An argument with the guest is the most undesirable thing that can happen to a staff member and the restaurant. With good training and a lot of practical experience with guests everyone can master the art of being nice to guests. Just keep one thing in your mind, that is, dissatisfying guest means a loss of potential future business.

Unit 12

Bar Service

 Learning Objectives

After this unit, you will be able to:
- ➤ tell the regular terms about beverages
- ➤ receive and chat with the guests
- ➤ take orders and serve wine
- ➤ get the bill paid

 Warming Up

I. Look at the pictures below and identify each one. Use the words from the list.

bar counter	wine glass	beer mug	screw pull	trays
straw	cocktail glass	bar stool	opener	

1_____

2_____

3_____

4 _____   5 _____   6 _____

7 _____   8 _____   9 _____

II. Look at the drinks menu below.

Drinks menu

Spirits	Wine	Soft Drinks	Hot Drinks
Brandies	Aperitifs	Mineral Water	Coffee
Scotch	White Wine	Coke	Hot Chocolate
Rum	Red Wine	Diet Coke	Milk
Gin	Rose Wine	Juice	Hot Tea
Vodka	Dessert Wine		
Tequila	Liqueurs		
	Sparking Wine		
Bottled Beers			
and Ciders	Cocktails		
	Champagne		

Now ask your partner what he or she wants to drink, like this:

A: What would you like to drink?

B: I'd prefer _____.

Situational Conversations

Pre-questions

Suppose you are a bartender in a hotel bar.

1. What do you usually do when the guest comes into the bar?

2. Could you have a chat with the guests?

3. How do you take orders?

4. Could you ask for tips from the guests?

Conversation 1   Take Beverage Order

(*A: Bartender   B: Guest*)

A: Good afternoon, Mr. Adams. How are you today?

B: Good. Thank you.

A: Your wife is not coming today?

B: Yes, she is. She will be here in a few minutes.

A: I see. You still prefer the smoking area?

B: As always.

A: This way, please. Is this table all right for you?

B: Yes. Thanks.

A: What would you like to drink today?

B: Local beer for me, please, and for my wife, a fresh orange juice.

A: One local beer and one fresh orange juice, am I correct?

B: Yes.

A: Do you want some snacks with the drink?

B: What snacks do you sell?

A: We have peanuts and potato chips. But the popcorn is free today.

B: OK, give me some popcorn.

(Later) Now how much do I owe you?

A: It's 40 Yuan plus 10% service charge. So the total is 44 Yuan.

B: Okay. Can I sign for it?

A: Certainly. Could you sign your name here, please? Thank you.

Conversation 2   Serving the Guest

(*A: Bartender   B: Ben Adams   C: Rooney Black*)

A: Good evening, Sir! Welcome to Lotus Bar.

B: Good evening.

A: What would you like to drink, Sir?

B: I'd prefer a brandy.

A: How do you like your brandy? Straight up or on the rocks?

B: With ice, thank you.

A: (Turn to Rooney Black) What about you, Sir?

C: I can hardly decide what to drink. What do you recommend?

A: I suggest you have a taste of Shanghai cocktail.

C: That's a good idea. I'll have a Shanghai cocktail.

A: Have you ever been in Shanghai?

B: No, not yet. This is our first trip to Shanghai.

A: It is quite difficult to get used to the time difference, isn't it?

C: Yes it is.

  (after a while)

A: Excuse me. Here are your drinks, a brandy with ice and a Shanghai cocktail.

B: Thank you. How much please?

A: The total is 60 Yuan, including 10% service charge.

Conversation 3 Serving the Guest

(*A: Guest   B: Barman*)

A: Is this bar open now?

B: Yes, Sir. We are open round the clock. But the bar is full now. Do you care to wait for about 20 minutes?

A: OK.

B: Would you like to read China Daily while waiting?

A: That's fine. Thank you.

(about 20 minutes later)

B: We have a table for you now, Sir. This way, please. We're very sorry for the delay.

A: That's all right.

B: Here is the drink list, Sir. Which do you prefer?

A: Are there any famous Chinese spirits?

B: What about Mao Tai?

A: I have no idea about Mao Tai. What kind of liquor is it?

B: It's one of the most famous liquors in China. It tastes good and never goes to the head. Many guests give high comments on the liquor.

A: Sounds great. I'd like to have a try. By the way, please book me a table tomorrow evening and here are tips for you.

B: I'd like to. But we don't accept tips. Thank you just the same.

Key Words & Expressions

brandy	['brændi]	*n.*	白兰地
cocktail	['kɔkteil]	*n.*	鸡尾酒
delay	[di'lei]	*n.*	延迟
liquor	[likə(r)]	*n.*	酒，烈性酒
local	['ləʊkl]	*adj.*	当地的
lotus	['ləutəs]	*n.*	莲花
owe	[əʊ]	*v.*	欠，应给予
peanut	['pi:nʌt]	*n.*	花生
popcorn	['pɔpkɔ:n]	*n.*	爆米花
snack	[snæk]	*n.*	小吃，零食
Chinese spirits			白酒
give high comments on			赞赏有加
get used to			适应，习惯
on the rock			加冰块
potato chips			薯片
round the clock			昼夜不停
straight up			不加冰块

Additional Useful Expressions

1. Asking what the guest wants to drink

    a. What would you like to drink today?

    b. What can I make for you tonight?

    c. What is going to be tonight?

    d. What can I offer you, Sir?

    e. What is your pleasure, Sir?

    f. We have a great variety of wines. Which kind do you prefer?

2. Asking guests what else they would like to order

    a. What else would you like to drink?

    b. Is there anything else I can do for?

    c. Do you want a double, Sir?

3. Recommending drinks

    a. Our special cocktail is quite good.

b. How about a non-alcoholic cocktail?

c. May I suggest a sweet Martini cocktail?

d. If you prefer something milder, we have rice wine.

e. They say that Shaoxing wine tastes very good.

f. I can recommend our special of the month.

4. Confirming details about beverages

a. Would you care for something a little stronger?

b. Would you like your beer draught or bottle?

c. With ice or without ice?

d. An aperitif or some red wine?

f. Would you like to have something to go with your wine?

5. Asking guests to wait to be served

a. Your drink will be ready soon.

b. Your wine will be served very soon.

c. You will be served soon.

d. Do you care to wait for about 20 minutes?

6. Serving guests

a. Here is the wine list, Sir.

b. I'll put the drink here, Sir.

c. How is the taste of the wine, Sir?

d. If we add more ice, the taste will be spoiled.

e. Please tell me if it is enough.

f. May I serve it to you now?

7. Asking guests if they have finished their drink

a. Have you enjoyed your drinks, Sir?

b. Is there anything you would like to try, Madam?

c. How is your drink?

d. Is everything to your satisfaction?

8. Asking guests to pay the bill

a. Do you want to start a tab, Sir?

b. One bill or separate bills?

c. How would you like to settle the bill?

d. Here is your bill, Sir.

_ Listening Practice _

I. Listen to the recording and complete the following conversation.

(*B: Barman   J: Jack   S: Sally*)

B: Good evening, Sir and Madam. 1._____ you tonight?

J: Sally, what do you prefer?

S: I don't know what I want. I'm not really a drinker.

J: It doesn't matter. I would like to look through the 2._____ .

B: OK, Sir. Here is the drink list.

J: An aperitif or some 3._____ ?

S: Sorry, I don't drink at all.

J: Man, what would you recommend for the lady?

B: How about our special 4._____ ? It is usually popular with ladies.

S: Is it non-alcoholic?

B: Certainly, Madam. It is a kind of 5._____ .

S: It sounds interesting. I'll take that.

B: Okay, madam. 6._____ for you, Sir?

J: I'm very thirsty. I'll have some beer.

B: Any special brand, Sir?

J: What about your local brew? I hear it's good.

B: It is Yan Jing Beer. Bottled or 7._____ ?

J: Let me try the draught.

B: Fine. One non-alcoholic cocktail for the lady and one draught Yang Jing Beer.

J: Yes, that's right. By the way, could we have some snacks?

B: Certainly, I'll get a fresh supply.

J: Thank you. How much do I owe you?

B: 86 Yuan. You can 8._____ if you like.

J: That's great.

II. Listen to the recording and choose the best answer with the questions.

1. What kind of day has it been for Mr. Jackson?

  a. relaxing day   b. stressful day   c. holiday

2. What's Mr. Jackson's first complaint?

    a. about his aching feet

    b. about his whiskey sour

    c. about the bartender taking so long

3. Which drink does Mr. Jackson order?

    a. a beer   b. a whisky sour   c. a glass of wine

4. What does Mr. Jackson need?

    a. a towel   b. an ashtray   c. a cigarette lighter

5. Why are Mr. Jackson's feet aching?

    a. He's been walking around town to get to meetings.

    b. He's been working out at the gym.

    c. He's been shopping.

6. What kind of snacks does the bartender have?

    a. Mini pizzas   b. Nuts and crackers.   c. Olives

7. What does Mr. Jackson ask for with his drink?

    a. a shot glass   b. stirrer   c. a napkin

8. What does Mr. Jackson complain about?

    a. the spicy peanuts   b. the tasty peanuts   c. the stale peanuts

9. What does the bartender offer to keep Mr. Jackson happy?

    a. a small sandwich   b. a drink on the house   c. a handshake

10. Which type of whisky would Mr. Jackson like in his drink?

    a. Smithson   b. Old Kentucky   c. Jack Daniel's

__ *Communicative Practice* __

I. Brainstorm the possible problems in a bar.

Assume you are a customer; please try to figure out as much complaint about the drink served in a bar as you can, like this:

1. Bartender, there is something in my drink.

2. _____

3. _____

4. _____

5. _____

6. _____

7. _____

8. _____

II. Role Play

Work in pairs or groups and create conversations according to the given situations.

Situation 1: Receiving the guest

A guest comes to the bar for a drink. Have a conversation between the guest and the bartender with the information given below.

Barman card
Greet the guest
Where ... from
Offer what
Introduce local beer
How to pay

Guest card
Name:Bob White
Nationality: America
Favorite drink: Beer
Special request: local brew
By cash

Situation 2: Taking orders

Guest

1. You want to know what House Specialty the bar has.

   You want to order some red wine.

   You also want to have some fruits.

2. You want to ask today's specialty.

   You also ask the clerk to give you some recommendation.

   You order chilled bottled beer.

Situation 3: Dealing with complaints

Guest

1. Your name is Nancy.

   You notice the glass is dirty in a bar.

   You ask for a clean one.

2. Your name is Jack.

   Your beer arrives. You find the glass with beer is not full.

   You ask for a full one.

Clerk

1. Ask the customer what happened.

2. Say "sorry".

3. Find a best way to cope with the complaints. For example, getting him another one, giving him a refund, or offering him a free drink.

Reading

Pre-reading questions

1. How do you think the work of bartending?
2. What does a bartender do when he is on duty?
3. What are the important qualities that a good bartender should have?

What Does It Take to Become a Good Bartender?

For a lot of people, bartending is considered a cool job. Especially for people who like going out and hanging out at bars. But bartending is not a job for all. If you want to become a good bartender, you must possess the necessary qualities that make a good bartender. Here are some skills and rules every bartender should follow.

- Have a good attitude

Being a good bartender starts out with you having a good attitude. You must leave all your problems at home. No one wants to hear all about your problems. Your customers want to feel comfortable and relaxed when they are in your bar.

- Look presentable

Always come to work clean and refreshed. Good hygiene is a must when you are working face to face with people. Hair, teeth, hands and clothing are the main points of interest to work on.

- Be friendly with your customers

Smile and ask some general questions to show your customers your care and make the customer feel more comfortable with you. When they are talking to you, try to use some eye contact if possible. If you have a lot of regular customers try to get to know them and their interests. They will feel like they know you on a more personal level.

- Know your drinks

Have a working knowledge of the popular drinks served in your area, as well as the usual list of favorites. A professional bartender doesn't give the customer a puzzled look when they take their drink order. There may be an occasional off the wall drink now and then, but 99% of the time you should have them memorized. This can make or break your tip jar.

- Keep your bar clean and stocked

Keep the bar clean at all times. This includes emptying ashtrays, place a new napkin under drinks, wipe up sticky stuff and pick up trash on floor and bar. Use clean towels to wipe the bar and get rid of empty glasses and beer bottles. Set up the bar and stock plenty of back up just in case, so that you don't run out of anything. Without proper preparation the bar will not run smoothly and end up being chaotic.

- Pay attention to details

When you are bar tending, you should constantly be looking around the bar. There are usually things you may have missed, for example, a coaster or a napkin. If you are busy with another patron and someone behind you is calling, you nod or tell them you will be right with them.

To sum up, always treat the customer the way you would want to be treated, if you were the customer.

Notes to the text

1. hang out   闲逛
2. presentable   得体的；像样的
3. Good hygiene is a must when you are working face to face with people.   当你与人面对面打交道的时候，良好的个人卫生是一定要的。
4. eye contact   目光交流
5. There may be an occasional off the wall drink now and then.   你偶尔也会碰到一些不太熟悉的酒精饮料。
6. tip jar   装小费的钱罐
7. emptying ashtrays   清理烟灰缸
8. wipe up sticky stuff   擦拭那些黏糊糊的东西
9. Set up the bar and stock plenty of back up...   为酒吧营业做准备，储备充足的备用品……
10. end up being chaotic   以慌乱告终
11. coaster   杯子垫
12. patron   老主顾，顾客

Follow-up questions

1. What is the difference between a Good Bartender or a Bad Bartender?

Read the following statements. Then, put G in the blanks for good bartenders' performance and B for poor performance.

_____Asks customers if they would like another drink when the glass is almost empty.

_____Knows what's going on in the area when asked by customers.

_____Doesn't wear full uniform.

_____Encourages friends to drink in the bar when he is on duty.

_____Lets the tap run for a second or two before placing the glass underneath.

_____Can explain the difference between different bottles of wine.

_____ Offers to carry the drinks to the table for you when necessary.

_____ Takes orders from customers in rotation, without leaving anyone waiting longer than others.

_____ Takes orders from the pretty girls first.

_____ Leaves the Cash Drawer open in the cash register.

1. Why does a bartender need to call a patron's name?
2. How do you understand the last sentence in the text?

Exercises

__Words exercises__

I. Test your vocabulary relating to interacting with customers in a bar. Fill in the blanks with the words from the box, change the form where necessary.

Call	water	tap
pitcher	mix	part
get	potent	bottle
serve	disturb	glass
cut	round	allow

1. Buying beer by the _____, is cheaper than buying it by the glass.
2. What kind of beer do you have on _____? (= on draught)
3. When the bartender says "Last _____!", it means that it's the last chance for customers to order drinks before the bar closes.
4. I'm warning you—This drink is really _____ ! (= strong)
5. It's two _____ orange juice and one part vodka.
6. I'm sorry but I can't _____ you since you're intoxicated (= drunk).
7. I've broken 5 _____ today.
8. What can I _____ you? = What would you like?
9. Would you like another _____ of drinks?
10. If a customer is "_____ off", it means that he/she is not allowed to order any more drinks (because of drunkenness, bad behavior, etc.)
11. We don't have any draught beer. We only have _____ beer.
12. I would never _____ down a drink. I would lose my job if I did.
13. It's a bad idea to _____ vodka with wine.
14. Smoking is not _____ anywhere inside the bar. You'll have to go outside to smoke.

15. Sir, please don't _____ the other customers.

II. Choose the best response for each question.

1. Can we run a tab?
    a. Sure, I'll start one for you.   b. That'll be $5, please.
    c. No, we don't have one.

2. When's last call?
    a. Yes, you can use our phone.   b. We open at 11:00 am.
    c. We don't close until the last customer leaves.

3. You got any appetizers/snacks?
    a. Our special today is Chicken Florentine.   b. We've got chips, fries, and peanuts.
    c. We have Guinness and Budweiser on tap.

4. A _____ is something you put under your drink so that the table doesn't get wet.
    a. round thing   b. coast   c. coaster

5. Can I pay with my bank card?
    a. Would you like to pay cash?   b. I already gave you your bill/check.
    c. Normally you can, but today our machine is broken.

6. What are your drink specials today?
    a. We've got Mojitos for £ 5.   b. I can make all kinds of special drinks.
    c. Yup, we've got have drink specials.

7. Can we get the bill?
    a. Would you like to pay?
    b. I'm sorry, but we only accept cash.
    c. Can I put you all on one bill, or would you like separate bills?

8. Do you serve pitchers of beer?
    a. You'd have to check the snack menu.   b. No, we only sell beer by the glass/mug.
    c. Yes, there's another bar across the street.

9. Why is the bar closing so early?
    a. We're closing.   b. We usually close early on Sundays.
    c. Thanks. Here is your bill.

10. Does the bartender make good drinks?
    a. Yes, she does. She's one of the best bartenders in the city.
    b. No, you have to place your drink order with me.
    c. Thank you. I'll let her know you like them.

___ *Grammar exercises* ___

Use some, any, something, anything, somebody and anybody to fill in the blank.

Example: There is no _____ wine in my glass?   <u>any</u>

        Can you do _____ for me?   <u>something</u>

1. Would you like to drink _____ beer?

2. Bartender, there is _____ in my drink.

3. _____ has taken my glass when I was answering the phone.

4. _____ could have taken your glass by mistake.

5. Would you like _____ else to eat?

6. I won't drink _____ alcoholic drink.

7. Do _____ of you have an idea about what to drink?

8. There must be _____ reason for her to drink like that.

___Translation ___

1. 先生，您要喝点什么？

2. 我想看一下酒水单？

3. 这种酒酒性很烈，但是不上头。

4. 先生，酒的味道如何？

5. 先生，您还需要其他饮料吗？

6. How would you like your scotch, straight or on the rock?

7. You can hold the payment of the bill until you decide to leave if you like.

8. I've got to go take care of my other customers. I'll be back to check on you.

9. I'm sorry, Sir. I can't serve you since you are drunk.

10. Would you like to put it on your hotel bill?

Learning Tips

The Classic Cocktails and Popular Drinks in a Bar

There are many different ways to prepare classic cocktails. Every bar or restaurant has rules about how much alcohol to put in a cocktail and how to build it. The following recipes do not contain specific amounts. Use them to learn the names of the cocktails, liquors, and mixes.

Black Russian	vodka, coffee liqueur, on ice (for a white russian-add milk)
Bloody Mary	vodka, tomato juice, tobasco sauce, worchestershire sauce, salt, pepper, celery salt, slice celery, on ice
Cosmopolitan	vodka, orange liqueur, cranberry juice, lime, on ice
Daquiri	light rum, lime juice, sugar, blended with ice
Long Island Iced Tea	vodka, gin, rum, orange liqueur, lemon juice, cola, on ice
Margarita	tequila, lime, salt, blended with ice

Martini   gin, dry vermouth, (garnish with olive)
Pina Colada   rum, coconut milk, pineapple juice, blended with ice
Screwdriver   vodka and orange juice, on ice
Tom Collins   gin, lemon juice, sugar, soda water, on ice

Common Liquor

Gin   Rum   Vodka   Whisky   Tequila
Liqueur (various sweet alcohol)

Beer and Coolers

Local (beer brewed nearby)   Cans (beer served in a tin)   Bottles
Draft (beer on tap)   Keg (beer in a large barrel)
Ciders   (alcoholic drink from apples or other fruit)
Coolers   (premixed and bottled alcoholic drinks)

Unit 13

Business Service

Learning Objectives

After this unit, you will be able to:

➤ get tickets for the guests
➤ offer secretarial service
➤ offer internet service
➤ provide telephone service

Warming Up

I. Look at the pictures below and identify each one. Use the words from the list.

stapler	laser printer	scanner	fax machine	photocopier
laptop	CD	USB flash drive	folder	

1_____

2_____

3_____

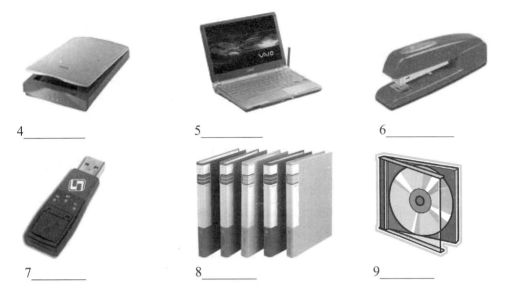

4_____   5_____   6_____

7_____   8_____   9_____

II. Working at the business center in a hotel, a clerk has to have a good command of basic names about secretarial service, reservation and telephone service. Now have a brainstorming to collect as many words or phrases as possible according to the following classification.

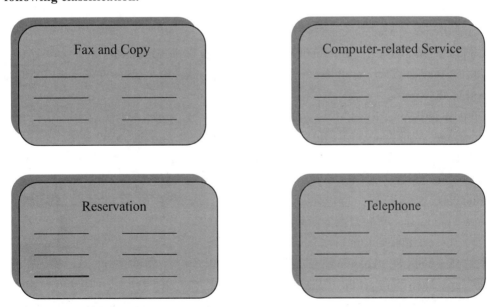

Fax and Copy
_____ _____
_____ _____
_____ _____

Computer-related Service
_____ _____
_____ _____
_____ _____

Reservation
_____ _____
_____ _____
_____ _____

Telephone
_____ _____
_____ _____
_____ _____

Situational Conversations

Pre-questions

Suppose you are a clerk of the business center in a hotel.

1. When guests come into the business center, what do you often do?

2. In the business center, if you are asked to introduce the services provided, what would you say?

3. While a guest is booking an air ticket, what kind of materials do you ask the guest to present?

4. If all tickets are fully booked, what will you give your guests advice?

5. If the original materials which the guest offered for copying is not clear enough, what will you do?

Conversation 1   Booking Flight

(*C: Clerk of Business Center   G: Guest*)

C: Good afternoon, Madam, can I help you?

G: Good afternoon. Is there any flight to Washington on September 24th?

C: Oh, let me see. There are three flights. The planes take off at about 9:00 a.m., 14:00 p.m. and 18:00 p.m..

G: I'll take 14:00 p.m. flight, then. Would you like to book a ticket for me?

C: Of course. Would you please fill in this form and present your passport?

G: OK. Here you are.

C: Which method do you want to fly, first class or economy?

G: First class, please.

C: To a window seat or an aisle one, which do you like?

G: An aisle seat, please. Can I pay cash now?

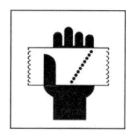

C: Yes, please pay 800 Yuan in advance.

G: OK, and when can I get the ticket?

C: We'll have the ticket sent to you on the morning of September 23th. Would you give me your phone number and address?

G: I'm now staying in Room 305. My telephone number is 13988322135. Thank you very much.

C: My pleasure.

Conversation 2　Copying and Typing

(C: Clerk　　G: Guest)

C: Good evening, Sir. What can I do for you?

G: Oh, I'd like to make these materials copied.

C: OK. How many copies do you want?

G: Three copies for each.

C: Oh, but your original is not very clear, would you mind making it a little darker by me?

G: All right. And would you copy these on both sides to the paper?

C: Certainly.

G: I'll leave the original here. Please phone me when the copies are ready.

G: OK.

(Two hours later)

C: Here you are, Sir.

G: Thank you very much. And can you type these materials for me?

C: Certainly. What font and size would you like?

G: Times New Roman, size 4, to A 4 paper.

C: I see. What time do you expect it?

G: The sooner, the better! I need it before 10 o'clock.

C: OK. I'll send it to your room as soon as I finish typing.

G: Thank you very much.

C: *(Bring the bill)* Please sign your name here!

G: OK.

Key Words & Expressions

aisle	[ail]	*n.* 过道
expect	[iks'pekt]	*v.* 期待
flight	[flait]	*n.* 航班
font	[fɔnt]	*n.* 字体
original	[ə'ridʒənl]	*n.* 原件
economy		经济舱
first class		头等舱
take off		起飞

Additional Useful Expessions

1. Ticket service

    a. Is there a non-stop flight to Paris?

    b. Which seats would you like?

    c. A window seat or an aisle seat?

    d. Is there a discount for company booking?

    e. Which train would you like to take?

    f. Do you have any tickets left for *King Lear*?

    g. I am afraid that flight/train/show is fully booked.

    h. Hard/soft berth tickets are not available now.

2. Copying

    a. I'd like to print this.

    b. Would you like to staple these for you?

    c. Shall I staple them on the left side or at the top?

    d. Shall I enlarge/reduce this to fit B5 paper?

    e. The paper is jammed.

    f. It's out of ink.

3. Typing

    a. Shall I make the space larger?

    b. Please indent the first line of each paragraph.

    c. Shall I save it on your disk?

    d. I'm afraid we can only save it on our disks, in case of any virus.

4. Sending a fax

    a. I want to send a fax, but I don't know where I can send it out?

    b. I want to fax my friend in Japan.

    c. What's the rate?

    d. To Shanghai it's 10 Yuan per minute, including service charge.

    e. The minimum chare is 10 Yuan.

    f. Please write down the country code, the area code and their number.

    g. We have received a fax for you.

5. Telephone

    a. I'd like to make a long distance call to New Zealand. Could you please tell me the rate for call New Zealand?

    b. The standard rate for calling New Zealand is 0.7 Yuan for every 6 seconds, excluding service charge.

    c. What's your service charge?

d. What time do the special rates apply?

e. We offer IDD and DDD service.

f. The mini charge will apply for the first three minutes, then each additional minute will be charged.

g. Can you put me through to Jack Hills in Room 1711?

h. The line is busy.

I. You're through.

6. Computer-related service

a. I want to know if you could provide internet service. I have to send an E-mail to my colleague.

b. You can get on the internet here.

c. The price for half an hour of connection is 15 Yuan.

d. We charge it on an hour basis.

Classroom Activities

__ Listening Practice __

I. Listen to the recording and complete the following conversation.

(C: Clerk   G: Guest)

C: Good morning, Mr. Black. What can I do for you?

G: Yes. I'd like to know whether you provide 1._____ here. I have to 2._____ to my boss.

C: Yes. Internet access is 3._____ in all guest rooms. The access is just 4._____ the standing lamp.

G: Yes. I know. But I forgot to 5._____. I just wonder whether I can send e-mails here.

C: Well, you can get on the internet here. The price for half an hour of connection is 6._____.

G: That's good.

(a few minutes later)

G: Your computer is very quick. 7._____

C: Pleased to hear that. For 8._____, we charge you 20 Yuan. We charge it on 9._____ basis.

G: I see. Can I 10._____ ?

C: Yes, Sir. May I look at your room card?

G: Here they are.

II. Listen to the recording and answer the questions.

1)

1. Where does the guest want to call?

2. What's the rate for that?

3. What's the service charge for a long distance call?

2)

1. What does the guest want to do?

2. Where does the guest want to send a fax?

3. What's the fax number?

4. How much does the guest pay for the fax?

5. How does he settle the bill?

 ___ *Communicative Practice* ___

Role Play

Work in pairs or groups and create conversations according to the given situations.

Situation 1: Booking a ticket

Mr. White is going to attend a meeting in Shanghai. Now he calls the Business Center in the hotel where he is living and wants to reserve a flight to Shanghai on December 5th. He is told there are two flights to Shanghai every day. Then he books an economy class ticket of the morning flight.

Situation 2: Typing and Printing

A guest from Room 1108 comes to the Business Center and wants a document of 10 typed. He will sign it to the room and the requirement for typing is as follows:

- Font: Times New Roman
- Size: 4
- space: double space, indent the first line
- Print: Black and White

The clerk explains the price according to price table below and the time it takes to finish it.

Situation 3: Sending a fax

A guest wants to send a fax to the headquarters of his company in Australia and the line is busy, so the clerk asks him/her to wait for a few minutes. Then the guest asks the price of sending a fax and he want to pay in cash. The clerk tells him the price according to the table below.

Business Center

Fax
- Incoming Faxes (Non-guest) $1.00pp
- Incoming Faxes (Guest)   Complementary
- Fax   Sending (Domestic) $3.00pp
- Fax   Sending (International) $8.00pp

Copies:
- Black & White Photocopies $0.25pp
- Laser Pages $0.25pp
- Color Pages $0.50pp
- Laminators $5.00pp
- Xerox Paper Per Ream Letter Size $20.00
- Xerox Paper Per Ream Legal Size $25.00

Computer/Printer:
- High Speed Internet Access $0.37 per minute
- Laptop Connection to Printer Connection Fee $5.00
- Black and White Printers $0.50 per page
- Color Printers $1.50 per page)

Binding:
- Small Book (<100 pgs) $7.00 per book
- Large Book(>100 pgs) $10.00 per book

*Reading*

Pre-reading questions

1. What facilities are there in the business center?
2. What services does the business center usually offer?

Welcome to Business Services

24-hour business center services at Four Seasons meet the needs of busy business guests.

One of the many ways that Four Seasons sets itself apart is through the exceptional business center services and amenities that it offers the business traveler. Whether you require business hotels in Tokyo and New York, or in virtually any other corner of the globe, you will find that 24-hour business services are a standard company-wide offering.

The business center at many Four Seasons hotels and resorts ensures that secretarial and translation services and business support – from computers, printers and scanners to high-speed Internet access, photocopying and faxing facilities – are readily available.

In addition, many other business services are offered, which generally include a 24-hour multilingual concierge service, airline reservations, Internet access in guest accommodations, complimentary newspaper and direct-dial multi-line telephones with voice mail, speaker and data port.

Hours

Weekdays: 7 a.m. - 6 p.m.

Weekends: 9 a.m. - 3 p.m.

During busy seasons, our hours are automatically extended based on the needs of guests and groups.

Copies

Fast, small or large volume, duplex, automatic stapling and sorting. A wide variety of paper stock is available including brights, pastels, cardstock, transparencies, and labels.

Fax

Receiving: Hotel guests may receive faxes at the hotel's Communications Department (operator) 24 hours-a-day at (808) 879-4077. Faxes are delivered to guest rooms approximately every hour. To receive a fax at The Business Center - to be picked up during our business hours only - fax to (808) 874-2488.

Sending: During our business hours, for the most part, guests are directed to us for sending faxes. A few suites in the hotel include a fax machine. We have available for rent as well if desired.

Computer and Internet Services

We offer both IBM and Macintosh systems. Standard software included on our systems is Microsoft Office 2019. This includes Word, Excel, Powerpoint and Access. All systems include a CD, ZIP, etc. At least one system has CD writing capability, and a Compact Flash / Smart Media Reader is also connected to enable easy emailing and printing of your special vacation pictures. We also have a scanner available in case you took your pictures "the old fashioned way".

Internet Access

Access to the Internet is via a fast T-1 line, so waiting for pages to load is minimal. Your email is usually accessible from our Internet portal page as long as you have your password and your email is not restricted somehow.

Printing

Our standard black and white printer is an HP 8100DN, printing at up to 32 pages per minute, up to 11×17, and with duplex capabilities up to 8.5×14. Our color output is on an HP 4500N Color Laserjet, and produces nice quality color images up to 8.5×14. High resolution color printing is available on HP Color Inkjet printers, up to 11×17.

Notes to the text

1. meet the needs of…　满足某人的需要

2. set apart　使……显得与众不同

3. exceptional business center services and amenities　出色的商务服务与设施

4. a standard company-wide offering　符合企业水平

5. multilingual concierge service　多语言的礼宾服务

6. complimentary newspaper　免费赠送的报纸

7. direct-dial multi-line telephones with voice mail, speaker and data port　具有语音信息、扬声器和接口的直拨多线电话

8. duplex, automatic stapling and sorting　双面打印、自动装订和分拣

9. A wide variety of paper stock is available including brights, pastels, cardstock, transparencies, and labels.　纸张齐全，包括复印纸、淡色纸、卡片纸、投影胶片和标签纸。

10. At least one system has CD writing capability, and a Compact Flash / Smart Media Reader is also connected to enable easy emailing and printing of your special vacation pictures. 至少每个系统都有刻录功能，可以插上闪存和读卡器，这样便于发送邮件和打印度假照片。

Follow-up questions

1. The business center of Four Seasons offers five types of services. What are they?

_____, _____, _____, _____,_____,

2. Can you mention at least four terms related to each service above?

*Exercises*

__*Words exercises*__

I. Test your vocabulary of Business Center. Fill in the blanks with words from the box.

printer	scanner	Fax machine
paper clip	business class	photocopier
webcam	E-mail	first class
economy class	typist	stapler

Secretarial Service in a Business Center

The person who works in an office typing letters and other documents is called a 1._____. The machine for printing text on paper, especially one connected to a computer is called a 2._____, The machine which quickly copies documents onto paper by photographing them is called 3._____.

If you don't like typing, you can use a 4._____ to do that, which is a piece of computer equipment that you use for copying a picture or document onto a computer

After printing or copying, a typist will hold loose sheets of paper together by either using a 5._____, a small piece of bent wire that is used to fasten papers together; or using a 6._____, a device that joins together sheets of paper or other similar materials by driving a thin metal staple through the sheets.

If you want to send documents to a partner in other cities, you can make use of a 7._____, a machine that sends and receives documents in an electronic form along telephone wires and then prints them.

Internet and E-mail Service

You can send an 8._____ to your friends or colleagues through the internet, a system of sending written messages electronically from one computer to another. Besides, you can chat with them through some chat software, and some business centers also connect the computer with a 9._____, a video capture device connected to a computer or computer network, so that you can see your partners.

Booking service

Most business centers provide booking service. When you book air tickets, you have three classes to choose from: 10._____, the best and most expensive seats or accommodation on planes; 11._____, the part of a plane where passengers have a very high level of comfort and service, designed for people travelling on business; 12._____, the lowest class of seating in air travel.

II. Choose the best answer.

1. You must _____ the first line of a new paragraph.

   a. indent   b. capitalize   c. bold   d. big letter

2. A _____ is an additional charge for a service for which there is already a basic fee.

a. tip   b. service charge   c. fare   d. change

3. I want to _____ a fax to the company.

    a. receive   b. send   c. mail   d. post

4. I can't find the documents I need. Maybe my computer is _____ with virus.

    a. get   b. spread   c. catch   d. infected

5. Mr. Lee, this is the Business Center of the hotel. We have _____ a fax from you company.

    a. received   b. sent   c. mailed   d. posted

6. If you are _____, you no longer have any of it.

    a. out of paper   b. no paper   c. short of paper   d. plenty of

7. The fax machine _____, it became fixed in position and cannot move freely or work properly.

    a. jammed   b. broke   c. damaged   d. didn't work

8. When a photo is _____, a bigger print of it is made.

    a. enlarged   b. big   c. improved   d. increased

9. A _____ is a flexible cover folded in the center and used as a holder for loose paper.

    a. box   b. cabinet   c. bag   d. folder

10. If a hotel, restaurant, or theatre is _____ or fully booked, it has no rooms, tables, or tickets left for a particular time or date.

    a. booked   b. booked up   c. booked   d. sold

___ *Grammar exercises* ___

Write the definition of the following words by using...*a machine/device/a piece of equipment for doing...*

Example: printer (print text on paper)

    The printer is a machine for printing text on paper.

1. photocopier (make copies of documents)

_____

2. scanner (copy a picture or document onto a computer)

_____

3. stapler (fasten papers together)

_____

4. fax machine (send and receive documents)

_____

5. staple remover (quickly remove a staple from a material without causing damage)

_____

6. camera (take photographs, make films, produce television pictures)

_____

7. telex (type messages to a distant point)

___Translation ___

1. I want to book a business class ticket to Paris for December 11th, please.

2. I'm sorry all the tickets for that date have been booked up.

3. I want to send a fax, but I don't know where I can send it out.

4. Please write down the country code, the area code and their number.

5. The paper is too thick. It may jam the printer.

6. The business center provides a word procession service, photocopying facilities, and an information desk near the conference hall.

7. Your original is not very clear. I can't guarantee the copy will be good.

8. We'll try to finish the typing of 20-page document before 5:00 this afternoon.

9. We'll have a lot of overseas businessmen who don't understand Chinese, so we need some qualified interpreters.

10. The interpreter is well experienced in business talk translation.

 *Learning Tips*

Business Center Service

Business Centers usually offer the following services:

- Facsimile transmissions
- Computer workstations
- Copy services
- Internet and email capabilities
- Secretarial services
- Shipping Services
- Printers
- Send/Receive FedEx

Unit 14

Shopping Arcade

 Learning Objectives

After this unit, you will be able to:
- greet guests politely
- give guests shopping advice
- introduce the commodities guests like
- praise guests with proper compliment

 *Warming Up*

I. Look at the pictures below and identify each one. Use the words from the list.

sandal fan	emerald	jade articles	sapphire
Four Treasure of Study		tri-chromatic glazed ware of Tang Dynasty	
pearl necklace	Chinese painting	hand-embroidered	

1_____

2_____

3_____

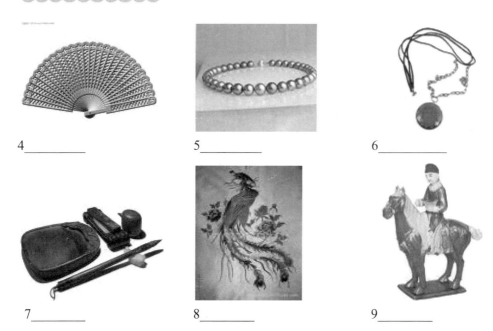

4 _____   5 _____   6 _____

7 _____   8 _____   9 _____

II. Working in a shopping arcade, a shop assistant has to have a good command of basic names about commodities. Now have a brainstorming to collect as many words or phrases as possible according to the following classification.

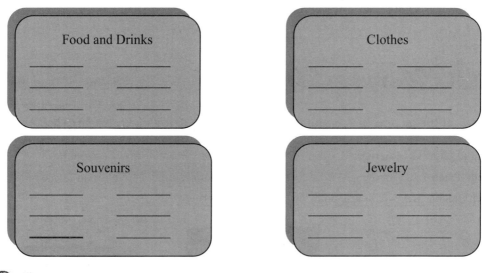

Food and Drinks

_____   _____

_____   _____

Clothes

_____   _____

_____   _____

Souvenirs

_____   _____

_____   _____

Jewelry

_____   _____

_____   _____

Situational Conversations

Pre-questions

Suppose you are a shop assistant of the shopping arcade.

1. When guests come into the shopping arcade, what do you often do?

2. If the guest doesn't know how to select, how would you give your guests advice?

3. To the guest who buys something for the first time, what kind of information would you offer?

4. If guests want to change the commodity without any reason, what should you do?

5. What would you say if the commodity is out of stock?

Conversation 1   Selecting a Gift

(*A: Assistant   G: Guest*)

A: Good afternoon, Madam. Welcome to our arcade.

G: Good afternoon. I want to buy a gift for my daughter.

A: Have you got an idea?

G: I'm afraid not.

A: Can I give you some advice?

G: Of course!

A: Why not give her a gift with Chinese feature?

G: Surely that's a good idea. What are they?

A: Things such as a pearl necklace, a silk blouse, a paper fan or the traditional Chinese paintings.

G: I think I'd better give her a pearl necklace. Is that OK?

A: Certainly. Girls always like beautiful jewelry, especially given by their mothers.

R: But I have never bought pearls before. Could you give me some suggestions on how to select the pearl necklace?

A: No problem, natural pearls are of higher value and cultured pearls can be made into more colors and designs and they have equal luster.

R: In my mind cultured pearls are more beautiful. What about the price?

A: The label price is RMB 4200.

G: It's a little high.

A: If you really want, you can get a discount of 20 percent. It's RMB 3360.

G: Are they real pearls?

A: Of course. Everything sold here is real. In this business, our Arcade has good reputation.

G: I'll take it.

A: So I'll wrap it for you with a beautiful ribbon.

G: Thank you very much.

A: My pleasure.

Conversation 2   About Chinese Arts and Crafts

(*A: Assistant   G: Guest*)

A: Good morning, Sir. What can I do for you?

G: Oh, yes. I want to select some presents for my friends.

A: What would you like? We have various traditional Chinese arts and crafts.

G: I have no idea about them. Could you give me some suggestion?

A: Surely, these are Chinese figure paintings. They are made with ink brushes, ink sticks, rice paper and ink slabs, which are called the Four Treasures of Study.

G: Excellent. Are they expensive?

A: The prices are from several hundred RMB to several thousand RMB.

G: What is the vase made of?

A: It is made of the traditional enamel ware cloisonné and the typical color is blue. But now we have all kinds of colors.

G: What about this tea set?

A: It is made by Jingdezhen, Jiangxi, which is the Porcelain Capital of China. From Tang Dynasty, the famous ware is tri-chromatic glazed ware.

G: On the tea sets, I can see so many beautiful pictures.

A: Not only tea sets, but also coffee sets and table wares are made by them. Celadon is more famous than white ware. Which one do you like?

G: So I choose a vase and a tea set.

A: OK. I will give them to you at a reasonable price.

C: Thank you.

Key Words & Expressions

arcade	[a:'keid]	*n.* 商场	jewelry	['dʒu:əlri]	*n.* 珠宝,珠宝类
cloisonné	[klwa:'zɔnei]	*n.* 景泰蓝	luster	['lʌstə]	*n.* 光泽
craft	[kra:ft]	*n.* 工艺	porcelain	['pɔ:səlin]	*n.* 瓷器
emerald	['emərəld]	*n.* 翡翠	ribbon	['ribən]	*n.* 缎带
enamel	[i'næml]	*n.* 瓷釉	reputation	[repju'teiʃn]	*n.* 声望
feature	['fitʃə(r)]	*n.* 特点	sapphire	['sæfaiə(r)]	*n.* 蓝宝石
Four Treasure of Study		文房四宝	traditional	[trə'diʃənəl]	*adj.* 传统的
hand-embroidered		手工刺绣	sandal fan		檀香扇
ink slab		砚			

Additional Useful Expressions

1. Complimenting

a. It looks good on you.

b. It suits you.

c. It makes you look thin.

d. It goes well with your shirt.

e. It matches your dress.

2. Recommending

a. Why not buy something with Chinese features?

b. This ring is very fashionable this season.

c. The price is reasonable and the style is new.

d. How about jewelry? Women always like them.

e. The price is a little high, but the clothes are very comfortable.

 *Classroom Activities*

 __ *Listening Practice* __

I. Listen to the recording and complete the following conversation.

(*A: Assistant   C: Customer*)

A: Welcome to Robinson's Shoes. We're _____.

C: That's great. I need some dress shoes. What do you have on sale?

A: Well, we have Silver Queens and Cool Holidays.

C: _____?

A: Well, Silver Queens are _____ Whereas, Cool Holidays are not as expensive and they're more comfortable.

C: _____?

A: With tax, the Silver Queens come to $47.00 and the Cool Holidays come to $39.00.

C: So that's about an $8.00 difference.

A: That's right.

C: I'll take the Cool Holidays.

A: _____?

C: I'll put it on my credit card.

A: All right, _____. Have a nice day.

C: Thanks.

A: My pleasure.

II. Listen to the recording again and answer the following questions.

1. What shoes are on sale?

2. Does the customer need dress shoes?

3. What does the assistant recommend?

4. Which shoes are more fashionable and with higher quality?

5. Which shoes are not as expensive and more comfortable?

6. Is there any difference in price between these two brands?

7. How much is the difference?

8. How would the customer like to pay?

 **_Communicative Practice_**

Role Play

Work in pairs or groups and create conversations according to the given situations.

Situation 1: At the Toy Counter

Mr. White is going to buy a birthday gift for his 5 years daughter Rose. Now he is at the toy counter. The shop assistant recommends A Barbie Doll to him. Mr. White has to accept it.

Situation 2: Changing porcelain

Mr. and Mrs. Green bought a tea set from the porcelain counter yesterday. They would like to give it to their friend. But today they learned that their friend liked other color, so they come back to change it. A different assistant receives the couple, solves their problem and make them satisfied.

Situation 3: Making complaints

Mr. Lee bought a pair of pearl earrings for his wife from the jewelry counter last evening. He found the pearls have different luster under the sunshine. He thought that the assistant didn't explain clearly to him. Now he makes complaints with the assistant. The assistant and manager ask the customer what happened, say "sorry", and find a best way to cope with the complaints.

*Reading*

Pre-reading questions

1. Where does a shop assistant work?

2. What does a shop assistant do, when he or she is on duty?

3. Do you want to be a shop assistant? And why?

Main Duties of Shop Assistants

As a shop assistant, the main purpose of his job is getting along well with other shop assistants, for the day to day service operation of a shop. He must retail a wide range of confectionery, newspapers, stationery, greeting cards and general goods in accordance with shopping center's policy and under the direction of the shop supervisor. The postholder will assist in ensuring that high standards of customer service are maintained.

Main Duties

1. Maintain a high standard of personal presentation and hygiene and wearing of staff uniform provided while on duty.

2. Be aware of security issues concerning stock and cash that may be targeted through shoplifting and theft and report any incidents to the shop supervisor.

3. Accepts and checks deliveries and stores appropriately and ensures the security of all stock.

4. Reports any stock delivery shortage immediately to the shop supervisor.

5. Prices stock under the direction of the shop supervisor.

6. Organizes and assists in stocking up of the shop throughout the day.

7. Ensures that stock is put away in rotation and also sold in rotation to minimize wastage through out of date stock.

8. Monitors stock levels of regular weekly ordered items.

9. Monitors all products in the shop and informs the shop supervisor of any items which are out, or going out of stock.

10. Operates a cash register and provide counter services, as necessary to ensure effective customer service.

11. Assist customers and deal with queries, problems, complaints, etc..

Supplementary Duties

1. Assists in the termly stock take, e.g. counting, listing stock.

2. Attend any relevant training courses as directed by the shop.

3. Ensures that shop areas are kept in a general state of cleanliness and that Health and Safety policies are enforced.

Notes to the text

1. retail   零售

2. confectionery   糕点, 糖果

3. termly   定期的

4. hygiene   卫生

5. in accordance with   依据，按照

6. be aware of   意识到

7. shoplift   入店行窃

8. prices stock   为商品标价

9. in rotation   按照次序

10. shop supervisor   店铺主管

11. cash register   收银机

12. deal with   处理

13. Health and Safety   健康与安全

14. He must retail a wide range of confectionery, newspapers, stationery, greeting cards and general goods in accordance with shopping center's policy.   他必须按照购物中心的规定出售糖果、报纸、文具、贺卡等种类繁多的普通商品。

15. The postholder will assist in ensuring that high standards of customer service are maintained.   领导在确保为顾客提供高水平的服务方面给予帮助。

16. Be aware of security issues concerning stock and cash that may be targeted through shoplifting and theft and report any incidents to the shop supervisor.   要意识到货物与现金的安全问题，它们可能成为入店盗窃的目标；要将一切问题汇报给店铺主管。

17. Ensures that stock is put away in rotation and also sold in rotation to minimize wastage through out of date stock.   要确保商品摆放有序，出售有序，把因商品过期造成的浪费降低到最小。

18. Monitors stock levels of regular weekly ordered items.   要检查每周常规订购的商品的库存量。

Follow-up questions

1. The following items are the duties of a shop assistant. Please judge them *True or False* according to the text above.

   (   ) A. A shop assistant ought to remain a high standard of personal presentation and wear staff uniform provided on duty.

   (   ) B. A shop assistant should be aware of security issues concerning stock and cash and needn't report any incidents to the shop supervisor.

   (   ) C. A shop assistant should accept and check deliveries and stores appropriately and ensures the security of all stock.

   (   ) D. A shop assistant needn't report any stock delivery shortage immediately to the shop supervisor.

   (   ) E. Pricing stock is the work of the shop supervisor.

   (   ) F. Shop supervisor should organize and assist in stocking up of the shop throughout the day.

(　　) G. A shop assistant should ensure that stock is put away in rotation and also sold in rotation to minimize wastage through out of date stock.

(　　) H. A shop assistant should monitor all products in the shop and informs the shop supervisor of any items which are out, or going out of stock.

(　　) I. The shop supervisor operates a cash register and provide counter services, as necessary to ensure effective customer service.

(　　) J. The shop supervisor should attend any relevant training courses as directed by the shop.

2. What's the job of the shop supervisor?

3. What' the job of the postholder?

 *Exercises*

__Words exercises__

I. Test your vocabulary of products in shopping arcade. Match the words in the left column with the proper Chinese equivalents in the right column.

1. calligraphy	a. 药房	
2. embroidery	b. 消费者	
3. tableware	c. 瓷器	
4. knitwear	d. 退款	
5. garment	e. 工艺品	
6. pharmacy	f. 书法	
7. consumer	g. 刺绣	
8. porcelain	h. 餐具	
9. refund	i. 针织品	
10. arts crafts	j. 服装	

II. Choose the best answer.

1. When your clothes are too _____, you need to go on a diet.

　　a. loose　　　　　b. cheap　　　　　c. tight　　　　　d. expensive

2. It's so cold today. A wool coat will make you _____.

　　a. colder　　　　b. warmer　　　　c. cooler　　　　d. hotter

3. A _____ friend is a friend who doesn't break their promises.

　　a. reliable　　　　b. powerful　　　　c. important　　　　d. strong

4. This is the latest style, which make you _____.

　　a. cozy　　　　　b. popular　　　　c. comfortable　　　d. fashionable

5. Fashion shoes are beautiful but not _____.

   a. roomy　　　　b. comfortable　　c. tight　　　　d. high

6. The precious gift needn't be the _____ things.

   a. expensive　　　b. cheap　　　　c. beautiful　　d. important

7. If a building has a lot of space, we say it is _____.

   a. high　　　　　b. low　　　　　c. roomy　　　　d. narrow

8. A _____ product is one that lasts for a long time.

   a. durable　　　　b. cozy　　　　　c. compact　　　d. precious

9. Chinese porcelain is also called _____.

   a. vase　　　　　b. bowl　　　　　c. tea set　　　d. china

10. If the customer doesn't want the goods he bought, he may require _____.

   a. change　　　　b. refund　　　　c. charge　　　d. complaint

___ Grammar exercises ___

Rewrite the following sentences with *more…than…and not as…as…*, according to the examples.

Example: This pair of shoes is fashionable.

     That pair is more fashionable than this pair.

     That pair is not as fashionable as this one.

1. The fur coat is so expensive.

   _____

   _____

2. This pearl's luster is unique.

   _____

   _____

3. The dress shoes are comfortable.

   _____

   _____

4. The red dress is beautiful on you.

   _____

   _____

5. The products of this brand are reliable.

   _____

   _____

6. The man is an important person in the company.

   _____

   _____

7. The pictures on the tea pot are wonderful.

_____

_____

8. The silk blouse is so colorful.

_____

_____

___ *Translation* ___

Translate the following sentences into Chinese.

1. Would you like us to <u>customize</u>（定制）that pair of earrings?
2. How bright the <u>sapphire</u>（蓝宝石）is!
3. I recommend you this pearl necklace.
4. This <u>emerald</u>（翡翠）is genuine.
5. This <u>sandal fan</u>（檀香扇）is of traditional Chinese design.
6. This table cloth is <u>hand-embroidered</u>（手工刺绣）with a tiger design.
7. Do you like these key rings with Chinese character?
8. I can tell you how to recognize glassware from the <u>jade articles</u>（玉器）.
9. Chinese <u>Four Treasure of Study</u>（文房四宝）are ink brushes, ink sticks, rice paper and ink slabs.
10. The famous ware is <u>tri-chromatic glazed ware of Tang Dynasty</u>（唐三彩）.

Learning Tips

What Is a Shop Assistant Going to Do

The shop assistants' main task is to determine the needs of the customer and show them the range of products available. They must be objective and advise the customer on size, color and price. Shop assistants must have a thorough knowledge of the articles they sell. They must be willing to work on Saturdays and sometimes Sundays. The shop assistants are sometimes exposed to demanding customers and must be able to handle them in a tactful way.

Unit 15

Recreation and Fitness

Learning Objectives

After this unit, you will be able to:

➤ be familiar with the services in clubs
➤ be familiar with the services in night bars
➤ introduce sports apparatuses in the gym
➤ introduce other sports in fitness center

Warming Up

I. Look at the pictures below and identify each one. Use the words from the list.

bar bell	dumb bell	chest expanders	Taiji	Yoga
rock and roll	spring-grips	race apparatus	Pilates	

1_____

2_____

3_____

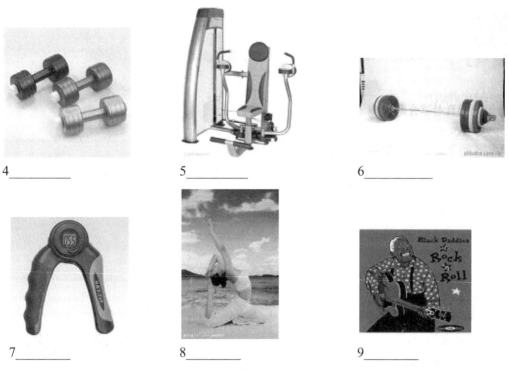

4_____

5_____

6_____

7_____

8_____

9_____

II. Working in a recreation and fitness center, a waiter or waitress has to have a good command of basic names about services. Now have a brainstorming to collect as many words or phrases as possible according to the following classification.

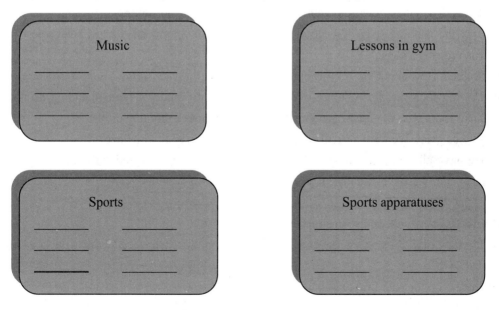

Music

_____ _____

_____ _____

_____ _____

Lessons in gym

_____ _____

_____ _____

_____ _____

Sports

_____ _____

_____ _____

_____ _____

Sports apparatuses

_____ _____

_____ _____

_____ _____

Situational Conversations

Pre-questions

Suppose you are a clerk working in the night club.

1. When guests come into your night club, what do you often do?

2. In your mind, what's the difference between karaoke hall and KTV rooms?

3. Do you know how much is it to sing a song in the common Karaoke hall?

4. Do you know what kind of songs can KTV rooms offer?

5. What kind of drinks does the night club provide to its guests?

Conversation 1   At Night Club

(*W: Waiter   G: Guest*)

W: Good evening, Madam and Sir. Welcome to our night club.

G: Good evening. We'd like to relax completely.

W: Here is your ideal place. We have karaoke hall and KTV rooms. Which one do you prefer?

G: It is the first time that we come here. Could you give us some advice?

W: Surely. The karaoke hall is equipped with super stereo and lightning systems. In a fashion style the dancing stage is decorated. Many Fashion Shows have been held here. It's 15 Yuan to sing a song.

G: Not bad. How about the KTV room?

W: The big room accommodating over 8 persons is 80 Yuan per hour including drinks, the small room with or under 8 persons is 50 Yuan per hour excluding drinks.

G: Sounds great. We want a small room. What kind of songs do you have?

W: We have all kinds including folk songs, pop songs, and rock and roll and so on. As for language, we have Mandarin songs, Cantonese songs, South Korean songs and English songs. You just name it.

G: OK. But how will we use this machine?

W: It's very easy. First, select the codes of the songs you choose; second, press the key "input", that's OK.

G: Thank you for your introduction.

Conversation 2   At Training Center

(C: Clerk   G: Guest)

A: Good evening, Sir. Can I help you?

G: Oh, yes. I want to do some exercises. Would you introduce your facilities to me?

A: Of course. We have a well-equipped gymnasium with the latest recreational sports apparatus. You can see that we have race apparatus, rowing machines, stationary bikes, muscle builder sets, chest expanders and spring-grips and so on.

G: Great! Are they safe?

A: No Problem. They are all made by the famous sports apparatus company.

G: Excellent. I wonder how to use these machines.

A: Our coach will tell you, moreover he will supervise all the activities.

G: Are there any other exercises?

A: Yes, We have Yoga lessons and Taiji lessons from 7 p.m. to 9 p.m. every evening.

G: Do you have any other sports rooms?

A: Well, we have a ping-pang room on the third floor and a bowling center and a game center on the fourth floor.

G: Is there a swimming pool?

A: The swimming pool is on the second floor under ground. It is 50 meters long and 2 meters deep, with security men on the bank.

G: Very good. Thank you, I will go to swim there.

Key Words & Expressions

apparatus	[ˌæpə'reitəs]	*n.* 设备	equip	[i'kwip]	*v.* 装备
exclude	[ik'sklu:d]	*v.* 除外	folk	[fəuk]	*a.* 民间的
gymnasium	[dʒim'neiziəm]	*n.* 健身房	karaoke	[ˌkæri'əuki]	*n.* 卡拉 OK
Mandarin	['mændərin]	*n.* 普通话	Yoga	['jəugə]	*n.* 瑜伽
bar bell		杠铃	race apparatus		跑步机
Cantonese song		粤语歌	rock and roll		摇滚乐
chest expanders		扩胸器	rowing machines		划式练力器
dumb bell		哑铃	stationary bikes		固定脚踏车

Additional Useful Expressions

1. Working in the recreation center

    a. This is the best place to relax.

    b. You can choose karaoke hall or KTV room to sing.

c. The karaoke hall is equipped with super stereo and lightning systems.

d. The big room is 100 Yuan per hour including drinks.

e. First, select the codes of the songs you choose and then press the key *input*.

2. Working in the fitness center

a. Let me show you around.

b. Our gymnasium is well- equipped with the latest recreational sports apparatus.

c. Our coach will tell you how to use the sports apparatuses.

d. We have Yoga lessons and Taiji lessons from 6 p.m. to 7 p.m..

e. We have a ping-pang all room and badminton room.

Classroom Activities

__ Listening Practice __

I. Listen to the recording and complete the following conversation.

(*C: Clerk   G: Guest*)

C: Good evening, 1._____ can I do for you?

G: My doctor advised me to keep in good physical condition. Could you tell me 2._____
   you have here?

C: Well, we have a well-equipped gym with all the latest 3._____, and we also have
   several sports courts to play tennis, badminton and ping-pang.

G: That's very good.

C: There is a 4._____ in our club. You can have a try.

G: Really? That's sound interesting. Is here a swimming pool?

C: Yes, of course. Our swimming pool is excellent.

G: Why do you say it's excellent?

C: First, it's big enough. It's 5._____, 20 meters wide and 2.5 meters deep.

G: And then?

C: Second, It's a 6._____ The water can keep a comfortable temperature all year round.
   You can swim in any season.

G: Anymore?

C: At last, you can relax with beer, juice and coffee 7._____.

G: Oh, it seems that I must spend some money here tonight.

C: 8._____ is very reasonable, I promise.

G: OK. Thank you for your information.

C: My pleasure, Sir. Have a nice time.

II. Listen to the recording again and answer the questions.

1. Why does the guest go to the health club?

2. How is the gym according to the clerk?

3. What sports can guests play in the sports courts?

4. Is there a sauna? How does the clerk describe it?

5. How big is the swimming pool?

6. Why can the swimming pool keep a comfortable temperature?

7. What other activities can the guests do beside the swimming pool?

8. Do you think the guest will relax in the club? How do you know?

9. Is the charge low or high in this club?

 ___ *Communicative Practice* ___

Role Play

Work in pairs or groups and create conversations according to the given situations.

Situation 1: At the Fitness Center

Mr. Black wants to relax after a busy day. The clerk in the fitness center is introducing the facilities to Mr. Black. At last, Mr. Black chooses swimming as the recreation manner.

Situation 2: At the ball room

Linda and her friends go to the ball room to have a dance. The waiter brings them to a table. Linda and her friends enjoy themselves very much. She pays the bill with 200 Yuan for the drinks and 100 Yuan for the fruit, plus 10% service charge.

Situation 3: At the KTV Room

Mr. and Mrs. Green invite some friends come to a karaoke hall to sing. The waitress receives the couple. She advices them to sing at a KTV room and shows them how to use the machine. Mr. and Mrs. Green accept his advice and order some drinks and fruit. After paying the bill, they give the waitress 50 Yuan as tip.

*Reading*

Pre-reading questions

1. Where can the guest in a hotel do the exercise?

2. What is the duty of the fitness worker?

3. How does the fitness worker help the guests do practice?

Job of the Fitness Worker

Fitness workers lead, instruct, and motivate individuals or groups in exercise, activities, including cardiovascular exercise, strength training, and stretching. They work in health clubs, country clubs, hospitals, universities, resorts and clients' homes. Increasingly, fitness workers also are found in workplaces, where they organize and direct health and fitness programs for employees of all ages. Although gyms and health clubs offer a variety of exercise activities such as weightlifting, yoga, cardiovascular training, and karate, fitness workers typically specialize in only a few areas.

Personal trainers work one-on-one with clients either in a gym or in the client's home. They help clients assess their level of physical fitness and set and reach fitness goals. Trainers also demonstrate various exercises and help clients improve their exercise techniques. They may keep records of their clients' exercise sessions to monitor clients' progress toward physical fitness. They may also advise their clients on how to modify their lifestyle outside of the gym to improve their fitness.

Group exercise instructors conduct group exercise sessions that usually include aerobic exercise, stretching, and muscle conditioning. Cardiovascular conditioning classes are often set to music. Two increasingly popular conditioning methods taught in exercise classes are Pilates and yoga. In these classes, instructors demonstrate the different moves and positions of the particular method; they also observe students and correct those who are doing the exercises improperly. Group exercise instructors are responsible for ensuring that their classes are motivating, safe, and challenging, yet not too difficult for the participants.

Fitness directors oversee the fitness-related aspects of a health club or fitness center. They create and oversee programs that meet the needs of the club's members. They also select fitness equipment, coordinate personal training and group exercise programs, hire, train, and supervise fitness staff and carry out administrative duties.

Fitness workers in smaller facilities with few employees may perform a variety of functions in addition to their fitness duties, such as tending the front desk, signing up new members, giving tours of the fitness center, writing newsletter articles, creating posters and flyers, and supervising the weight training and cardiovascular equipment areas. In larger commercial facilities, personal trainers are often required to sell their services to members and to make a specified number of sales. Some fitness workers may combine the duties of group exercise instructors and personal trainers, and in smaller facilities, the fitness director may teach classes and do personal training.

Notes to the text

1. weightlifting 举重

2. karate　空手道

3. modify　修正，改正

4. aerobic exercise　有氧运动

5. cardiovascular exercise　心肺训练

6. Pilates　普拉提课程

7. newsletter　新闻通讯

8. posters and flyers　海报和传单

9. Fitness workers lead, instruct, and motivate individuals or groups in exercise, activities　健身工作者带领，指导并激发个人和团体锻炼、活动

10. they organize and direct health and fitness programs for employees of all ages　他们为不同年龄的员工安排和指导健身项目

11. Cardiovascular conditioning classes are often set to music　心肺训练课通常伴随音乐进行

12. Group exercise instructors are responsible for ensuring that their classes are motivating, safe, and challenging　团体训练指导要确保他们的课程有活力，安全，有挑战性

13. supervising the weight training and cardiovascular equipment areas　监管荷重训练区和心肺训练器材区

14. personal trainers are often required to sell their services to members and to make a specified number of sales　私人教练要给会员提供有偿服务，同时要完成指定销售量

Follow-up questions

1. The following items are the duties of a waiter or waitress. Please find out the right procedure according to the text above.

(　　) A. Fitness workers lead, instruct, and motivate individuals and groups in exercise.

(　　) B. Fitness workers work in health clubs, country clubs, hospitals, universities and resorts but not in clients' homes.

(　　) C. Fitness workers typically specialize in several areas, such as weightlifting, yoga, cardiovascular training, and karate.

(　　) D. The trainers help clients assess their level of physical fitness and set and reach fitness goals.

(　　) E. Fitness workers require their clients to modify their lifestyle outside of the gym to improve their fitness.

(　　) F. Group exercise sessions usually include aerobic exercise, stretching, and muscle conditioning.

(　　) G. Two increasingly popular conditioning methods taught in exercise classes are Karate and yoga.

(　　) H. Fitness directors select fitness equipment, coordinate personal training and group exercise programs.

(   ) I. Fitness workers in smaller facilities with few employees may perform a variety of functions.

(   ) J. In larger commercial facilities, personal trainers are only required to sell their services to members.

Right order: 1._____   2._____   3._____   4._____   5._____

             6._____   7._____   8._____   9._____   10._____

2. What do the personal trainers do except selling their services to members in larger commercial facilities?

3. What do fitness workers in smaller facilities do in addition to their fitness duties?

 *Exercises*

__Words exercises__

I. Test your vocabulary of recreation and fitness. Match the words in the left column with the proper Chinese equivalents in the right column.

A	B
1. sauna proper	a. 美容厅
2. ball hall	b. 微型高尔夫
3. beauty salon	c. 康乐服务生
4. body building	d. 桑拿浴室
5. indoor tennis	e. 调音师
6. recreation attendant	f. 有氧操
7. aerobic	g. 室内网球场
8. bowling center	h. 保龄球馆
9. mini golf	i. 舞厅
10. D.J.	j. 健身

II. Choose the best answer.

Fill in the blanks with the proper words given below, changing the form where necessary.

apparatuses	items	trainer	consumption	ball
song	minimum	computer	highlight	partner

1. You can go to the disco with your _____.

2. The _____ of the party is the dance of jazz performed by a group of young boys.

3. The _____ charge at the Karaoke bar is 200 Yuan, including drinks.

4. You may consult the song book for the _____ you want.

5. Guests may use the _____ to order the songs they like.

6. The minimum _____ here is 100 Yuan, excluding drinks.

7. If you need a _____, please write down your name and room number on the form.

8. We prepare all kinds of sports _____ for our guests.

9. Our hotel is equipped with the latest recreational sports _____.

10. The concert will be opened at the _____ room.

___ Grammar exercises ___

Rewrite the following sentences with *What and How,* without changing their meanings.

Example: The swimming pool is so comfortable.

　　　　What a comfortable swimming pool it is!

　　　　How comfortable it is!

1. All the sports apparatuses are so useful.

   _____

2. The dancing stage is so fashionable.

   _____

3. The music is so nice.

   _____

4. The Yuga lessons are so wonderful.

   _____

5. Pilates are very excellent.

   _____

6. The girl is a perfect dancer.

   _____

7. Ice cream is very delicious.

   _____

8. They are really great singers.

   _____

___ Translation ___

Translate the following sentences into Chinese.

1. The karaoke hall is equipped with super stereo and lightning systems.

2. The room for more than 6 persons is 100 Yuan per hour including drinks.

3. As for language, we have Mandarin songs, Cantonese songs, South Korean songs and English songs.

4. We have a well- equipped gymnasium with the latest recreational sports apparatus.

5. The coach will tell you how to use sports apparatus.

6. The swimming pool is on the second floor under ground. It's 25 meters long and 2 meters deep, with security men on the bank.

7. We have a bowling center and a game center on the fourth floor.

8. We have Yoga lessons Qigong lessons and Taiji lessons from 6 p.m. to 7 p.m. every afternoon.

9. We have folk songs, pop songs, rock and roll, and so on.

10. The charge is very reasonable, I promise.

Tips for Keeping Fit

Here are some tips to keep fit to enjoy a longer life: Take a walk of 10 to 30 minutes every day. Sleep for 7 hours. Make time to practice meditation, yoga and prayer or contemplation. These provide us with daily fuel for our busy lives. Eat more food that grow on trees and plants and eat less food that is manufactured. Drink plenty of water. Don't waste your precious energy on gossip. Eat breakfast like a king, lunch like a prince and dinner like a beggar. Smile and laugh more.

Unit 16

Meeting Service

 Learning Objectives

After this unit, you will be able to:
> introduce the meeting facilities
> introduce the meeting service
> arrange a conference
> arrange catering for a conference

 *Warming Up*

I. Look at the pictures below and identify each one. Use the words from the list.

projector	recording pen	digital camcorder	Slide	Microphone
function hall	flip chart	whiteboard	hi-fi AV	

1_____

2_____

3_____

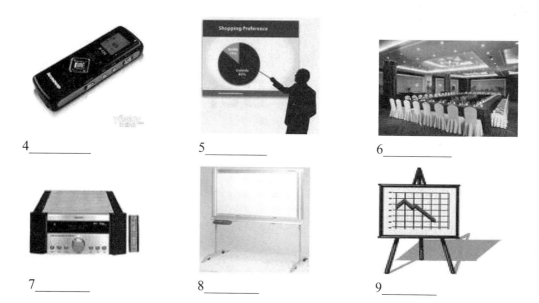

4 _____   5 _____   6 _____

7 _____   8 _____   9 _____

II. Working as a clerk at the meeting center has to have a good command of basic names about meeting facilities and services. Now have a brainstorming to collect as many words or phrases as possible according to the following classification.

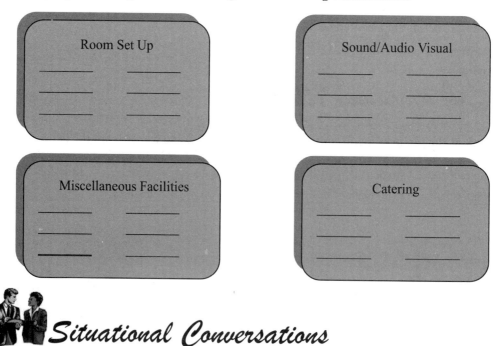

Room Set Up

Sound/Audio Visual

Miscellaneous Facilities

Catering

Situational Conversations

Pre-questions

Suppose you are a clerk at the Meeting Service in a hotel.

1. When customers book the conference hall, what do you usually do?

2. What kind of message would you offer to the guest who arranges to have a conference?

3. What kind of facilities do you think are necessary to the video-conference?

Conversation 1   Arranging a Conference

(*P: Conference planer   M: Manager of the Meeting Service*)

P: Good afternoon, Sir.

M: Good afternoon. Welcome to our hotel. Can I help you?

P: Our firm is going to hold a video-conference next month. Would you please give me an introduction about your conference facilities?

M: OK. Our hotel is one of the best convention hotels in the city. We have 20 meeting rooms with the most modern equipment, video-conference and simultaneous translation system. So what size of conference will you have?

P: There will be 300 guests attending the convention. And the conference lasts 4 days from 20th to 23rd in August.

M: I see. What kind of facilities would you need?

P: We need a large conference hall with video-conference facilities and eight smaller meeting rooms. How much are they?

M: 2000 Yuan for the large conference hall and 300 Yuan for each smaller room per day.

P: Great. Besides that, we also want to reserve one suite for our office and 150 double rooms for the guests to the convention. Could you give me the rate, please.

M: 650 Yuan per night for a standard suite and 350 Yuan for a double room.

P: Now shall we talk about the meals? We want to host the guests buffet every day.

M: Could you give me more details about your requirements for the breakfast and buffet, such as the meal time?

P: I think the breakfast's time is 7:00 a.m. and buffet is 12:00 at noon and 6:30 p.m.. Can I know the terms?

M: Yes. The cost for the breakfast is 30 Yuan per person and 120 Yuan each for the buffet. Would you like tea and some snacks to be served in the meeting rooms?

P: That seems fine. You're so considerate. And I don't think there's anything else.

M: OK. We're looking forward to your guests.

Conversation 2   Booking Meeting Facilities

(*C: Clerk   G: Guest*)

C: Good afternoon. Can I help you?

G: Good afternoon. Because we're going to hold a meeting on next Sunday, I want to book some facilities and personnel for it.

C: Next Sunday…it is November 15th, isn't it?

G: Yes. We need a conference hall for 200 people and six smaller rooms for discussion.

C: I see. We have some multi-function halls that can accommodate from 100 to 400 guests at the meeting and for buffet and cock-tail parties. And we also have several smaller meeting rooms which can seat about 50 people.

Grand Ballroom

G: Great. What basic equipment do you offer?

C: The basic equipment includes such as recorders, microphones, loudspeakers.

G: That's great.

C: By next Wednesday everything will be ready. And you can come and check it then.

G: OK. Thanks.

Key Words & Expressions

accommodate	[əˈkɔmədeit]	*n.*	容纳
attend	[əˈtend]	*v.*	出席
conference	[ˈkɔnfərəns]	*n.*	会议
considerate	[kənˈsidərit]	*adj.*	考虑周到的
equipment	[iˈkwipmənt]	*n.*	设备
loudspeaker	[ˌlaudˈspi:kə(r)]	*n.*	扩音器
messenger	[ˈmesindʒə(r)]	*n.*	勤务员
personnel	[ˌpə:səˈnel]	*n.*	人员
slide	[slaid]	*n.*	幻灯片
simultaneous translation system			同声传译

Additional Useful Expressions

1. Asking the client what he/she needs

a. What size of conference do you have in mind?

b. What kind of facilities would you need?

c. What time should we expect you, Sir?

d. Could you give me more details about your requirements for the conference?

2. Asking about the meeting facilities and expressing the requirements

a. We're going to have/hold a three-day conference next week.

b. I'd like to book some facilities and personnel for it.

c. We need a simultaneous interpreter for the meeting.

d. We'll finalize the numbers by next week.

e. What's the capacity of the hall?

f. Do you have closed circuit TV?

g. I'd like to get some information on the prices for hiring personnel and renting equipment for our convention.

3. Introducing the conference facilities

a. Our conference hall is multi-purpose.

b. It can be used as several smaller rooms divided up by soundproof folding partitions.

c. The conference can comfortably seat/accommodate 100 guests.

d. We're fully equipped with modern facilities such as overhead projector, slides and hi-fi AV.

e. We have a multi-function hall that can accommodate one hundred people at meeting and for holding buffet or cock-tail parties.

f. Here are the convention brochures showing the details about meeting facilities.

g. The drop curtains and side curtain are electronically operated. Press the red button and the curtain is raised.

h. A roving microphone will come in handy.

i. Each participant is provided with a cordless headset receiver.

j. We have some brand new equipment which costs around 20 Yuan an hour.

4. Catering for a meeting

a. Could you give me more details about your buffet parties, such as the number of guests and the exact time?

b. The cost for the breakfast is 60 Yuan per person and 168 each for the buffet.

c. Do you want to have the buffet lunch on Friday?

d. Would you like tea to be served in the meeting rooms?

e. Every dinner will start at 6:30 p.m.. Will that do?

f. How would you like your banquet to be served?

Classroom Activities

_ Listening Practice _

I. Listen to the recording and complete the following conversation.

Conveniently located in the 1._____ of midtown New York City, the Roosevelt Hotel gives you the unique opportunity to plan an intimate meeting to a stunning gala by 2._____ a vast choice of meeting rooms.

Meeting:

Wayport High Speed Internet access is available in all 3._____ square feet of our function and 4._____, as well as in all of our 5._____ guest rooms. Also, WiFi 6._____ access is available in all common areas of the hotel.

In addition, the flexibility of 7._____ well-appointed breakout rooms complete with direct phone lines and PC compatibility, our on-site audio visual company and outstanding video conferencing abilities, makes the Roosevelt Hotel the ideal location in New York City to hold your next corporate event of 8._____ people.

Accommodation:

Each of our 9._____ luxurious guest rooms, including the 10._____ suites, combine the 11._____ of yesterday with all the 12._____ of today.

Each guest room has new HD 13._____,wireless internet access, dual telephone lines with voice mail, dataport capabilities, individual climate control, 14._____ and hairdryers, and irons and boards to assure that you have all the comforts of home.

For New York City business travelers, each of our guest rooms has15._____, desk lamp with Internet and DC plugs, an ergonomic desk chair and 16._____ Internet access so you're able to be productive away from the office.

The Roosevelt Hotel Presidential Suite boasts a square footage of 17._____ with eight rooms. That includes 18._____ bedrooms, a complete kitchen, formal 19._____, and an expansive wrap-around terrace with a panoramic 20._____.

II. Listen to the recording and answer the questions.

1. What does Robby want to do in the hotel?

2. How many people can be seated in the center?

3. How big is the center stage?

4. How can the audience take part in the discussion?

5. Does Robby hire an interpreter?

6. How much is the multi-function hall?

 **_Communicative Practice _**

Role Play

Work in pairs or groups and create conversations according to the given situations.

Situation 1: Reserving a convention hall

Mr. White wants to reserve a large hall for a convention and 40 guest rooms for the delegates to the convention. The manager of Meeting Service is receiving him.

Situation 2: Arranging catering

Mr. Lee would like to order a reception for 100 guests. He is meeting with the F&B Manager to talk about terms for ordering buffet and reception.

Situation 3: Renting equipment and personnel

Mr. Green comes to a hotel to reserve a convention hall for the conference to be held next month. Now he is talking with the Manager of the Meeting Service about the conference facilities and price about them. (using the given words to help you)

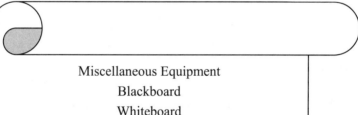

Miscellaneous Equipment
Blackboard
Whiteboard
Flipchart
Banner
poster
Pads/Pens

Sound/Audio Visual
Projector
Slide
Screen
Standing Mike
Roving Mike
Head set
Electronic Pointer
Hi-fi AV

Pre-reading questions

1. What facilities are needed for an audio conference?
2. What facilities are needed for a video conference?
3. What facilities are needed for a web conference?
4. What are the advantages and disadvantages of these three kinds of conference calling service?

How to Choose the Right Conference Call Service

There are several different types of conference calling services available for all types of businesses, whether they are large corporations or small to medium sized businesses.

Audio Conferencing

This conference call service has been available for quite a long time. It is very popular due to its cost effectiveness and allowing communication from all over the world.

All that is required for an audio conference is a telephone for each person attending the conference.

Those in the call are able to hear each other instantly, as if they were all in the same room.

One of the main problems with an audio conference call is not being able to see the other people you are talking to or instantly to share images or information directly related to the business.

Video Conferencing

It's a conference call service that has been available to businesses for around ten years. Due to the cost of equipment, only larger companies used video conferencing.

Recently, due to changes in technology and cheaper equipment, video conferencing is now readily available to smaller businesses.

The equipment needed for a video conference is a camera and television on each end of the conference. This allows all of the participants in the conference call to hear and see each other.

Video conferencing is very effective and is ideal for those wishing to have conferences on a regular basis, although it is quite difficult to set up and trouble shoot the equipment. Regular maintenance by a professional is required to keep video conferencing equipment working correctly.

Web Conferencing

Web conferencing is the newest of the three types of conference calling services. This new technology uses the Internet to hold the conference or meeting.

The real bonus with web conferencing is that those attending can share files, visual aids and text messages instantly.

Web conferencing has all of the benefits of a traditional audio or videoconference meeting. Those attending can still hear and see each other in real time over the Internet, without the need for overly expensive equipment.

The best way to choose a conference call service provider is to shop around and find the package that best suits your needs. For example, if your budget is low and you only require verbal communication to communicate, audio is most probably the best option.

If you require whiteboard sharing and face to face meetings, video is ideal. Web conference calling services are the most expensive of all of the services, but will allow you to share files and communicate on a much higher level with those included in the business conference call.

Notes to the text

1. conference calling services　电话会议服务
2. audio conferencing　音频会议
3. due to its cost effectiveness　由于其成本效益
4. on a regular basis　定期
5. although it is quite difficult to set up and trouble shoot the equipment.　尽管设备的安装与故障的处理有很大难度。
6. The real bonus with web conferencing is that those attending can share files, visual aids and text messages instantly.　网络会议的真正好处就是与会人员可以同时共享文件、视觉辅助材料和文本信息。
7. shop around and find the package that best suits your needs.　（对多家酒店的会务服务）进行比较，选择最符合需要的全套服务。

Follow-up questions

1. The following table is about the three types of conference calling services. Please find out the proper information according to the text above.

Types	Facilities needed	advantage	disadvantage
Audio Conferencing			
Video Conferencing			
Web Conferencing			

2. How can a client choose the conference call service he needs?

Exercises

__Words exercises__

I. Test your vocabulary of Meeting Service. Fill in the blanks with words from the box.

theater Style	U-Shape	screen
over projector	microphones	poster
classroom Style	lectern	banner
wireless microphone	recorders	tier
conference or Boardroom Style		

Conference Room Set up

A Conference room set up should be carefully designed so that the message may reach every body.

1._____: Seats or chairs in rows facing a stage area, head table, or speaker (with no conference table). This is the most efficient set-up when the attendees will act as an audience. This set-up is not recommended for food events or if note taking is required.

2._____: A series of conference tables set in the shape of the letter U, with chairs around the outside. This layout style is often used for meetings where there is a speaker, audio-visual presentation or other focal point.

3._____: Rows of conference tables with chairs facing the front of a room (and usually a speaker), providing writing space for each person. This room set-up is ideal for note taking, meetings requiring multiple handouts or reference materials, or other tools such as laptop computers. This is the most comfortable set-up for long sessions and allows refreshments to be placed within reach of each attendee.

4._____: A rectangular or oval table set up with chairs around all sides and ends. Used for This table layout is often used for Board of Directors meetings, committee meetings, or discussion groups.

Sound/Audio Visual:

Usually on the wall of the Convention Center is 5._____, a flat vertical surface on which pictures or words are shown; and in front of it is 6._____, a machine that projects films or slides onto a screen or wall. In addition, Convention Centers also provide the basic equipment such as 7._____ a machine for recording sound or pictures or both; 8._____ which is used for making your voice louder when you are speaking to an audience. If you want to interact with the audience, you can use 9._____, which is free from cables.

Miscellaneous Equipment

A 10._____ is usually put in the lobby of the hotel, which is a large, usually printed notice, or announcement to advertise or publicize something. In the convention hall, guests can see some 11._____ , a piece of cloth bearing a name, motto or slogan, as of a meeting. The speaker will stand behind a 12._____, which is a stand that serves as a support for the notes or books of a speaker. In some grand convention hall, the center stage can be raised or lowered in 13._____.

II. Choose the best answer.

1. The hotel provides you _____ all conferencing services available for your business or family needs.

   a. with   b. to   c. by   d. at

2. This conference technology with internet enables you to easily and instantly _____ information with your associates.

   a. tell   b. exchange   c. say   d. spread

3. Video and web conferencing services are usually more _____ solutions.

   a. expensive   b. cheap   c. so so   d. accepted

4. We are going to _____ a news press next week.

   a. make   b. show   c. hold   d. rent

5. Would you please come with me to the _____ to arrange the guest rooms for you?

   a. Room Service   b. Landry   c. Recreation Center   d. Front Desk

6. I want to reserve rooms for the guests _____ the meeting.

   a. making   b. coming   c. going   d. attending

7. We need an auditorium that can _____ 100 guests.

   a. accommodate   b. make   c. attend   d. put

8. Could you give me more _____ about your requirements for the meeting?

   a. details   b. news   c. things   d. informations

9. A _____ is designed to hold activities of various kinds, such as performance shows, exhibitions, large and small size business meetings, seminar and press meeting.

   a. multi-function hall   b. convention hall

   c. meeting room   d. auditorium

10. _____ is mainly required for a conference. While a speaker is making a speech, the interpreter interprets the speaker's speech into a specified language, which will be transferred to the other attendees via earphone.

   a. Interpreter   b. Simultaneous interpretation

   c. Translator   d. Software

___Grammar exercises ___

Inquire about meeting service politely *using Would you*

Example: I want to know some information about the conference facilities then.

   Would you please give some information about the conference facilities then?

1. What is the capacity of the hall?

   _____

2. What office support service do you offer?

   _____

3. What's the technical equipment for the hall?

   _____

4. I'd like to know the price for renting equipment for the convention.

   _____

5. Do you have a hall that can seat 500 guests?

   _____

___Translation ___

1. We're going to have a five-day seminar in the middle of next month.
2. We'd like to reserve some facilities and personnel for the training.
3. Due to the cost of equipment, only larger companies used video conferencing.
4. Video conferencing is very effective and is ideal for those wishing to have conferences on a regular basis,
5. The best way to choose a conference call service provider is to shop around and find the package that best suits your needs.
6. We're fully equipped with things like overhead projectors, slides, recorders, soundproof folding partitions and remarkable hi-fi AV.
7. There will be about 100 film makers and actors attending the awarding ceremony.
8. Our conference hall can be used either as one big conference hall or as several smaller rooms divided up by folding partitions.
9. Sign me up for the personnel and the equipment and thanks for you suggestions.
10. Do you have closed circuit TV? How much is it?

Conventional Room Set up

Hollow Square Setup

The participants are seated surrounding a Hollow Square. This is often called a closed "U".

Cluster Setup

In this setup style the participants are seated in groups within the meeting-room. Each group can be designated as a team or can be from a specific department. This setup is used in such cases where the instructor presides group sessions or group problem solving sessions.

Octagon Setup

In this setup style the participants are seated around tables arranged in an octagon. The seating arrangement permits each participant to view others.

Keys to Exercises

Unit 1   Hotel Basics

Warming Up

I. Look at the symbols below and identify each one. Use the words from the list.

1. Restaurant on premises   2. Meeting facilities   3. 24-hour airport shuttle bus

4. Valet parking   5. Indoor swimming pool   6. Satellite or cable TV

7. Exercise facilities available   8. Laundry service   9. 24-hour room service

II. Words for hotel basics

Hotel departments: Front Office, Housekeeping, Food & Beverage, Business Center, Fitness and Recreation, Shopping Arcade, Engineering and Maintenance, Security …

Hotel services: room reservation, reception, bell service, check-in, operation, currency exchange, room service, laundry service, room cleaning, catering service, wake-up call, check-out…

Hotel amenities: swimming pool, wheelchair accessible, business center, wireless internet, restaurant, lounge bar…

What guests needs: (open)

Classroom Activities

Listening practice

I. Listen to the recording and complete the following passage.

1. location   2. leisure   3. attractions   4. shopping

5. Internet access   6. reserve   7. service staff   8. at home

II. Listen to the recording and answer the questions.

1. having his operational and managerial internship

2. 6 months

3. Front Office

4. He'll be a reservation agent, receptionist, bellman, informant, operator and cashier. He'll have the most direct contact with foreign guests.

5. Housekeeping

6. Public Area cleaner

7. try his best to make every customer know better about Chinese cuisine

8. It's a big challenge.

Reading

Follow-up questions

1. "Green" Hotels are environmentally-friendly properties whose managers are eager to institute programs that save water, save energy and reduce solid waste—while saving money—to help PROTECT OUR ONE AND ONLY EARTH!

2. The goal of this association is to reduce the amount of energy and water consumed by the lodging industry. GHA provides hotels around the world with easy access to environmentally friendly products and ideas…

3. b c f h i j

 （注：a. not any, it should be non-toxic

 d. not individual packages, it should be bulk organic soap and amenities

 e. the bins should be recycling

 g. hotels should offer On-site transportation with green vehicles to the guests）

Exercises

Words exercises

I. Test your vocabulary of Restaurant and Food.

| 1. towels | 2. sheets | 3. low-flow | 4. bulk | 5. turn off |

 6. unoccupied 7. recycler baskets 8. recycling bins 9. lower

 10. Minimize 11. glass 12. encourage 13. eco-friendly

 14. leftover 15. replace

II. Choose the best answer.

 1-5 B D C B C   6-10 C A C B D

Grammar exercises

 1. a 2. the 3. a 4. the 5. a. 6. the 7. a. 8. the 9. an 10. a

Translation

1. Glad to be of service. Please feel free to contact us anytime.

2. There is no hurry, Sir. Take your time.

3. That won't be necessary, Sir, but thank you all the same.

4. I'm sorry I cannot guarantee, but I'll do my best.

5. My pleasure, I'm happy everything was to your satisfaction.

6. 很抱歉，我不是很明白。我能让我经理过来吗？

7. 它确实物有所值。

8. 您能说慢些吗？

9. 我们期待能再次服务您。并祝您一路平安。

10. 请替我向您的家人问好。

Unit 2　Room Reservation

Warming Up

I. Look at the pictures below and identify each one. Use the words from the list.

1. standard single room　　2. standard suite　　3. presidential suite

4. lake-view room　　　　5. adjoining room　　6. connecting room

7. banquet hall　　　　　8. meeting room　　　9. game room

II. 略

Classroom Activities

Listening practice

I. Listen to the recording and complete the following conversation.

1. the travel schedule　　2. in whose name　　3. the date　　4. September 15th

5. another party　　　　6. my boss.　　　　7. cancel Mr. White's reservation

8. another chance

II. Listen to the recording and answer the questions.

1. Group Reservation.

2. Five days.

3. Double rooms with twin beds.

4. Yes, they are.

5. Yes, there is a 10 per cent discount.

6. The reservationist wants to know the flight number in case the plane's late?

7. No, she doesn't.

8. They'll have a meeting on the 25th.

9. Yes, it is.

Reading

Follow-up questions

I. His/Her duties are: answering questions, concerning reservations, booking and assigning rooms for guests who request rooms in the hotel. He/She also takes reservations, cancellations and revisions and writes and sends out the hotel's letters of confirmation.

II. Advance reservations can be made by telephone, fax, letter, telegraph and internet, or by the guest in person.

III. (The answer is open).

Exercises

Words exercises

I. Test your vocabulary of hotel types, bed types and hotel facilities.

1. Hostels	2. youth hostels	3. Motels	4. resorts hotels
5. Long boys	6. queen beds	7. rollaway	8. Hide-a-beds
9. the front desk	10. Lobbies	11. Lounges	12. Suites
13. Meeting rooms	14. Game rooms	15. Gift shops	

II. Match the room types and the definitions.

1-5   B IGEC   6 – 10   JFDHA

Grammar exercises

1. will…be staying	2. will…be arriving	3. will be meeting
4. will be leaving.	5. will be paying	6. will…be coming
7. will be bringing	8. will…be seeing	

Translation

1. 这段时间有房间，您需要两个单人房间，对吗？

2. 我们盼望下周二见到您。

3. 你要订房吗？

4. 我需要你的名字和信用卡号码。

5. 请别挂断好吗，我来查一下是否有空房间。

6. 好的先生，我们会为您登记一间有大号床的房间。

7. 您一行有多少人？

8. 单人房每晚 80 美元外加 10% 的税金和 10% 的服务费。

9. 我们酒店为贵公司提供特价。单人房可以打 8.5 折。

10. 很抱歉因为是旺季，那段时间的客房都被订光了。

Unit 3   Bell Service

Warming Up

I. Look at the pictures below and identify each one. Use the words from the list.

1. bellman	2. luggage or baggage	3. elevator	4. parcel
5. bell	6. trolley/luggage cart	7. backpack	8. baggage receipt
9. Reception desk			

II. Words for Bell Service

Special services: bell service, laundry service, a morning call service, food delivery, buying something for a guest, introducing room facilities, asking to clean the room, extra bed…

Room facilities: central heating, bath tub, bedclothes, bedside lamp, bedspread, bench, blanket, carpet, clothes-hanger, cold and hot water taps, curtain, desk. dressing table, pillow, sheet, stool, thermos, towel, toilet paper, wardrobe, TV set, remote control, mini-bar, telephone, wireless internet access....

Delivered items: luggage or baggage, trunk, suitcase, briefcase, newspapers, messages, faxes...

Deposited items: passport, camera, jewellery, luggage, handbag, visa, watch, parcel, briefcase, backpack…

Classroom Activities

Listening practice

I. Listen to the recording and complete the following conversation.

1. Welcome to　　　　2. How many pieces　　　3. two suitcases and one briefcase

4. the Front Desk　　　5. check-in　　　　　6. key card

7. elevator　　　　　　8. Watch your step

II. Listen to the recording and answer the questions.

1. on the reception desk

2. She has something important to do.

3. She is going to the post office to get some stamps for her best friend

4. She is going to leave the luggage at the Porter Section and get it back an hour later.

5. Yes, it is.

6. They can take care of her luggage until she is back.

7. An hour later

8. To put this claim tag on her luggage

9. Storage receipt

10. To get her luggage back an hour later

Reading

Follow-up questions

I. Right order: 1. F　　2. E　　3. C　　4. D　　5. B　　6. A

II. The answer is open, but most complaints may be involved with bellboy, including planking down the guests' baggage, breaking into the guests' room without knocking at, sending the wrong luggage to the guest and asking guests for tip.

III. Say sorry to the guests or apologize sincerely if you do something wrong and listen attentively with concern and don't argue with the guests.

Exercises

Words exercises

I. Test your vocabulary of bell service.

1. bellman	2. porter	3. luggage	4. bell	5. Bellboy
6. bellhop	7. concierge	8. safe box	9. luggage tag	10. items
11. remote control	12. wake up	13. bathroom	14. laundry	15. surf

II. Choose the best answer.

1-5　A DDDB　　　6-10　　BDCBD

Grammar exercises

1. If you like history, you can have a day trip to the castle.

2. If the traffic is good, it will take you about 25 minutes.

3. I can/will get you a 10% discount If you like to have dinner.

4. I'll order a taxi for you if you come to see me tomorrow.

5. If you follow the signs to the museum, you can/will get to the central business district.

6. If we'd like tickets for the water park for tomorrow, we can have 15% off the face value.

7. You will/can learn a lot about our history if the tour guides are very knowledgeable.

8. If you prefer a trip to the countryside, a tour guide will show you the local wildlife.

Translation

1. 能不能派一位门房上来？

2. 这位旅馆服务员会带您去您的房间。

3. 行李员会把大家的行李送到车上。

4. 这是您房间的钥匙，旅馆服务员会把您的行李送上楼。

5. 到时可否派人上来帮我提一下行李？

6. 如果您准备好了，服务员就带您去您的房间。

7. 当 VIP 客人到达酒店时，行李员和门童及时主动为客人开车门，并且面带微笑迎接客人，称呼客人姓名。

8. 您的行李可以寄存在行李部。

9. 团队抵达酒店前行李领班安排行李员和门童准备迎接客人。

10. 您可以拿行李牌去行李部取包。

Unit 4　　Reception

Warming Up

I. Look at the pictures below and identify each one. Use the words from the list.

　1. assistant manager　　2. hotel directory　　3. lost property　　4. key card

　5. passport　　　　　　6. registration form　　7. receptionist　　8. hotel lobby

　9. room service

II. Words for Receptionist

Room type: Single Room, Double Room, King -Size & Queen -Size bed Room, Three
　　　　　　room/Triple room, Business/Commercial/Executive Room, Business/Commercial/

executive suite presidential suite, deluxe suite, standard suite, adjoining room, connecting room…

Hotel services: housekeeping service, business service, checking-in and checking out, Serving dishes, dealing with complaints, health and recreation service, post service, pick-up service,…

Hotel amenities: Banquet facilities, Laundry facilities, Business centre, Lobby, Cocktail bar, Gymnasium, Conference facilities, Currency exchange, dining hall, ladies' room and men's room, Lounge, reception desk, elevator, hotel rooms, massage room, swimming pool. beauty salon…

Hotel type: motel, designated hotel, stated guest house, holiday village, youth hotel, international hotel, joint-venture hotel, lodge, lower-grade hotel, mom-and-pop hotel, starred hotel, State hotel, villa hotel…

Classroom Activities

Listening practice

I. Listen to the recording and complete the following conversation.

| 1. a bath | 2. fortnight | 3. check − in | 4. vacant |
| 5. form | 6. one hundred yuan | 7. a receipt | 8. deluxe suites |

II. Listen to the recording and answer the questions.

1. No, they don't.　2. Everything is so nice.　3. Yes, they did.

4. In cash.　5. It was ￥880.

Reading

Follow-up questions

I. Right order:　1.F　2. E　3. A　4. C　5. B　6. G　7. D　8. H

II. The answer is open, but most complaints may be involved with room services, hotel services or something wrong with the room facilities. For example, a guest wanted a wake-up call, but he/she didn't get one. The staff members are rude or the guests are not happy with the facilities. They also make a complaint about lost articles.

III. The receptionist should listen to them, apologize for the trouble, clarify what the exact problem is and let them know you understand. Tell them what you can do or pass it on to your manager.

Exercises

Words exercises

I. Test your vocabulary of Hotel Reception.

1. checks　2. receptionists　3. Cashiers　4. registration card　5. signature

6. passport　7. destination　8. payment　9. prior reservation

10. obligation   11. occupancy   12. the other hotel

II. Choose the best answer.

1-5   B A B C A   6-10   C A B D D

Grammar exercises

1. where   2. where   3. that /which   4. that/which

5. who   6. who   7. who   8. whom

Translation

1. 请将贵重物品随身携带。

2. 如果您有什么特殊要求请告诉我。

3. 非常感谢您的合作和谅解。

4. 您可以拿行李牌来行李部取包。

5. 我们将比日程安排时间晚半小时到。

6. 请填写您的姓名和详细的地址，然后在这里签名。

7. 我们可以给团体入住打一些折扣。

8. 您是饭店的客人，可以免费使用行李寄存室。

9. 您在我们酒店预订了一套房，现在要延长两天您的住宿，是吗，先生?

10. 这是酒店服务资料册，有我们服务的详细资料。

Unit 5   Switchboard

Warming Up

I. 1. long distance call   2. hotel directory   3. switchboard

   4. operator   5. wake up call   6. message form

   7. information desk   8. leaving a message   9. sign of phone service

II. 略

Classroom Activities

Listening practice

I. Listen to the recording and complete the following conversation.

International HOTEL

Message for Mr. Borkman Wood

Room No.   2122

Caller's name: Grace Wang

Telephone No: 55219181

   She is going to meet him tomorrow evening in the coffee bar at this hotel around 7:30.

II. Listen to the recording and answer the questions.

1. His calls were cut off.　　2. 1208　　　　　　　　3. He rang his boss in London

4. Twice　　　　　　　　5. About thirty seconds.　　6. 0044-020-5556728

7. She is awfully worried for that, and wants to find out the cause of the problems.

8. No, she isn't.

Reading

Follow-up questions

1. The operator should invite the caller to "hold the line" "ring back" or "leave a message".

2. Their duties will include the receiving of all incoming calls, connecting them with the required extension and dealing with outgoing calls. In addition, the switchboard offers the services such as reserving for the room, table, conference, making a morning call, paging a guest, answering service, leaving a message, etc..

3. Because sending a telegram over the telephone cannot be done by the meter.

Exercises

Words exercises

I. Test your vocabulary of telephone service.

　　1. Person-to-person call　　　2. Area code　　　3. A collect call　　4. Pay phone

　　5. Switchboard　　　　　　　6. External call　　7. International Direct Dialing (IDD)

　　8. DDD: Domestic Direct Dial　9. Telephone directory

　　10. Station-to-station call　　　11. international prefix　　　　12. Country code

II. Choose the best answer.

　　1-5　CBCCA　　　　　6 – 10　CABAB

Grammar exercises

　　1. can't　　　2. May　　　3. Shall　　4. Can

　　5. must　　　6. Would　　7. can't　　8. Could

Translation

1. 饭店的电话系统有国际长途直拨功能。

2. 对不起，我不能告诉您客人的房号。这是饭店的规定。

3. 使用国际直拨电话，首先，请拨打酒店的长途电话代码 0，然后拨打国际字冠；其次是国家代码，再拨地区号码，最后拨所要电话号码。

4. 我要从我的房间打个本地电话。

5. 请你别挂机。我可以将电话转到他的房间。

6. 这里是客房预约处，我帮您转接到餐厅预约柜台。

7. 不好意思，这是直拨电话。我们无法为您转接中式餐厅。请您改拨 2234-1156 好吗？

8. 不好意思，您打错电话了。

9. 请放心。我会在明早 8:00 准时叫醒您。

10. 请告诉我您的名字和电话，好吗？

Unit 6   Information Service

Warming Up

I. Look at the pictures below and identify each one. Use the words from the list.

1. sign of Information   2. tourists attractions   3. tour guide

4. taxi   5. tour bus   6. sign of airport

7. brochure   8. direction   9. weather report

II. Words to express weather, direction, temperature and transportation

Weather: sunny, windy, rainy, chilly, cool, hot…

Transportation: bus, car, taxi, subway, train, plane…

Indirection: left, right, west, north, east, south…

Temperature: high, low, average, centigrade, Fahrenheit, maximum…

Classroom Activities

Listening practice

I. Listen to the recording and complete the following conversation.

Conversation 1   Introducing restaurants

1. if you could recommend to me a good local restaurant

2. The restaurant serves very good Roast Duck.

3. I would suggest that you'd better take a taxi there.

4. how much we should pay the taxi-driver for the trip?

Conversation 2   Searching for guests

1. if he is in the hotel?

2. There are a lot of Blacks here today

3. Please wait a moment

4. Step this way

II. Listen to the recording and answer the questions.

1. He wants to call to Beijing, China.

2. 13 hours. But I don't know what time it is in Beijing now. Could you tell me?

3. No, it's not urgent.

4. After 19:00.

5. It's 10:00 p.m. on July 5th in New York.

Reading

Follow-up questions

1. When guests check in: B C E F H

   When guests check out: A D G I J

2. Keep an inventory of room reservations; respond to reservation inquiries; answer telephones and take messages; handle guest mail; Handle guest mail; record guest comments; deal with customer complaints or refer dissatisfied customers to a manager.

3. In large hotels, hotel desk clerks usually specialize in a particular area such as keys, reservations, or information. Hotel desk clerks who work in small hotels are responsible for more general operations. They usually process mail, collect payments, record accounts, handle reservations, operate the telephone switchboard, and do bookkeeping.

Exercises

Words exercises

Choose the best answers for responding.

1-5　ACBCB　　6-10　CBACB

Grammar exercises

1. for　2. since　3. for　4. since　5. for　6. for　7. since　8. for

Translation

1. 请你给我介绍一下交通情况。
2. 酒店的旅行社提供去天津的各种旅游。
3. 您能否帮我推荐一家供应北京烤鸭的当地好饭馆。
4. 怀特先生留言给 1223 房间的李先生。
5. 我在找我的朋友布莱克先生。请问他在酒店吗？
6. 你们想要带空调的巴士吗？
7. 北京和纽约的时差是 13 小时。
8. 出电梯朝左，你会看到它就在走廊尽头。
9. 我试图联系 1223 房间的李先生，但是他出去了。
10. 直向前走，经过大堂，咖啡店就在电梯左侧。

Unit 7　Foreign Exchange and Cashier's

Warming Up

I. Look at the pictures below and identify each one. Use the words from the list.

1. foreign currencies	2. cashier	3. coins
4. bill	5. ATM	6. credit card
7. cheque	8. credit card swiper	9. cash

II. The kinds of foreign currencies, credit cards, cheques and coins.

Foreign currencies: Australian Dollar, Canadian Dollar, British Pound, Euro, Indian Rupee, Japanese Yen…

Credit cards: Visa, MasterCard, Discover, American Express, Diners Club, Sears…

Cheques: certified cheque, payroll cheque, personal cheque, bad cheque, blank cheque, treasurer's check…

Coins: one cent, five cents, one dime, quarter dollar (US Dollar)

one cent, two cents, five cents, ten cents, 50 cents, one Yuan (Chinese Yuan)

Classroom Activities

Listening practice

I. Listen to the recording and complete the following conversation.

1. I'd like to change some money.

2. we have a change limit of 500 dollars

3. Can't you make an exception for me?

4. our cash supply runs out

5. Why do you keep a change limit?

II. Listen to the recording and answer the questions.

1. He lives in room 102.

2. His flight will leave at five thirty.

3. He wants to keep the room this afternoon.

4. He needs to pay half of the rate.

5. He can leave it to the Bell Captain's Desk.

Reading

Follow-up questions

1. Right order: C   A   E   B   D   F

2. Check if the guest has paid a reservation deposit. Check with the guest if he is entitled to any kind of discount or complimentary rate. Remind the guest to return his room key to the reception before he leaves the hotel. If the guest settles his account in traveler's check, make sure that he countersigns the check in front of you.

3. If the guest settles his account in traveler's check, make sure that he countersigns the check in front of you. Do not accept checks that have already been countersigned. Then compare the two signatures carefully. When a traveler's check is suspected to be a counterfeit, one first look at the check closely and see if the portraits and patterns are clearly printed. Then feel the check with your hand. With some traveler's checks, the cashier can look for watermarks by holding the check against the light or look for the special ink color by putting the check under an ultraviolet light.

Exercises

Words exercises

I. Test your vocabulary of cashier's.

1. cash	2. bill	3. change	4. currency	5. coins
6. clerk	7. discount	8. bank card	9. charge	10. checkout

Grammar exercises

1. how I can get to the post office?

2. which kind of currency you want to change?

3. how many coins you want?

4. what your way of payment is, Sir, please?

5. how much you want to change?

6. where the best place for guests to wait is?

7. what your room number is?

8. How much total cost is?

Translation

1. 请问您的名字和房号？

2. 先生，我们恐怕不接受未兑现的货币，您到外汇银行兑换好吗？

3. 这是您的零头和收据。

4. 对不起，先生，这的确是个错误。我们马上把这笔账从你的账单上减去。

5. 我叫个行李员给您搬行李，好吗？

6. 您要用现金支付差额吗？

7. 我们在晚上限制现金兑换额是出于安全原因。

8. 能帮我换些硬币吗？

9. 我们根据今天的兑换率兑换外币。

10. 劳驾，我们今天要离店了。我希望现在就把账结清。

Unit 8　Housekeeping（Ⅰ）

Warming Up

I. Look at the pictures below and identify each one. Use the words from the list.

1. towel	2. lamp	3. pillow	4. bathroom
5. coffeemaker	6. remote	7. bathtub	8. mini-bar	9. safe

II. Words for hotel furnishings

Bedroom Furniture: wardrobe, dressing table, carpet, sofa, tea table, curtain

Electric Appliance: desk lamp, wall lamp, floor lamp, telephone

Toilet Facilities: bath tub, washbasin, water closet, waste-paper basket

Other Facilities: bath towel, bathrobe, pillow case, slipper, water tap, toilet soap

Classroom Activities

Listening practice

I. Listen to the recording and complete the following conversation.

1. room facilities　　2. temperature adjuster　　3. bathrobes　　4. minibar

5. night stand　　6. bathroom　　7. shampoo　　8. shower cap

II. Listen to the recording and answer the questions.

1. His room was in a mess.

2. The bed sheets needed changing, the bathtub was full of water, there was no soap and the tower was dirty.

3. She apologized for that and changed the room for the guest.

4. Yes, he did.

5. Yes, he was.

Communicative Practice

II. Choose the most natural-sounding response.

1. a　2. a　3. c　4. b　5. a　6. b　7. c　8. c　9. a

Reading

Follow-up questions

1. d f j

2. room maids　→　to do the actual cleaning of the guest rooms.

　housemen →to deal with the heavy work, such as the moving of the furniture or heavy linen baskets and trolleys.

　linen-room keepers　→　to store/sort/check/issue/repair all the linens

　housekeepers　→　to allocate and supervise all the work of the staff.

3. Housekeeping Department is the backbone of a hotel. It is responsible for neatness and cleanliness of all the guestrooms for the Front Office to sell. Without the Housekeeping Department, a hotel cannot operate.

Exercises

Words exercises

I. Match each word or phrase in the column at the left with its meaning in the column on the right.

1. b　2. g　3. f　4. h　5. c　6. d　7. e　8. a

II. Choose the best answer

1-5　BBDAB　　6-10　CCDBA

Grammar exercises

1. It is ***this picture*** that I want to show you.

2. It was *by the end of September* that the weather began to cool down.

3. It was *Mike and Mary* who helped the old man several days ago.

4. It was *after he got what he had desired* that he realized it was not so important.

5. It was *our being late* that caused him to serve dinner an hour later than usual.

6. It was *not until his wife came back* that he went to bed.

7. It was *Li Ming* that I met at the railway station yesterday.

8. It was *in the World War I* that he was captured by the enemy.

Translation

1. 放在毛巾架上的毛巾意味着"（不用更换）继续使用"。

2. 房间打扫好了，还有什么可以为您做的吗？

3. 如果我十一点再来，您方便吗？

4. 您要我什么时候收拾您的房间呢？

5. 当您需要清理房间时可以给前台打电话。

6. 相信我们一定会进一步提高我们的服务质量。

7. 当然可以，女士。我会转告夜班服务员。

8. 为了清洁书桌，我可以移动您桌子上的物品吗？

9. 这是饭店服务指南，上面印着有关您所在房间的情况及饭店服务项目。

10. 我们有许多用品可供客人借用，您可以参考"客人手册"。

Unit 9 Housekeeping（II）

Warming Up

I. Look at the pictures below and identify each one. Use the words from the list.

1. hair dryer　　　2. electric iron　　　3. clothes hanger

4. wardrobe　　　5. bed spread　　　6. bedside table

7. blanket　　　　8. toilet roll　　　　9. dressing table

II. Words for Restaurant

Hotel business service: Business center, conference room, multi-function room, IDD, Fax, Internet access

Bedding: pillow case, bed sheets, bed spread, bed skirts, blanket, quilt

Laundry items: normal shirt, blouse, jacket, T-shirt, jeans, pajamas

Room facilities: wardrobe, electric iron, clothes hanger, dressing table, floor lamp, wall lamp

Classroom Activities

Listening practice

I. Listen to the recording and complete the following conversation.

1. I'm always at your service　　2. an extra bed　　3. the Front Office　　4. hangers

5. enjoying your stay with us   6. a pillow   7. a stain   8. see to it

II. Listen to the recording and answer the questions.

1. It was so noisy during the night.

2. She apologized for it and changed room for the guest.

3. Yes, he was.

Communicative Practice

II. 1. a   2. c   3. a   4. c   5. c

Reading

Follow-up questions

I.   1. T   2. F   3. T   4. F   5. T

II. 1. A   2. D   3. B   4. C   5. D

III. 客房服务员与客人密切接触。客人可能会要求服务员在特定的时间整理他的房间，或者表明他完全不希望被人打扰，或想在他的房间里用餐。

Exercises

Words exercises

I. Test your vocabulary of Restaurant and Food.

1. valet service   2. towels   3. Room service   4. rates   5. pillow case

6. lobby   7. front desk   8. damage charge   9. cots   10. complimentary

11. amenities   12. bellboy   13. linens   14. housekeeping 15. concierge

II. Choose the best answer.

1-5   c c b d d   6-10   b b c b a

Grammar exercises

1. is   2. were   3. needs   4. is   5. was   6. is   7. is   8. does   9. were   10. was

Translation

1. 如果你们洗衣时损坏了衣服怎么办?

2. 我马上通知维修部和客房部。

3. 我会叫经理来处理你的要求。

4. 本项服务对本店客人免费。

5. 酒店为客人提供免费的擦鞋服务。

6. 我们提供快洗服务，加收 50% 的额外费用。

7. 如果您有问题，请随时找我们。

8. 赔偿金额最高不超过洗衣费的 10 倍。

9. 你们的客房送餐服务还供给其他品种的早餐吗?

10. 费率表就在您化妆台抽屉里的文具折叠小册子上。

Unit 10 Maintenance and Safety

Warming up

I. Look at the pictures below and identify each one. Use the words from the list.

  1. faucet   2. showerhead   3. wash basin   4. soap

  5. shower curtain 6. repairman   7. fire safety sign

  8. toilet   9. hair shampoo and conditioner

II. Words for repair and maintenance

  Electric facilities: TV set, air conditioner, floor/ table lamp, switch, electric coffee maker,
             hair drier …

  Bathroom facilities: wash basin, toilet, toilet paper, tissue, bathtub, towels

             Soap, shampoo and conditioner, body shampoo, lotion…

  Common problem: Something doesn't work. Faucet is leaking…

  Emergency in hotel: fire, injury, broken bone, illness…

Classroom Activities

Listening practice

I. Listen to the recording and complete the following conversation.

  1. locked   2. duplicate   3. It doesn't matter.   4. picture

  5. electrician   6. Maintenance   7. By all means   8. remote

  9. tips   10. nice stay

II. Listen to the recordings and then fill in the form.

	What's the trouble?	Solution
Conversation 1	Smoke detector is flashing	Stop smoking and be fined
Conversation 2	The water tap drips	Replace some parts
Conversation 3	The light is too dim	Replace it
Conversation 4	Air conditioner is out of order	The repair takes time. Ask the guest to move to a new room

Reading

Follow-up questions

1. not answer the door/not open the door until the guest can make sure the visitor's identification

2. inform the front desk immediately

3. keep it in the hotel save deposit box

4. use the main entrance of the hotel

5. close the room door and lock inside

6. telephone the front desk for help

7. not use his or her guestroom

8. report to the operator immediately

9. use credit card

10. go out of the hotel room and find a authorized smoking area

Exercises

Words exercises

I. Test your vocabulary of maintenance.

1. taking place   2. fixtures   3. checking   4. dripping   5. toilet seat

6. make a note   7. instructions   8. meeting rooms   9. hazard   10. lower

II. Choose the best answer.

1-5　D B C B A　　　6-10　D C B D C

Grammar exercises

1. meet   2. had had   3. were   4. drop   5. told

6. had   7. had seen   8. may be

Translation

1. What seems to be the problem?

2. Your TV remote is out of battery. I will replace that for you.

3. The toilet of your room is all right. You may use it.

4. Some part needs to be replaced. I will be back soon.

5. If there is anything more you need, please let us know.

6. 如果您不满意我们的住宿和服务，请马上通知前台，我们会及时更正。

7. 饭店提供的有线和无线的互联网接入使你的旅途像在家一样舒适。饭店为客人提供的高速网络连接是免费的。

8. 饭店装备了最新式的防火设备和警报系统。

9. 饭店致力为有残疾的旅行者提供无障碍设施。如果你在住店期间遇到任何障碍，请直接联系当班经理。

10. 要选凉风，按高冷或低冷键。此外，把温度钮转到左边，调到想要的温度。

Unit 11　Restaurant service

Warming Up

I. Look at the pictures below and identify each one. Use the words from the list.

1. a napkin   2. a knife, fork and spoon   3. a cup and saucer

4. a plate   5. a bowl   6. salad

7. cheeseburger   8. pizza   9. bacon and eggs

II. Words for Restaurant.

Meat: pork, bacon, ham, venison, veal, beef, mutton, lamb…

Vegetables: cabbage, broccoli, cucumber, asparagus, carrot, pepper…

Drinks: beer, wine, juice, mineral water, tea, cola…

Tableware: chopstick, spoon, fork, knife, wineglass, bowl…

Classroom Activities

Listening practice

I. Listen to the recording and complete the following conversation.

    1. How   2. a table for one   3. today's specials   4. mushroom soup

    5. fish and chips   6. starter   7. green salad   8. mineral water

II. Listen to the recording and answer the questions.

    1. Her coffee is too weak.

    2. Yes.

    3. It is not fresh.

    4. She is not happy about it.

    5. The waiter promises to look into the matter.

    6. The waiter offers the guest something replaced, if she'd like a change.

    7. No. She doesn't want to trouble anyone.

    8. Give the restaurant another chance to make up.

    9. The guest said, "I hope so."

Reading

Follow-up questions

I. Right order: I C D A F H E B G

II. The answer is open, but most complaints may be involved with food, drink, service and environment of the restaurant. For example, food is too spicy, or the restaurant is too smoky.

III. Be patient and tactical when dealing with demanding customers. Do not exchange words with them. If you do something wrong indeed, you have to say "sorry" to your customers, explain why and tell them what you can do to remedy.

Exercises

Words exercises

I. Test your vocabulary of Restaurant and Food.

    1. waiter   2. cook   3. chef   4. dishwasher   5. tip

    6. breakfast   7. lunch.   8. dinner   9. brunch   10. appetizer

11. soup	12. salad	13. dessert	14. fancy	15. fast-food
16. buffet	17. bar	18. smoking	19. non-smoking	

II. Choose the best answer.

   1-5 B D A C A   6-10 B C B D A

Grammar exercises

1. So am I.

2. So do I.

3. Neither can I.

4. Neither do I.

5. So have I.

6. Neither will I.

7. So am I.

8. Neither have I.

Translation

1. 先生，我们现在没有空座位。

2. 您是否介意和别人共用一张台？

3. 您要浓茶还是淡茶？

4. 我是否可以介绍一下我们饭店的招牌菜？

5. 您的菜上齐了，请慢用！

6. 您这里有素食菜吗？

7. 我们餐厅主要提供粤菜。

8. 这道菜听起来很吸引人。是怎么做的？

9. 中餐讲究色、香、味三要素。

10. 按中国习俗，我们先上菜，后上汤。如果您喜欢，我们可以先给您上汤。

Unit 12　Bar service

Warming Up

I. Look at the pictures below and identify each one. Use the words from the list.

1. trays	2. straw	3. bar counter	4. screw pull
5. opener	6. bar stool	7. cocktail glass	8. wine glass
9. beer mug			

Classroom Activities

Listening practice

I. Listen to the recording and complete the following conversation.

1. What may I offer	2. drink list	3. white wine	4. cocktail

5. soft drink   6. What can I make   7. draught

8. hold the payment of the bill until you decide to leave

II. Listen to the recording and answer the questions.

1-5 BCBBA   6-10   BBCBC

Communicative Practice

I. 1. The possible problems with the drink in a bar.

2. The drink is not what I ordered.

3. You are overcharged me with the bill.

4. Your wine has a peculiar smell.

5. There is lipstick on my glass.

6. The coffee is weak.

7. My drink is not cold enough.

8. I have kept waiting so long. May I take my order now?

Reading

Follow-up questions

I. GGBBB   GGGBB

II. You can make your customers know your care and make them feel more comfortable with you.

III. All the customers want to be treated nicely. So being a server, what you can do is to make the customers satisfied.

Exercises

Words exercises

I. Test your vocabulary relating to interacting with customers in a bar.

1. pitcher	2. tap	3. call	4. potent	5. parts
6. serve	7. glasses	8. get	9. round	10. cut
11. bottled	12. water	13. mix	14. allowed	15. disturb

II. Choose the best answer.

1-5 ACBCC   6-10   ACBBA

Grammar exercises

| 1. some | 2. something | 3. somebody | 4. Anybody |
| 5. anything | 6. any | 7. any | 8. some |

Translation

1. What would you like to drink, Sir?

2. I would like to look through the drink list.

3. The wine is rather strong, but never goes to the head.

4. How is the taste of the wine, Sir?

5. Would you like to have other drinks?

6. 您想怎样喝苏格兰威士忌，加不加冰？

7. 您可以在离开前在结账。

8. 我需要照顾一下其他客人，等一下我会再回来。

9. 对不起，先生。您已经醉了，我不能再给您添酒了。

10. 您是否愿意记账？

Unit 13　Business Service

Warming Up

I. Look at the pictures below and identify each one. Use the words from the list.

1. a laser printer　　2. a fax machine　　3. a photocopier

4. a scanner　　5. a laptop　　6. a stapler

7. a USB flash drive　　8. folders　　9. CD

II. Words for Business Center

Fax and copy: a fax machine, copy, original, stapler, file, ink, paper…

Computer-related service: laptop, internet, printer, word-processing, e-mail, website, anti-virus…

Reservation: air ticket, economy class, single room, theatre, cinema, concert…

Telephone: long distance call, line, extension, switch board, operator, international call…

Classroom Activities

Listening practice

I. Listen to the recording and complete the following conversation.

1. internet service　　2. answer an E-mail　　3. available　　4. next to

5. bring my laptop with me.　　6. 20 Yuan.　　7. I've done everything I wanted.

8. 25 minutes　　9. half an hour　　10. sign it to my room

II. Listen to the recording and answer the questions.

1)

1. He wants to make a long distance call to France

2. 0.7 Yuan for every 6 seconds.

3. 15%.

2)

1. He wants to send a fax.

2. Taiwan.

3. (886) 02-2396-9795

4. 15.5Yuan.

5. He wants to pay in cash.

Reading

Follow-up questions

I. copies, fax, computer and internet services, internet access, printing

II. copies: duplex, stapling, sorting, paper stock…

    fax: receive a fax, deliver a fax, pick up a fax...

    computer and internet services: software, floppy drive, CD writing capability, PPT

    internet access: password, email, load page, internet portal page…

    printing: black and white printer, laserjet, inkjet, color printing…

Exercises

Words exercises

I. Test your vocabulary of Restaurant and Food.

1. typist	2. printer	3. photocopier	4. scanner	5. paper clip
6. stapler	7. fax machine	8. e-mail	9. webcam	10. first class
11. business class	12. economy class			

II. Choose the best answer.

    1-5　A B B D A　　　6-10　A A A D B

Grammar exercises

1. The photocopier is a machine for making copies of documents.

2. The scanner is a machine for copying a picture or document onto a computer.

3. The stapler is a device for fastening papers together.

4. The fax machine is a machine for sending and receiving documents.

5. The stapler remover is a device for quickly removing a staple from a material without causing damage.

6. The camera is a device for taking photographs, making films and producing television pictures.

7. The telex is a machine for typing messages to a distant point.

Translation

1. 我想要预订一张 11 月 11 日去巴黎的机票，要商务舱的。

2. 很抱歉，那天所有的票都卖完了。

3. 我想要发份传真，可是不知道该去哪里发。

4. 请写下（传真）发往的国家代码、地区代码和传真号码。

5. 纸太厚了，可能会卡打印机的。

6. 商务中心提供文字处理服务，复印设备，在会议厅旁边还设有咨询台。

7. 您的原件不清楚，我很难保证复印效果。

8. 我们会尽量在下午五点前打完这 20 页的文件。

9. 我们有很多海外客商，他们不懂汉语，所以我们需要一些能力很强的翻译。

10. 这个翻译在商务会谈方面很有经验。

Unit 14   Shopping Arcade

Warming Up

I. Look at the pictures below and identify each one. Use the words from the list.

1. Chinese painting　　　2. emerald　　　3. jade articles

4. sandal fan　　　5. pearl necklace　　　6. sapphire

7. Four Treasure of Study　　　8. hand-embroidered

9. tri-chromatic glazed ware of Tang Dynasty

II. Words for Business Center

Fax and Drinks: Sandwich, hamburger, milk, tea, juice, biscuit…

Clothes: sweater, overcoat, underwear, blouse, jacket, dress, trousers…

Souvenirs: photo album, necklace, dictionary, watch, medal…

Jewelry: diamond, ruby, nephrite, agate, emerald, crystal…

Classroom Activities

Listening practice

I. Listen to the recording and complete the following conversation.

1. having a sale on dress shoes　　　2. What do you recommend?

3. more fashionable and with higher quality　　　4. What's the difference in price?

5. How would you like to pay?　　　6. here's your receipt

II. Listen to the recording and answer the questions.

1. Dress shoes.　　　2. Yes, he needs.　　　3. Both Silver Queens and Cool Holidays.

4. Silver Queens.　　　5. Cool Holidays.　　　6. Yes, there's difference.

7. That's about an $8.00 difference.　　　8. The customer will put it on his credit card.

Reading

Follow-up questions

1. A. T　　　B. F　　　C. T　　　D. F　　　E. T

 F. T　　　G. T　　　H. F　　　I. F　　　J. F

2.

1) Directing and lead the shop to run according to shopping center's policy;

2) Being aware of incidents from security issues concerning stock and cash that may be targeted through shoplifting and theft reported from assistants;

3) Knowing the reports any stock delivery shortage;

4) Directing the prices stock;

5) Monitoring all products in the shop.

3. Assisting in ensuring that high standards of customer service are maintained.

Exercises

Words exercises

I. Test your vocabulary of products in shopping arcade.

1. f	2. g	3. h	4. i	5. j
6. a	7. a	8. c	9. d	10. e

II. Choose the best answer.

1. tight	2. warmer	3. reliable	4. fashionable	5. comfortable
6. expensive	7. roomy	8. durable	9. china	10. refund

Grammar exercises

1. The fur coat is more expensive than that one.

   The fur coat is not as expensive as that one.

2. This pearl's luster is more unique than that one.

   This pearl's luster is not as unique as that one.

3. The dress shoes are more comfortable than that pair.

   The dress shoes are not as comfortable as that pair.

4. The red dress is more beautiful than other one on you.

   The red dress is not as beautiful as other one on you.

5. The producats of this brand are more reliable than that one.

   The producats of this brand are not as reliable as that one.

6. The man is more important person than any other one in the company.

   The man is not as important as any other any other one in the company.

7. The pictures on the tea pot are more wonderful than those ones.

   The pictures on the tea pot are not as wonderful as those ones.

8. The silk blouse is more colorful than the other one.

   The silk blouse is not as colorful as the other one.

Translation

1. 我想让我们定制那对耳环吗？

2. 蓝宝石多么明亮！

3. 我建议你要这个珍珠项链。

4. 这颗翡翠是真的。

5. 这款檀香扇采用中国传统设计。

6. 这块桌布是老虎图案的手工刺绣。

7. 你喜欢这些带有中国特色的钥匙环？

8. 我可以告诉你如何从玉器中识别玻璃器皿。

9. 文房四宝是笔、墨、纸和砚。

10. 这个著名的器物是唐三彩。

Unit 15　Recreation and Fitness

Warming Up

I. Look at the pictures below and identify each one. Use the words from the list.

1. Taiji 　　　　2. Pilate 　　　　3. race apparatus

4. dumb bell 　　5. chest expanders 　6. bar bell

7. spring-grips 　8. Yoga 　　　　9. rock and roll

II. Words for Restaurant

Music: classical music, pop music, folk music, rock and roll, jazz…

Lessons in gym: Taiji, Yuga, Qigong, Pilate…

sports: race, ping-pang, badminton, tennis, golf, swim…

sports apparatuses: bar bell, dumb bell, chest expander, race apparatus, spring-grips…

Classroom Activities

Listening practice

I. Listen to the recording and complete the following conversation.

1. what 　　　　　2. what facilities 　　3. recreational sports apparatus

4. wonderful sauna 　5. 25 meters long 　　6. heated swimming pool

7. beside the pool 　8. The charge

II. Listen to the recording again and answer the questions.

1. His doctor advised him to keep in good physical condition.

2. The gym is well-equipped with all the latest recreational sports apparatus.

3. He can play tennis, badminton and ping-pang ball.

4. Yes. It is a wonderful sauna.

5. It's 25 meters long, 20 meters wide and 2.5 meters deep.

6. It's a heated swimming pool.

7. Guests can relax with beer, juice and coffee 7 beside the pool.

8. Yes, because the guest says he must spend some money here tonight.

9. The charge is very reasonable

Reading

Follow-up questions

1. TFFTFTFTTF

2. In larger commercial facilities, personal trainers are often required to sell their services to

members and to make a specified number of sales. Some fitness workers may combine the duties of group exercise instructors and personal trainers.

3. Fitness workers in smaller facilities with few employees may perform a variety of functions in addition to their fitness duties, such as tending the front desk, signing up new members, giving tours of the fitness center, writing newsletter articles, creating posters and flyers, and supervising the weight training and cardiovascular equipment areas.

Exercises

Words exercises

I. Test your vocabulary of Restaurant and Food.

  1. d   2. I   3. a   4. j   5. g   6. c   7. f   8. h   9. b   10. e

II. Choose the best answer.

1. partner	2. highlight	3. minimum	4. song	5. computer
6. consumption	7. trainer	8. items	9. apparatuses	10. ball

Grammar exercises

1. What useful sports apparatuses they are!
   How useful they are!

2. What a fashionable dancing stage it is!
   How fashionable it is!

3. What nice music it is!
   How nice it is!

4. What wonderful Yuga lessons they are!
   How wonderful they are!

5. What excellent Pilates they are!
   How wonderful they are!

6. What a perfect dancer she is!
   How perfect she is!

7. What delicious ice cream it is!
   How delicious it is!

8. What great singers they are!
   How great they are!

Translation

1. 卡拉 OK 厅配有超级音响和照明系统。

2. 六个人以上的大房间每小时 100 元，包括饮料。

3. 按语言分，我们有普通话、广东话、韩语和英语歌曲。

4. 我们有设备优良的体操馆，配有最新的娱乐体育器材。

5. 教练会告诉你如何使用这些体育器材。

6. 游泳池在地下二层，长 20 米，宽 25 米，身 20 米，池边有安全保障人员。

7. 在四层，我们有保龄球中心和游戏中心。

8. 每天下午6点到7点，我们有瑜伽课和太极课。

9. 这里有民歌、流行歌、摇滚等。

10. 我敢肯定，收费非常合理。

Unit 16   Meeting Service

Warming Up

I. Look at the pictures below and identify each one. Use the words from the list.

1. a digital camcorder   2. a projector   3. a microphone

4. a recording pen   5. a slide   6. a function hall

7. hi-fi AV   8. a whiteboard   9. a flip chart

II. Words for Restaurant

Room Set up: conference, theater, U-shape, T-shape, schoolroom, rounds…

Sound/Audio Visual: Mike, laptop, projector, slide, recorder, screen…

Miscellaneous Facilities: whiteboard, flipchart, blackboard, pads, pens, flag…

catering: banquet, buffet, afternoon tea, snack, coffee, wine…

Classroom Activities

Listening practice

I. Listen to the recording and complete the following conversation.

1. heart   2. offering   3. 30,000   4. meeting space   5. 1,015

6. wireless Internet   7. 19   8. 10 to 500   9. 1,015   10. 52

11. classic styling   12. modern conveniences   13. flat screen TVs

14. cable television   15. a sofa chair   16. high-speed

17. 3,900   18. 2   19. living and dining area   20. city view

II. Listen to the recording and answer the questions.

1. His company is going to hold a conference next month. And he wants to reserve some meeting rooms.

2. 400 people

3. 200 square meters

4. They are provided with wireless microphones.

5. No, he doesn't. There is a simultaneous translation system in the meeting room.

6. 2000 for the multi-function hall.

Reading

Follow-up questions

I.

Types	Facilities	advantage	disadvantage
Audio Conferencing	A telephone	Hear each other instantly Cheapest among the three	not able to see the other people not able instantly to share images or information directly related to the business.
Video Conferencing	a camera and television on each end of the conference.	effective and ideal for regular meetings	difficult to set up and trouble shoot the equipment.
Web Conferencing	Internet	share files, visual aids and text messages instantly hear and see each other over the internet	Most expensive

2. The best way to choose a conference call service provider is to shop around and find the package that best suits your needs and also take your budget into consideration.

Exercises

Words exercises

I. Test your vocabulary of Restaurant and Food.

1. theater style   2. U-shape

3. Classroom style   4. conference or boardroom Style

5. Screen   6. projector   7. recorders   8. microphone

9. wireless microphone   10. poster   11. banner

12. lectern   13. tier

II. Choose the best answer.

1-5   A B A C D   6-10   D A A A B

Grammar exercises

1. Could you please tell me the capacity of the hall?

2. Could you tell me what office support service you offer?

3. Could you tell me what the technical equipment is for the hall?

4. Could I get the price of renting equipment for the convention?

5. Could you tell me whether you have a hall that can seat 500 guests?

Translation

1. 下个月中旬我们计划召开为期 5 天的研讨会。

2. 我们想为培训租一些设备和工作人员。

3. 由于设备费用大，只有大型公司才召开视频会议。

4. 视频会议是召开定期会议的有效方式。

5. 选择声像会议场所的最好方法就是货比三家，选择最适合自己的服务。

6. 我们设备齐全，有投影仪、幻灯片、录音设备、隔音折叠屏风和高保真视听设备。

7. 将有 100 位导演和演员出席这个颁奖晚会。

8. 我们的会议厅可以用作一个大型的会议厅或用折叠屏风隔成几个小的会议室。

9. 我们签署租用设备和人员的协议吧。也谢谢你的建议。

10. 有闭路电视吗？费用是多少？

Transcripts of the Conversations

Unit 1 Hotel Basics

Situational Conversations

Conversation 1 The Sense of Service

Zhou Wang, a fourth-year student majoring in Hotel Service and Management in a tourism institute, is doing his internship in Crown Plaza Shenzhen. The training manager is talking to him about the sense of service.

(*M: The Hotel Training Manager   Z: Zhou Wang*)

M: Good morning, Mr. Zhou. Welcome to our hotel. You're going to spend 3 months on having your operations intern here. Are you ready for that?

Z: Yes, Sir. I'm so excited and a bit upset.

M: That's for sure. After all, it's your first full-time job. Could you tell me why you choose Hotel Service and Management as your major?

Z: I enjoy dealing with people. In a hotel, we can meet and serve people from all walks of life and I have a real liking for guests and a warm desire to them.

M: That's great. Then, could you tell me what makes you feel unease?

Z: I don't have much experience to communicate with strangers.

M: Great! I understand. Take it easy. I will tell you what you can do, but before that, please tell me what you think of the hotel business?

Z: A hotel is an establishment that provides paid lodging, usually on a short-term basis and it is also a home away from home for all the travelling guests.

M: Good idea. Then, what about hotel service?

Z: I think hotel service is a very decent and honorable occupation and it is understanding, anticipating and fulfilling needs of others.

M: Right. Good service is a blending of courtesy and efficiency without either familarity or servility. Do you happen to know what the word "SERVICE" stands for?

Z: Sorry, Sir. What do you mean?

M: Actually, service is the SERVICE. As you can see, each of its letters is rich in meaning. S stands for smiling, E for excellent, R for ready, V for viewing, I for inviting, C for creating and the last E for Eye. In other words, we should keep smiling all the time, everything we do should be excellent, be ready to treat every guest with hospitality, view every guest as a special, invite guests to return, create a warm atmosphere and show our care with eye contact.

Z: Oh, I see. You are telling me how to treat the guests. Well, I'll regard every guest as a VIP.

M: Good. I do hope you can bear in mind our hotel's mission—Crown Plaza is the business hotel that is focused on delivering the important services and facilities for formal and informal meetings consistently and completely. In addition, pay particular attention to your behavior and language, as well as be aware of the cultural diversity.

Z: Thank you, Sir. We did have such training courses for courtesy English, and service etiquette.

M: Terrific! Besides, remember we are one business, and we all work as a team to lead and win.

Z: Yes, I'll try my best to be a good team player.

Conversation 2   Choosing Your Hotel

Li Yang will have a business trip to Canada, but she doesn't have any idea about how to choose a proper hotel. Robert Goldfield, a Canada hotel manager, is giving Li Yang some advice.

(*Li: Li Yang   R: Robert*)

L: Robert. What types of rooms are offered by hotels in Canada?

R: In Canada, Hotel guest rooms are usually divided into two kinds–a room and a suite. The specific room types offered are as the following: single room designed for one person; double room, containing one king-size or queen-size bed; twin room, with two single beds; triple room, containing three single beds or a standard room with an additional single bed; while a suite is subdivided into several types as follows: Standard Suite, also named junior suite or family suite, Deluxe Suite, Executive Suite and Presidential Suite, which usually is the best accommodation in a hotel. However, if you want to find a single room, you should always check through whether you're booking into a hotel that has a shared bathroom, because some people are very uncomfortable doing that.

L: Can I get any discount if I make a room reservation on hotel's website?

R: It depends on the time you go. I mean the full price "rack rates" can vary from peak season to off-season.

L: What is the "rack rates"?

R: A hotel's rack rate, or its brochure rate, is usually the maximum room charges published by hotels when occupancy is high. In fact, I think that to get the best hotel room rate is over the telephone. You have to telephone the hotel directly, and you need to be very aggressive about asking what the specials are, what the discounts are, and if there are any special rates for membership.

L: Good idea. My next question is if there are the standard rules for tipping hotel personnel. You know tipping is not popular in China.

R: Tipping is always at the discretion of the traveler. However, generally speaking, you should tip the doorman, the bellman and the person who valet parks your car. I think a $2 tip is probably appropriate.

L: It's very kind of you, Robert. I do appreciate your information.

Classroom Activities

_ Listening Practice _

I. Listen to the recording and complete the following passage.

Welcome to Holiday Inn DIAMOND BAR

With a breathtaking view overlooking the San Gabriel Mountains our hotel's location is near Anaheim, downtown Los Angeles and a number of attractions and businesses making it the premier place to stay for business and leisure travelers.

Leisure travelers love that our hotel is near Disneyland® and many other local attractions including the Big League Dreams sports park and outdoor activities like golf and tennis. In addition, we are close to a variety of shops at the Ontario Mills which easily can meet all of your shopping needs.

Corporate guests of our hotel enjoy being near Anaheim businesses and appreciate the 24-hour business center that has fax, copy Internet access and print services. In addition, over 5,000 square feet of meeting space is available for our guests. Feel free to reserve one of our 13 rooms and take advantage our technical amenities and helpful service staff who can ensure that your next meeting or social event is a success.

Whether you're looking for hotels near Disneyland and Los Angeles or those near local corporations, we are the perfect choice. You'll feel right at home here as you relax by our outdoor pool and soak up the sun or as you burn off some steam in the fitness center. And, when it's time for a meal, you can eat right on our property at the on-site restaurant, DB's Bar and Grill, where kids eat free! Choose us — the name you can trust.

II. Listen to the recording and answer the questions.

(M: Hotel training manager   G: George , a college student during his internship)

M: Good morning, Gorge. You're going to spend 6 months on having your operational and managerial internship in our hotel. Right?

G: Yes. If possible, I'd like to work and learn in every department of both the front of the house and the back of the house.

M: Why not? First of all, you'll be a Front Office clerk. You'll be a reservation agent, receptionist, bellman, informant, operator and cashier. You'll have the most direct contact with foreign guests.

G: Great! Thank you. What then?

M: Then, you'll be a room attendant, a laundryman, a PA cleaner in the Housekeeping Dept.. You'll have a section of 14 rooms every day. That might cause you quite some physical labor.

G: No problem. I'd love to.

M: After that, you'll be put at the Food and Beverage Dept..

G: Fine. I'd try my best to make every customer know better about Chinese cuisine.

M: In addition, you still have chance to work as a shop assistant in our hotel's Shopping Arcade, a clerk in our Recreational Dept., a sales representative in Sales Dept., and a maintenance man in our Engineering and Maintenance Dept. to learn something of everything.

G: Oh, that's a big challenge.

Unit 2   Room Reservation

Situational Conversations

Conversation 1   Making a Reservation

(R: Receptionist   G: Guest)

R: Good Morning, Hilton Hotel, Room Reservations. Can I help you?

G: Yes, I'd like to book a room.

R: Thank you, Sir. For which day and how many people will there be in your party?

G: Next Friday and Saturday night. Just my son and myself.

R: What kind of room would you like, Sir?

G: A suite, please. I'd appreciate it if you could give me a room with a view over the lake.

R: Hold on please. I'll check our room availability…. Thank you for waiting, Sir. We do have a deluxe suite on the 8th floor with a really splendid view.

G: Fine. What's the room rate per night?

R: $100 per night, will that be all right?

G: OK, I'll take it.

R: May I have your name and telephone number, please?

G: Sure, my name is Goldfield, Tony Goldfield, and my telephone number is 8363-5252.

R: Could you spell it, please?

G: G-O-L-D-F-I-E-L-D.

R: Thank you , Mr. Goldfield. May I know your arrival time, please?

G: At about 6 p.m. next Friday.

R: That's fine. Thank you, Mr Goldfield. You'd like to have a deluxe suite next Friday and Saturday night. Is that right?

G: Yes, it is. Thank you.

R: Thank you for choosing Hilton Hotel and we are looking forward to your arrival. Goodbye.

G: Goodbye.

Conversation 2 Desired Room Being Fully Booked

(R: Receptionist   C: Caller)

R: Good afternoon, Sir. What can I do for you?

C: Good afternoon, I'd like to book a double room with a bath for this weekend.

R: Just a moment, please. Let me have a check…. I'm sorry, Sir, all the double rooms are fully booked for the weekend and there is no vacancy.

C: Oh, that's too bad.

R: Is it possible to change another date?

C: Oh, I'm afraid not.

R: Would you like me to contact some nearby hotels to see if they have vacancies?

C: But my wife prefers to stay here and she always appreciates your service.

R: Oh, I see. Don't worry, Sir. We sometimes may have cancellations. Would you like us to put you on our waiting list and call you in case we have a cancellation?

C: Thank you. That's very kind of you. Could you let me know as soon as possible if you do have any cancellation?

R: Yes, of course. Besides, would you like to have a standard room? It is also nice and comfortable for a weekend.

R: That's fine. How about the rate per night for a standard room?

R: Well, there is a minimum price for off-season stay and a maximum price for peak-season stay. A standard room at the moment would run you $40.

C: That's fine and I will talk with my wife and call you later. Thank you for your kindness.

R: You are welcome and wish you a nice day.

C: Thank you so much for your help. Good-bye.

R: Good-bye and thank you for calling us.

Classroom Activities

__ Listening Practice __

I. Listen to the recording and complete the following conversation.

(C = Clerk, G = Guest)

C: Room Reservations. May I help you?

G: Yes. I'd like to cancel a reservation, because the travel schedule has been changed.

C: That's OK. Could you tell me in whose name was the reservation made?

G: White. W-H-I-T-E.

C: And what was the date of the reservation?

G: From September 15th for 3 nights.

C: Excuse me, but is the reservation for yourself or for another party?

G: It's for my boss.

C: Well, may I have your name and phone number, please?

G: Yes, it's Ellen Green, and my number is 245-3971.

C: Thank you, ma'am. I will cancel Mr White's reservation for September 15th for 3 nights. My name is Wang Ying and we look forward to another chance to serve you.

C: Thank you the same. Miss Wang.

G: It's my pleasure.

II. Listen to the recording and answer the questions.

A Group Reservation

Scene: The telephone rings. the Reservationist (R) answers the phone.

R: Reservations, May I help you?

Client(C): Yes, the Australia New-way Education Delegation will be visiting Beijing at the end of this month. I'd like to reserve 10 double rooms with twin beds for five days.

R: For which dates?

C: For July 23rd, 24th... and 27th.

R: One more moment please, Sir.

(The reservationist checks to the list.)

Yes, we can confirm 10 rooms for five days.

C: Thank you. Is there a special rate for a group reservation?

R; Yes, there is a 10 per cent discount.

C: That's fine.

R: By the way, how will they be getting to Beijing? Will they be coming by air?

C: Yes.

R: Could you give me the flight number, please, in case the plane's late?

C: Oh, sorry. I don't know the flight number, but I'll let you know by phone tomorrow.

R: Thank you, Sir.

C: Oh, yes. According to the program, they'll have a meeting on the 25th. Have you got a big conference hall?

R: Yes, Sir. we have a very nice multi-function hall.

Unit 3   Bell Service

Situational Conversations

Conversation 1   Showing the Guests to Their Rooms

A car pulls up in front of a Star Hotel. A doorman goes forward to meet the guests, and opening the door of the car for them.
(D: Doorman   G1: Guest1   G2: Guest2)

D: Good evening, Sir and Madam. Welcome to West Lake State Hotel.

G1: Good evening.

D: May I help you with your luggage?

G2: Thank you.

D: (Opening the trunk, taking out the baggage and looking at the name on the baggage tags.)
   So, you have got altogether three pieces of baggage.

G1: Oh, no. Four pieces in all.

D: Four? Oh, sorry. Let me have a check again…. But here just three pieces.

G2: Oh, no. Always poor memory! We've got only three.

G1: I see. (To the doorman) Sorry, boy. You're right. Three pieces.

D: Never mind, Sir. Now I will show you to the Front Desk. This way, please.

G1: Thank you.

(After checking in a few minutes…)

D: Now I will show you to your room. May I have your room number, please?

G2: Sure and thank you. My room number is 1820.

D: This way, please.

G1: Thank you.

D: Here we are. Room 1820. May I have your key card, please?

G2: Sure. Here you are.

   (After entering the guestroom)

D: Sir and Madam, may I put your suitcases here?

G1 and G2: Sure. Just put them anywhere.

D: Is there anything else I can do for you?

G1: Yes, I'd like a wake–up call at 7 a.m. tomorrow morning.

D: Yes, I'll make sure you get one.

G2: Ok. Thank you very much indeed. By the way, could you tell me something about the hotel service?

D: Sure, our hotel is one of the first-class 5-star hotels in Beijing. There are all kinds of guestrooms here and we offer Chinese and Western cuisine in the two restaurants on the second floor. Also there is a 24-hour bar for you to have a chat with your friends.

G 2: That sounds perfect and do you have a Directory of Services?

D: Yes, here it is. It contains various services and information of our hotel. Here is the remote control for TV and this is the channel selector.

G2: Good! That's very kind of you. Now I want to know if I can surf on Internet in the room.

D: Sure you can.

G2: OK. Have you got a swimming pool here?

D: It is on the top floor of the hotel with a beautiful view of the city and there is also a beauty salon, a souvenir shop and a business center on the first floor which will provide all the necessary services for you.

G1 and G2: All right. Thank you very much, young man.

D: You are always welcome. Please call Front Desk if you need any further services.

Conversation 2　Depositing Some Items

A guest wants to deposit some valuable items and then go shopping and sightseeing with his family.

(A: Attendant　G: Guest)

A: Good morning, Sir. What can I do for you?

G: Yes, do you have somewhere I can keep my valuables safe?

A: Sure things. You can put them in the safe at reception or you can use the safe deposit box in your room.

G: Can you show me how to use the safe in my room?

A: Certainly Sir. If you want to use the safe, please go to the service center first and fill out a signature card, then the clerk there will give you an activation pin..

G: Activation pin? What's the use of it?

A: Once you get the pin, please plug in and open the door of the safe, insert the pin, then "open" will be indicated on the door.

G: How can I lock the safe?

A: You close the door of the safe, enter a code of your choice and it will lock. Just enter the code to open it again.

G: That's very easy. Can other people open it?

A: Unless they know the code. The safe will not unlock if you put in the wrong code, and it will show "ERROR".

G: Well, it's very safe.

A: I think so. But be sure not to forget the code you set. Otherwise, you have to contact the Service Center and ask the clerk to open it for you.

G: Oh, I see. Thank you very much.

A: It's my pleasure. One more thing, if you stop using the safe, please remove the activation pin and return it to the service center.

G: Sure. Thank you again. Good-bye.

A: Good-bye, Sir. Wish you a pleasant journey.

Listening Practice

I. Listen to the recording and complete the following conversation.

(B: Bellman   G: Guest)

B: Good afternoon, Sir! Welcome to the Lake View Garden Hotel.

G: Thank you.

B: How many pieces of luggage do you have?

G: Just two pieces.

B: Two suitcases and one briefcase. Is that correct?

G: Yes. That's all.

B: I'll show you to the Front Desk. This way, please.

G: I see. Thanks.

B: I will take care of your luggage when you do the check-in.

G: OK.

... On the Way to the Room

B: Let me see your key card, Sir.

G: That's it. Room 1203.

B: Your room is on the 12th floor. Let's take the elevator over there.

G: OK. By the way, where is the bar?

B: It's on the third floor. It opens around the clock.

G: It's very kind of you. Thank you.

B: You are welcome. The elevators on the right are for the guests of the hotel. You can take it up to the 12th floor. The elevators on the left are for the staff and luggage. I will take the elevator on the left up to your floor with your luggage. Your elevator is right here. Watch your step, Sir.

G: Thank you.

B: See you later!

G: Sure.

II. Listen to the recording and answer the questions.

(A guest has already checked out but she suddenly remembers that she has something important to do. So she wants to leave the luggage at the Porter Section and get it back an hour later.)

(A: Bellman　　B: Guest)

B: Excuse me.

A: Yes. What can I do for you?

B: I have already checked out. But I suddenly remembered that I have something important to do. I have to go to the post office to get some stamps for my best friend, Ann. She is a stamp collector. So I want to leave the luggage at the Porter Section and get it back an hour later. Is that Okay?

A: Sure. We can take care of your luggage until you are back.

B: Great! Here is my luggage.

A: Would you please put this claim tag on your luggage, Madam? And this is your storage receipt.

B: Do I have to pay?

A: No. you don't have to.

B: Thank you very much.

A: You are welcome.

Unit 4　Reception

Situational Conversations

Conversation 1　Checking in Guest with a Reservation

Mr. Arthur Henry checks in at the Reception Desk in the afternoon.

(A: Arthur Henry　　R: Receptionist)

R: Good afternoon, Sir. What can I do for your?

A: I booked a single room for 4 nights the day before yesterday and I would like to check in. I'm Mr. Arthur Henry.

R: Just a moment, please, Mr. Henry. I'll check the reservation list (after a while…). Sorry to have you kept waiting, Sir. Yes, we do have a reservation for you, Mr. Henry. Would you please show me your passport or some photo ID?

A: Here you are.

R: Thank you, Sir. One moment. You're saying for 4 nights, is that correct?

A: That's right.

R: How would you like to settle the deposit, in cash or by credit card?

A: By credit card.

R: OK, I'll need to swipe your credit card.

A: Here you are.

R: Please sign our guest book and fill out this form while I prepare your key card for you?

A: Well, what should I fill in under room number?

R: You can skip that. I'll put in the room number for you later on.

A: (After he completed the form) Here you are.

R: Let me see…name, address, and nationality, forwarding address, passport number, signature and date of departure. Now everything is OK. Mr. Henry. Your room number is 1820. Here is your key card. Would you like someone to take your bags to your room?

A: No, thank you, I can manage.

R: Very well, enjoy your stay.

A: That's for sure.

Conversation 2   Helping a Walk-in Guest

(G: Guest   R: Receptionist)

R: Good afternoon, Sir. Welcome to Marriott Hotel.
   What can I do for you?

G: Yes, I'd like to check in, please.

R: Do you have a reservation?

G: I'm afraid not. Is there a vacant room here?

R: Just a moment please… Let me see if there is a room available. What kind of room do you want?

G: I'd like a double, non-smoking room.

R: You're luck, we have one free. It's high season at the moment so we're very busy.

G: How much do you charge for the room?

R: It's $60 per night for a double room.

G: Would you give me some discount?

R: Certainly, Sir. We give 5% discount for one week, 10% for two weeks and over. How long do you intend to stay?

G: For a week.

R: Then we can give you 5% discount.

G: All right.

R: May I have your name, please?

G: I'm Tony Green.

R: Could you fill out the registration form, please?

G: Fine.

R: How will you be paying, Mr. Green?

G: By Visa Card.

R: May I take a print of your card?

G: Sure, here you are.

R: Thank you, Mr. Green. Your room number is 1622. A bellboy will show you to your room. Enjoy your stay here, please.

G: Thank you.

Listening Practice

I. Listen to the recording and complete the following conversation.

(A: Receptionist   B: Guest)

A: Good morning! Can I help you?

B: I want a double room with a bath. How much a day do you charge?

A: It is a hundred Yuan a day including breakfast but excluding service charge.

B: It's quite reasonable.

A: How long do you intend to stay in this hotel?

B: I shall leave in a fortnight.

A: Have you got through with the check-in procedure?

B: Oh, yes, I'm going to fill in the form of registration right now. By the way, I'd like check in a suite room for my friend tomorrow morning.

A: Sorry, we have no vacant room for your friend tomorrow morning. But tomorrow afternoon is OK.

B: That sounds very good! Can I book the air ticket here?

A: Please go to the CAAC office to book your air ticket. If you want to book train ticket or ship ticket, you'd better go to the Shanghai International Travel Service.

(Next afternoon)

B: Can I check in a suite room for my friend beforehand as he will arrive in Shanghai this evening?

A: Sure. Here is the form for you, Sir. Would you mind filling in this form and pay 100 Yuan in advance for him.

B: All right. This is five hundred Yuan to pay.

A: Thank you. This is a receipt for paying in advance. Please keep it.

B: Could you tell me how many kinds of rooms do you have?

A: There are single rooms, double rooms, suites and deluxe suite in our hotel. Every room is equipped with a telephone and a TV set.

B: Oh, I see. Thanks.

A: You are welcome.

II. Listen to the recording and answer the questions.

(R: Receptionist   G: Guest)

R: Good morning, Sir. May I help you? Are you checking out now?

G: Yes. Sorry, I know we're a few minutes late. My name is Mr. Bell and I was in room 1111.

R: That's no problem. It's always really busy at check out time anyway.

G: Oh, really. The last hotel we stayed in charged us for a late check out.

R: The room isn't booked this week, so it's not a problem. How was everything?

G: The room was great. The beds were really comfortable, and we weren't expecting our own fridge.

R: I'm glad you liked it.

G: The kids were disappointed that the pool wasn't open this morning, though.

R: I apologize for that. We often have the water changed in the swimming pool on Monday morning until 10 a.m..

G: Well, we had a nice swim last night.

R: Will you be putting this on your credit card?

G: No. I'll pay cash.

R: Have you used any hotel services since breakfast?

G: No, we haven't.

R: OK. So the total comes to ￥986.78, including tax.

G: I thought it was ￥880. That's what they said yesterday when we checked in…Oh, I forgot. My husband ordered a plate of nachos. Sorry.

R: No problem. So...from ￥1000, here's your change. Now, I'll just need to ask you for your room key.

G: Here you are!

R: Thank you for your coming. Please drop in again. Good-bye.

Unit 5   Switchboard

Situational Conversations

Conversation 1   Receiving a Phone Call

(O: Operator   G: Guest)

O: Hello, International Hotel. How can I help you?

G: Hello, I'd like to be put through to Mr. Smith and his room number is 1208.

O: I'll put you through, madam…I'm sorry the number is engaged. Would you care to hold on please?

G: Of course.

O: Sorry, there is no reply from Mr. Smith. No one is picking up. Would you like to leave a message?

G: Could you try again?

O: Certainly, Madam. Just a moment, please…Thank you for waiting. I'm afraid there is still no reply. Maybe he is not in the room at the moment.

G: May I leave a message?

O: Of course, Madam.

G: Please tell him that the meeting will be at 4 p.m..

O: Ok, the message is – the meeting will be at 4 p.m..

G: That's correct.

O: Can I take you name, please?

G: Yes, it's Mary Banks.

O: Ok, I'll make sure he gets the message.

G: Thank you, Good-bye.

O: You are welcome. Good-bye!

Conversation 2   Explaining the Way to Make Phone Calls

(O: Operator   G: Guest)

O: Good evening, Holiday Inn. What can I do for you?

G: Good evening. I'd like to know how to make a call?

O: For room to room calls, dial room number directly please. For local calls, first dial 9, then the number you want.

G: Thank you. I'd like to make an international call to New York. What can I do then?

O: You may call directly from your room. Dial 9 first, then the country code and area code and last the number you want.

G: I see. Thanks a lot.

O: The call charges will be added to your bill.

G: I see. By the way, what time is it in New York now?

O: There is a time difference of 13 hours. It's 8 o'clock in the morning.

G: I'd like to make a call now. You are so helpful.

O: You are welcome, sir. I'm always at your service.

Conversation 3   Placing a Morning Call

(O: Operator   G: Guest)

O: Good evening. Operator speaking. May I help you?

G: Good evening. I'm leaving for New York tomorrow and I have to wake up early to catch a plane.

O: We can give you a morning call to wake you up.

G: That's great! I need a morning call for 5 a.m..

O: OK. We will give you a wake-up call at 5 a.m..

G: Oh, yes. I'd like to inform my girl-friend in New York of my return. May I use the phone in my room?

O: Certainly, Sir. Just dial the country code, the area code and the number you want.

G: Thank you for your information. Please don't forget. It's very important that I don't miss my plane.

O: Don't worry. We won't forget.

G: Thanks, Goodnight.

O: Goodnight.

Classroom Activities

__ *Listening Practice* __

I. Listen to the recording and complete the following conversation.

(A: Operator   B: Guest)

A: Good afternoon, International Hotel. May I help you?

B: Good afternoon. I have made an appointment with Mr. Brookman Wood from the America. He is staying in this hotel.

A: Oh, do you know his room number?

B: Yes, room 2122.

A: Let me try his extension for you… Sorry, there is no answer form room 2122. May I take a message for him?

B: Yes, please tell him that my name is Grace Wang and I'm from the Business Center General Electric China. I'd like to meet him tomorrow evening in the coffee bar at this hotel around 7:30. Ask him to phone me at this number 55219181.

A: Yes, I'll make sure that Mr. Brookman Wood gets your message.

B: Thank you so much.

II. Listen to the recording and answer the questions.

A: Good morning. Operator. May I help you?

B: Morning. This is Billy calling from Room 1208. I've tried to ring my boss in London twice this morning and both times I was cut off.

A: I am sorry to hear that. Did you actually speak to the person in London, Mr. Billy?

B: Yes, it was the same both times. We spoke for about thirty seconds and then the connection was broken.

A: I am awfully worried for that, Mr. Billy. That certainly should not have happened. May I have his number?

B: Yes, the number is 0044-020-5556728.

A: All right, Mr. Billy. Let me try the number again and see if the fault is in their equipment or in ours. I'll call back as soon as I can.

B: Good. Thank you very much.

A: You are welcome.

Unit 6　Information Service

Situational Conversations

Conversation 1　Information for Shopping & Sightseeing

(G: Guest　　C: Clerk)

G: Excuse me, I'd like to ask you a few questions about the city.

C: Ok, ask away.

G: My wife wants to take the children shopping, where is the best place to go?

C: I would recommend the mall, it's about 15 minutes south in a taxi. It has a wide range of shops and restaurants.

G: Thank you. Also, we'd like to do some sightseeing while we're in town. Can you recommend some local attractions?

C: How old are your children?

G: I have a 7-year-old boy and a girl who is 9.

C: I would recommend a day at the zoo. It's fun for all the family. There is also a water park just outside the city if you would like a day trip.

G: That sounds great.

C: Have a look in the rack by the entrance. We have a selection of leaflets about local tourist attractions. If you find something you like I can help you get discounted tickets and I can arrange transport for you.

G: That's great. Thank you for your help.

C: You're welcome.

Conversation 2　Giving Directions to Hotel

(C: Clerk　T: Taxi Driver)

C: Hello, Hotel International. How can I help you?

T: Hi. I have two of your guests in my cab but I don't know where to find you. How do I get there?

C: Where are you now?

T: I'm at the airport.

C: Take the highway from the airport to the city center.

T: OK.

C: Follow the signs to the museum until you get to the central business district.

T: OK, I know where that is.

C: Take the first left after the Microsoft building and then take the third right.

T: Got it.

C: We're just on the right after the park.

T: OK, thanks for that.

C: That's OK. It should take you about 20 minutes if the traffic is good.

T: Thanks, bye.

Conversation 3   Taking a Message

(R: Receptionist   G: Guest)

R: Good evening! This is the Information Desk. What can I do for you?

G: Good evening. I tried to contact Mr. Black in Room 1602, but I failed. I'd like to be put through to him.

R: Hold on, please…

G: OK.

R: There is no reply form Mr Black. No one is picking up. I'm afraid he is not in. Would you like to leave a message?

G: Yes, thank you. When he gets back, please let him know that Jane called and I need him to call me back.

R: Does he have your number?

G: He does. But I'll give it to you again, 5-2-6-4-4-5-3-6.

R: That was 5-2-6-4-4-5-3-6, right.

G: Yes. Thank you very much.

R: You are welcome.

Classroom Activities

__*Listening Practice*__

I. Listen to the recording and complete the following conversation.

Conversation 1   Introducing restaurants

(C: Clerk   G: Guest)

C: Good morning. What can I do for you?

G: Good morning. I'm planning to take a friend of mine to dinner. You see, we both love Beijing Roast Duck. I'm wondering if you could recommend to me a good local restaurant where I can taste Beijing Roast Duck.

C: I'd love to, if Beijing Roast Duck is what you are looking for, there is no other place in the whole city that will please your appetite better than Qian Men Roast Duck Restaurant. The restaurant serves very good Roast Duck. You might want to try there.

G: How far is it from here?

C: It is on Qian Men Street, near Tian'anmen Square. I would suggest that you'd better take a taxi there.

G: Thank you very much. One more thing, could you write down the name of the restaurant on this piece of paper so that I can show it to the taxi-driver?

C: Yes, here you are.

G: By the way, do you know how much we should pay the taxi-driver for the trip?

C: Perhaps 50 Yuan is OK.

G: Thank you for your information. Good bye.

C: You are welcome. Bye-bye.

Conversation 2   Searching for guests

(C: Clerk   G: Guest)

C: Good afternoon. What can I do for you?

G: Good afternoon. I'm looking for a friend, Mr. Black. Could you tell me if he is in the hotel?

C: Mr. Black? Just a minute, please. I'll see if he is registered.

G: OK, thank you.

C: Black, Mr. Black? There are a lot of Blacks here today... Mr. David Black, Mr. Charles Black...

G: Mr. David Black from Canada. Isn't he staying at this hotel?

C: Oh, yes, here's his name Mr. and Mrs. David Black and family. They are in Room 203. Please wait a moment, let me phone him... Mr. Black said he's waiting for you in his room.

G: OK. Step this way, please. Here it is.

C: Thank you.

G: It's my pleasure.

II. Listen to the recording and answer the questions.

(C: Clerk   G: Guest)

C: Good afternoon, Sir. Can I help you?

G: Yes. I'd like to make an international call to Beijing, China. But I don't know what time it is in Beijing now. Could you tell me, please?

C: Of course, Sir. The time difference between Beijing and New York is 13 hours.

G: Is New York time earlier or later than Beijing time?

C: Sorry, Sir. Beijing time is 13 hours earlier than New York time. You see, the local time in New York now is 14: 30. Then the time in Beijing should be 3:30 in the morning. Have you got it?

G: Yes, Madam. That means now is people's sleeping time in Beijing. I'd better wait for half day to call.

C: If it is not urgent, you can make the call after 19:00.

G: OK, thank you very much.

C: You are welcome.

Unit 7 Foreign Exchange and Cashier's

Situational Conversations

Conversation 1 Exchanging Money

(C: Clerk   G: Guest)

C: Good morning, Sir. What can I do for you?

G: Good morning. I'd like to change some money. Can you do that for me?

C: Of course, Sir. How much?

G: 200 US dollars, please. What's the exchange rate today?

C: Today's exchange rate is 6.37 Yuan to the dollar.

G: Is it the same rate as the bank gives?

C: Exactly the same. Could you give me your name, room number and show me your passport, Sir?

G: Here is my passport. I'm Mark Sheridan in Room 1130.

C: Fine. Mr. Sheridan, would you please sign your name on this memo?

G: Sure. Is it all right?

C: That's all right. Here are your RMB and passport.

G: Thanks a lot. What should I do with the RMB left with me?

C: You have to go to the Bank of China or the airport exchange office.

G: Thank you very much.

C: It's my pleasure.

Conversation 2 Changing Coins

(C: Clerk   G: Guest)

C: Good morning. Can I help you?

G: Good morning. I'm leaving this night, but I still have some RMB here. Could you please help me to change them back into US dollars?

C: I'm sorry. I can't exchange your RMB for US dollars. You can only do it at the Bank of China or the Foreign Exchange Bank at the airport.

G: In that case I'll change my money at the airport.

C: What else could I do for you then?

G: Could you change some coins for me, please? I'm a coin collector.

C: Certainly. How many coins do you want?

G: Can I have 40 Yuan coins?

C: All right. How would you like them?

G: 10 Yuan for 1-Yuan coins, 10 Yuan for 50-cent coins and 20 Yuan for 10-cent, 5-cent, 2-cent and 1-cent coins. Will that be all right?

C: Yes of course. Here you are.

G: Thank you very much.

Conversation 3 Checking Out

(C: Clerk   G: Guest)

C: Good morning, Sir. May I help you?

G: I'm Tom Chan, in Room 123. I'd like to check out. Can I have my bill now?

C: Of course, Sir. Just a moment, please.

G: Thank you.

C: Did you have breakfast this morning at the hotel or have you used any hotel services since breakfast?

G: Yes, I had breakfast, but I paid cash, and I haven't used any services.

C: Fine. The total including service charge for two days is one thousand five hundred and thirty dollars. Please check it.

G: Okay. I can't find any miscalculations.

C: Thank you, Sir. How would you like to pay, by cash or by credit card?

G: Credit card. Here you are.

C: Thank you. Could you sign your name here, please?

G: Fine.

C: Thank you and here is your receipt. Please drop in again. Good-bye.

G: Bye-bye.

Classroom Activities

__ Listening Practice __

I. Listen to the recording and complete the following conversation.

(*C: Clerk   G: Guest*)

C: Good evening, Madam. May I help you?

G: Yes, I'd like to change some money.

C: How much would you like to change?

G: Let me see. I'll need about 700 dollars.

C: I'm afraid we have a change limit of 500 dollars between 9 p.m. and 8 a.m..

G: Well, I'll be leaving at 7:00 a.m. on an all day tour tomorrow and I'll need at least that money. Can't you make an exception for me?

C: I'm afraid that we have to place a limit on exchange for the benefit of all our guests. If we change large amounts, our cash supply runs out and we are unable to oblige our other guest.

G: Why do you keep a change limit?

C: We restrict the amount of cash kept at night for security reasons.

G: Well, I suppose it can't be helped.

II. Listen to the recording and answer the questions.

C: Good morning. May I help you?

G: I'm Peter Lee in room 102. I'm checking out now. But my flight will leave at five thirty and I don't want to wait around at the airport all day. Could I keep the room this afternoon?

C: Certainly, but it's the hotel policy. The check-out time is twelve at noon. You'll have to pay half of the rate more, if you leave after twelve.

G: Never mind, then. Can I just leave my luggage somewhere until three?

C: Certainly, Sir. Please leave it to our Bell Captain's Desk over there. He'll take care of it.

G: Thank you.

C: It's my pleasure.

Unit 8   Housekeeping (Ⅰ)

Situational Conversations

Conversation 1   Cleaning the Room

(*A: Housekeeping Attendant   B: Guest*)

A: Housekeeping. May I come in?

B: Yes, please.

A: Good morning. I'm sorry to disturb you, Sir.

B: It doesn't matter.

A: We'd like to clean the room. Can we do it now?

B: Well, I'm busy typing my report. Could you come back later?

A: Certainly, Sir. What time would it be convenient?

B: Let me see. Could you come around 11:30 a.m.?

A: Sorry, I'm afraid no cleaning can be done from 11:30 a.m. to 1:30 p.m.. May I come between 1:30 p.m. and 2:30 p.m.?

B: I think so. I'll be out then.

A: Let me press the "Do Not Disturb" button for you. If you want me to make up your room, please turn off the "DND" sign or dial 8 to the floor service desk. I'll be back to your service right away.

B: Thank you very much.

A: You're welcome. I'm always at your service.

Conversation 2   Turn-down Service

(A: Housekeeping Attendant   B: Guest)

A: Turn-down service. May I come in?

B: Come on in, please.

A: Good evening, Sir. May I do the turn-down service for you now?

B: Turn-down service? What do you mean by that?

A: It's a kind of chamber service done by the Housekeeping Department in the afternoon. It includes taking away bedspread, tidying up quilt and blanket, drawing curtain, switching on some lights, cleaning bathroom, emptying dustbin, adding or changing boiled water, etc.

B: I see. Well, would you please tidy up the bathroom? I've just taken a bath and it is quite a mess now.

A: Certainly, Sir. I'll clean the bathroom, and then make up the bed.

B: That's fine. Could you change the bath towels for me? They are a little bit dirty.

A: Right away. I'll place some fresh towels there.

B: Yes, that would be nice.

（*Having done all on request*）

A: It's getting dark. Would you like me to draw the curtains for you, Sir?

B: Why not? That would be so cozy.

A: May I turn on the lights for you?

B: Yes, please. I'd like to do some reading.

A: Is there anything I can do for you, Sir?

B: No more. Thank you very much.

A: Pleased to be at your service. Have a very pleasant evening.

Classroom Activities

_ Listening Practice _

I. Listen to the recording and complete the following conversation.

(*A: Clerk   B: Guest*)

A: Good afternoon. Welcome to the tenth floor.

B: Good afternoon, I have just checked in. My room number is 1016.

A: Let me show you to your room…. Here we are.

B: Thank you very much.

A: Now, Sir. May I introduce the room facilities to you? Here is the light switch and this is the temperature adjuster. The wardrobe is here and the cotton bathrobes are inside of it. Beside the wardrobe is the minibar, and there is a mini safe in the wardrobe.

B: Great. Now can you tell me something about the TV programs?

A: Well, the television provides satellite channels plus pay movies, with TV channels in Chinese and English. You can watch news from CNN and BBC. By the way the panel on the night stand between the beds controls the facilities.

B: It's amazing. Oh, by the way, I need a shower after such a long flight.

A: The bathroom is over there with hot water supplied round the clock. You can find all you may need: soap, shampoo, toothpaste and toothbrush, shower cap, comb, razor and shaving cream. If you have any laundry, just put it in the laundry bag. It will be picked up every morning.

B: Thank you very much. You have made me feel welcome.

II. Listen to the recording and answer the questions.

(*A: Clerk   B: Guest*)

A: Good afternoon. May I help you?

B: Yes, This is Room 1102 and I checked in about 15 minutes ago.

A: Yes, Sir. What can I do for you?

B: My room is in a mess. The bed sheets need changing and the bathroom is in a terrible mess. The bathtub is full of water, there is no soap and the tower is dirty.

A: I'm sorry to hear that. How come that happened? Room 1102, let me check…

B: OK.

A: Well, Sir. I do apologize for that. We have made a mistake. Room 1102 is not ready for new guests. The housekeeping should have checked the room. Would you please move to Room 903. That room is clean and neat.

B: All right.

A: Please get your luggage ready and the porter will help you to move.

B: That's very kind of you.

Unit 9　Housekeeping　（九）

Situational Conversations

Conversation 1　Laundry

（A: Laundry clerk　　B: Mrs. Bell）

A: What can I do for you?

B: Could you send someone up for my laundry, please? Room 908, Bell.

A: Certainly, Mrs. Bell. A valet will be up in a few minutes.

B: Good. I also have a silk dress which I don't think is color-fast. Will the color run in the wash?

A: We'll dry-clean the dress. Then the color won't run.

B: You're sure? Good! And the lining of my husband's jacket has come unstitched. It might tear over further while washing.

A: Don't worry, Madam. We'll stitch it before washing.

B: That's fine. Now, when can I have my laundry back?

A: Usually it takes about two days to have laundry done. But would you like express service or same-day?

B: What is the difference in price?

A: We charge 50% more for express, but it only takes 5 hours.

B: And for same-day, will I get the dress and skirt back this evening?

A: Yes, Madam.

B: I'll have same-day service then.

Conversation 2　Room Service

（A: Waiter　　B: John Smith）

A: Good evening, Room Service. This is Peter speaking. How may I assist you?

B: I want to order dinner for two. We will start with soup. What is the soup of the day?

A: The soup of the day is cream of corn.

B: OK. Two soup of the day. For main course, we'd like two fried noodles.

A: And for dessert?

B: Two apple pies with ice cream.

A: What would you like to drink?

B: A bottle of red wine, please.

A: Would you like French or American?

B: No. The local Dynasty wine is fine.

A: All right. Let me repeat your order, two cream of corn, two fried noodles, two apple pies with ice cream and one bottle of Dynasty red wine. Am I correct?

B: Right. When will it be served?

A: In about 25 minutes.

B: Very good. Thank you.

A: May I have your name and room number, Sir?

B: This is John Smith, room 1806.

A: OK, Mr. Smith, your order will be ready soon. Good-bye.

Conversation 3　Morning Call

(*A: Room attendant　　B: Mr. Jackson*）

B: Good evening! This is Mr. Jackson in Room 815.

A: Good evening, Mr. Jackson. What can I do for you?

B: This is my first visit to China. I wonder if your hotel has the morning call service.

A: Yes, sir. Anyone who stays in our hotel can ask for the service. Would you like a morning call?

B: Yes, I must get up earlier tomorrow. I want to go to the Bund to enjoy the morning scenery there. You know this is my first visit to Shanghai. People say there is a marvelous view of a poetic yet bustling life at the Bund just at dawn.

A: That's true. At what time do you want me to call you up, Sir?

B: At 6:00 sharp tomorrow morning, please.

A: What kind of call would you like, by phone or by knocking at the door?

B: By phone. I don't want to disturb my neighbors.

A: Yes, Sir. I'll tell the operator to call you up at 6:00 tomorrow morning. Anything else I can do for you?

B: No. Thanks. Good night.

A: Good night, Sir. Sleep well and have a pleasant dream.

Classroom Activities

__ *Listening Practice* __

I. Listen to the recording and complete the following conversation.

(*F: Floor attendant　　G: Guest*)

G: Good morning. Would you please do me a favor?

F: Yes, Sir. I'm always at your service.

G: My friend is coming here tonight for two days. Could I have an extra bed?

F: Please contact the Front Office first. I'll get you the extra bed with their permission.

G: Have you any idea how much an extra bed costs?

F: It's $30 for one night.

G: By the way, could you get us a few more hangers? I have so many clothes. I am long-staying guest, as you know.

F: Yes, Sir. We are happy to have you. We do hope you are enjoying your stay with us.

G: Thanks. Could you change a pillow for me? This one is too thin, and with a stain on it.

F: Certainly, Sir. I'll see to it right away. I do wish we had known earlier.

G: How nice of you to say so!

F: It's my pleasure. I'll be back in a minute, Sir.

II. Listen to the recording and answer the questions.

(A: Guest   B: Clerk)

A: Excuse me. My room number is 201.

B: Yes, Sir. What can I do for you?

A: I don't mean to make trouble, but I have to say that it was so noisy during the night that I kept awake last night.

B: Oh, I'm very sorry to hear that.

A: There is a lot of noise from the street and a construction site nearby.

B: Yes, I'll see if I can find another quieter room for you… Got it! You may move to room 812. It's higher up and at the backside.

A: That would be better. Thank you for your kindness.

B: Please bring your key card to the reception and the receptionist will help you to make the change.

A: Thank you very much.

B: You are welcome. Just let me know if there is anything I can do for you?

Unit 10   Maintenance and Safety

Situational Conversations

Conversation 1   The TV Doesn't Work

(A: Housekeeper   B: Maintenance man   C: Guest)

A: Housekeeping. Can I help you?

C: Yes. The TV doesn't work in my room. Could you send someone to fix it?

A: I'm sorry to hear that. What's your room number, please?

C: 808.

A: OK. Just a moment, I'll send the maintenance man to your room at once.

B: (after knocking at the door) Maintenance, may I come in?

C: (open the door)

B: Good afternoon, I've come to fix your TV set.

C: Oh, great. Come in.

B: What's wrong with the TV set?

C: The picture is blinking and the sound is not clear.

B: (After examining the TV) Don't worry. There is nothing wrong with the TV set. The cable TV is under examination and repair today. It probably will be fine this evening.

C: Ok, I see. By the way, is there an internet connection in my room?

B: Yes, there is. You can find it right behind the dressing table. It's RMB 100 for 24 hours and 2 RMB per minute.

C: Oh, that is expensive.

B: We also have wireless internet access. It is free of charge.

C: That's terrific. Shall I input the pin number or password?

B: Not necessary. It's user-friendly.

C: Great. Thank you very much.

B: It's my pleasure.

Conversation 2   Changing a Noisy Room

(A: Housekeeper   B: Guest)

A: Good morning, sir. Is there anything I can do for you?

B: I'm Louis Palmer. I'm in Room 1046. Can you change the room for me? It's too noisy. My wife was woken up several times last night by the noise from elevator. She said it was too much for her.

A: I'm awfully sorry, Sir. I do apologize. Room 1046 is at the end of the corridor and close to the elevator. It's possible that the noise is heard early in the morning when all is quiet.

B : Anyhow, I'd like to change our room.

A: No problem, Sir. We'll manage it, but we don't have any room available today. Could you wait till tomorrow? One group will be leaving tomorrow morning. There'll be some rooms for you to choose from.

B: All right. I hope we'll be able to enjoy our stay in a quiet room tomorrow evening and have a sound sleep.

A: Be sure. I'll make a note of that. Everything will be taken care of. And if there is anything more you need, please let us know.

Conversation 3　Asking for a Duplicate Key

(A: Room attendant　B: Electrician　C: Mrs. Green)

A: Hello, Mrs. Green. What can I do for you?

C: I've locked myself out of the room. May I borrow a duplicate key?

A: Don't worry. I'll open the door for you.

C: Thank you very much. Sometimes I'm quite absent-minded.

A: It doesn't matter, Mrs. Green. What else can I do for you?

C: Ah, I'm afraid there's something wrong with the light bulb. One of the light bulbs is burnt out.

A: I'm sorry. I'll send for an electrician from the Maintenance Department. We can have it repaired. Please wait just a few minutes, Mrs. Green.

　(She leaves the room. Ten minutes later, there is a knock on the door.)

B: May I come in?

C: (Opening the door) How do you do?

B: How do you do? The light bulb is out of order, isn't it, Mrs. Green?

C: Yes, it is.

B: Would you show me which one?

C: Yes, the one in the bathroom.

B: I'll change it immediately. (He finishes the repairing and checks other electric facilities in the room.) Mrs. Green, everything is OK now.

C: Thank you, young man. You are very helpful.

B: You are welcome. Enjoy your stay, Mrs. Green.

Classroom Activities

_ *Listening Practice* _

I. Listen to the recording and complete the following conversation.

(H: Housekeeper　　G: guest　　E: Electrician)

G: I have locked myself out of my room? May I borrow a duplicate key.

H: Don't worry, Madam. I'll open the door for you.

G: Thank you very much indeed. Sometimes I'm quite absent-minded.

H: It doesn't matter, Madam. What else can I do for you?

G: Well, I'm afraid there's something wrong with the TV. The picture is not clear.

H: I'm sorry. May I have a look at it?

G: Sure. Come on in.

(The housekeeper tried to fix it but in vain)

H: I'll send for an electrician from the maintenance department. Please wait just a few minutes,

Madam.

G: That's very kind of you.

...

E: (Knocking at the door.) Maintenance. May I come in?

G: Come in, please.

E: Thanks, Madam. I'm here to check and fix your TV.

G: By all means.

E: Let me have a look … Madam, everything is OK. Please have a try. Here is the remote.

G: What efficiency! Thanks a lot. (Taking out some money) This is for you.

E: Oh, no. We won't accept tips but thank you anyway. We wish you a nice stay with us, Madam.

II. Listen to the recordings and then fill in the form.

Conversation 1

(H: Housekeeper   G: Guest)

H: Housekeeping. May I come in?

G: Yes, what's the matter?

H: Your smoke detector is flashing, Sir. Is there anything burning in your room?

G: No. I've been smoking. That's all.

H: May I look around?

G: Go ahead.

H: Thank you very much. But I have to tell you our hotel is "Green" hotel. Our policy is whoever smoking inside hotel will be fined…

Conversation 2

(H: Housekeeper   G: Guest)

H: Maintenance. May I come in?

G: Come in.

H: What's the trouble?

G: The water tap drips all night long. I can hardly sleep.

H: I'm so sorry. Some parts need to be replaced. I'll fix it as soon as possible. It will not take too much time.

Conversation 3

(H: Housekeeper   G: Guest)

H: Good evening. Did you call for service? What can I do for you?

G: Yes. The light in this room is too dim. Please get me a brighter one.

H: Certainly, Sir. I'll be back right away.

Conversation 4

(H: Housekeeper   G: Guest)

G: My air conditioner is out of order and it makes too much noise.

H: I'm sorry, Sir. Let me take care of it.

G: Go ahead.

H: Excuse me, Sir. The filter of the machine is too dirty. We have to clean it.

G: Then how long shall I have to wait? It's so hot in the room.

H: If you like, we can help you to move to a new room.

Unit 11   Restaurant Service

Situational Conversations

Conversation 1   Receiving Guests

(A: Receptionist   B: Guest)

(A couple are waiting to be seated in a crowded restaurant)

A: Good evening, Sir and Madam. Welcome to our restaurant.

B: Good evening. Do you have a table for two?

A: Do you have a reservation, Sir?

B: I'm afraid not. I've just arrived with my wife.

A: Are you staying at our hotel?

B: Yes. We're in room 312.

A: I'm sorry, Sir. The restaurant is full now. You have to wait for about half an hour. Would you like to have a drink in the lounge while you are waiting? We'll call you as soon as we have a table.

B: No, thanks. We'll come back later. May I reserve a table for two now?

A: Yes, of course. May I have your name, please?

B: Victor Johnson. By the way, can we have a table by the window?

A: We'll try to arrange it but I can't guarantee, Mr. Johnson.

B: That's fine.

A: Do you prefer smoking or non-smoking area?

B: Non-smoking. Thank you.

 (Half an hour later, the couple comes back.)

A: Your table is ready, Mr. Johnson. Please step this way.

B: Okay.

A: Would you like to take your seat, Sir? Here's the menu. The waiter will come in a few minutes to take your order.

Conversation 2   At the Western Restaurant

(A: Waitress   B: Mr. Smith   C: Mrs. Smith)

A: Good evening, Mr. and Mrs. Smith. How are you today?

B: Oh, very nice. Today we visited Nanshan. We're starving now, and we decided to end our day with a nice and quiet dinner.

A: I will be at your service this evening.

B: Thank you.

A: Then, may I suggest starting with a nice glass of wine? We have a very nice Californian wine as our specialty of month.

B: That's a good idea. Let's have a nice bottle of wine with dinner.

A: Do you prefer red or white wine?

B: We both prefer red wine.

A: All right, a bottle of red Californian red wine. And have you made a choice for the main course yet?

B: Yes. We have. I'd like the sirloin steak served with roast potatoes.

A: Which sauce do you prefer, black pepper, mushroom or Bearnaise?

B: For me the black pepper sauce, please.

A: And for you, Mrs. Smith?

C: I'd like the tenderloin with mushroom sauce, please...

A: How would you like your steak done?

C: Well done, please.

A: And while you are waiting for your main course may I suggest a soup? Our seafood chowder is very good.

B: Well, I'd like to try the soup.

C: No, not for me. Thank you.

A: Would you like to order dessert now or later?

B: Later.

A: May I repeat your order? A bottle of Californian red wine. Furthermore for Mr. Smith, one seafood chowder and the sirloin steak served with roast potatoes and black pepper sauce. For Mrs. Smith the tenderloin steak with mushroom sauce.

B: That's right. Thank you very much.

Conversation 3   At the Chinese Restaurant

(A: Waiter   B: Guest)

A: Are you ready to order now?

B: Yes. I'd like to try some local specialties. What do you recommend?

A: I recommend poached chicken. It is very famous in Hainan.

B: Good. What pork dishes do you have?

A: Do you like sweet and sour food? Many Guests like the sweet and sour pork.

B: Well, I do, but my wife doesn't. So I think it is better to order something else.

A: Maybe pan fried lamb. It is the local specialty in Hainan.

B: Yes. We will try that one.

A: Would you care for a soup too?

B: Where are the soups listed?

A: On the next page.

B: Oh here, I see. Yes, we'll take the bean curd soup with seasonal vegetable.

A: Certainly. Do you want some vegetable?

B: No, thank you.

A: And noodles?

B: No. rice is OK.

Classroom Activities

_ Listening Practice _

I. Listen to the recording and complete the following conversation.

(*W: Waiter   G: Guest*)

W: Good afternoon, how can I help you today?

G: I'd like a table for one, please.

W: Right this way. Here you are.

G: Thank you. Can I have a menu?

W: Here you are. My name's Alan and I'm your waiter today. Would you like to hear today's specials?

G: Certainly.

W: Well, we have a wonderful mushroom soup to start off with. Today's main course is fish and chips.

G: Fish and chips? Is the fish fresh?

W: Certainly, Madam. Fresh off the docks this morning.

G: Alright, I'd like the fish and chips.

W: Would you like to have a starter?

G: Hmmm, I'm not sure.

W: Our salads are excellent, Madam.

G: I'd like a green salad.

W: Very good. Would you like something to drink?

G: Oh, I'd like some mineral water, please.

W: OK. So that's a green salad, fish and chips and mineral water.

G: Yes, that's right.

W: Thank you and enjoy your lunch.

G: Thank you.

II. Listen to the recording and answer the questions.

(*W: Waiter   G: Guest*)

G: Waiter.

W: Yes, Madam?

G: This coffee is too weak.

W: I'm sorry, Madam. I'll get you another one. Is everything all right?

G: No, this fish was recommended, but it is not fresh.

W: Oh! Sorry to hear that. This is quite unusual as we have fresh fish from the market every day.

G: Who knows? It is not fresh and I am not happy about it.

W: I'm terribly sorry, Madam. I'll look into the matter. I can give you something replaced, if you'd like a change. That would be our treat, of course.

G: It is very kind of you, but I suffered too much here. All that I need is fresh and healthy food. I don't want to trouble anyone. No more, thanks.

W: Just feel ease, Madam. Please give us another chance. I'm sure everything will be all right again the next time you come.

G: I hope so.

W: Thank you very much, Madam.

Unit 12   Bar Service

Situational Conversations

Conversation 1   Take Bverage Order

(*A: Bartender   B: Guest*)

A: Good afternoon, Mr. Adams. How are you today?

B: Good. Thank you.

A: Your wife is not coming today?

B: Yes, she is. She will be here in a few minutes.

A: I see. You still prefer the smoking area?

B: As always.

A: This way, please. Is this table all right for you?

B: Yes. Thanks.

A: What would you like to drink today?

B: Local beer for me, please, and for my wife, a fresh orange juice.

A: One local beer and one fresh orange juice, am I correct?

B: Yes.

A: Do you want some snacks with the drink?

B: What snacks do you sell?

A: We have peanuts and potato chips. But the popcorn is free today.

B: OK, give me some popcorn.

   (Later) Now how much do I owe you?

A: It's 40 Yuan plus 10% service charge. So the total is 44 Yuan.

B: Okay. Can I sign for it?

A: Certainly. Could you sign your name here, please? Thank you.

Conversation 2   Serving the Guest

(A: Bartender   B: Ben Adams   C: Rooney Black)

A: Good evening, Sir! Welcome to Lotus Bar.

B: Good evening.

A: What would you like to drink, sir?

B: I'd prefer a brandy.

A: How do you like your brandy? Straight up or on the rocks?

B: With ice, thank you.

A: (Turn to Rooney Black) What about you, Sir?

C: I can hardly decide what to drink. What do you recommend?

A: I suggest you have a taste of Shanghai cocktail.

C: That's a good idea. I'll have a Shanghai cocktail.

A: Have you ever been in Shanghai?

B: No, not yet. This is our first trip to Shanghai.

A: It is quite difficult to get used to the time difference, isn't it?

C: Yes it is.

 (after a while)

A: Excuse me. Here are your drinks, a brandy with ice and a Shanghai cocktail.

B: Thank you. How much please?

A: The total is 60 Yuan, including 10% service charge.

Conversation 3 Serving the Guest

(A: Guest   B: Barman)

A: Is this bar open now?

B: Yes, Sir. We are open round the clock. But the bar is full now. Do you care to wait for about 20 minutes?

A: OK.

B: Would you like to read China Daily while waiting?

A: That's fine. Thank you.

(about 20 minutes later)

B: We have a table for you now, Sir. This way, please. We're very sorry for the delay.

A: That's all right.

B: Here is the drink list, Sir. Which do you prefer?

A: Are there any famous Chinese spirits?

B: What about Mao Tai?

A: I have no idea about Mao Tai. What kind of liquor is it?

B: It's one of the most famous liquors in China. It tastes good and never goes to the head. Many guests give high comments on the liquor.

A: Sounds great. I'd like to have a try. By the way, please book me a table tomorrow evening and here are tips for you.

B: Id like to. But we don't accept tips. Thank you just the same.

Classroom Activities

__ *Listening Practice* __

I. Listen to the recording and complete the following conversation.

(B: Barman   J: Jack   S: Sally)

B: Good evening, Sir and Madam. What may I offer you tonight?

J: Sally, what do you prefer?

S: I don't know what I want. I'm not really a drinker.

J: It doesn't matter. I would like to look through the drink list.

B: OK, Sir. Here is the drink list.

J: An aperitif or some white wine?

S: Sorry, I don't drink at all.

J: Man, what would you recommend for the lady?

B: How about our special cocktail? It is usually popular with ladies.

S: Is it non-alcoholic?

B: Certainly, Madam. It is a kind of soft drink.

S: It sounds interesting. I'll take that.

B: Okay, Madam. What can I make for you, Sir?

J: I'm very thirsty. I'll have some beer.

B: Any special brand, Sir?

J: What about your local brew? I hear it's good.

B: It is Yan Jing Beer. Bottled or draught?

J: Let me try the draught.

B: Fine. One non-alcoholic cocktail for the lady and one draught Yang Jing Beer.

J: Yes, that's right. By the way, could we have some snacks?

B: Certainly, I'll get a fresh supply.

J: Thank you. How much do I owe you?

B: 86 Yuan. You can hold the payment of the bill until you decide to leave if you like.

J: That's great.

II. Listen to the recording and choose the best answer with the questions.

(J: Mr. Jackson   B: Bartender)

J: Bartender, could I have a drink? What's taking so long?

B: Excuse me, Sir. Yes, what can I get you?

J: I'd like a whiskey sour.

B: Certainly Sir, I'll get that straight away.

J: What a day! My feet are aching! Where's an ashtray?

B: Here you go, Sir. Did you have a busy day?

J: Yes, I had to walk all over town to get to meetings. I'm exhausted.

B: I'm sorry to hear that, Sir. Here's your drink. That should help.

J: (takes a long sip)

   That's what I needed. Much better. Do you have any snacks?

B: Certainly, here are some peanuts and some savory crackers, and a napkin.

J: Could I have a stir stick?

B: Coming up... Here you are.

J: Thanks. You know, I'm sorry to say this, but these snacks are awful.

B: I'm terribly sorry about that, Sir. What seems to be the matter?

J: The peanuts are stale!

B: I apologize, Sir. I'll open a fresh can immediately.

J: Thanks. Sorry to be in such a bad mood.

B: That's quite alright. Can I get you another drink? This one's on the house.

J: That's kind of you. Yes, I'll have another whiskey sour.

B: Right away, Sir. Do you have any preferences on the whiskey?

J: Hmmm, what's that bottle over there?

B: That's Jack Daniel's—aged 12 years.

J: That sounds good. I'd like to smoke...

B: Just a moment, here's an ashtray.

J: Thanks. So how long have you worked at this bar?

B: It's been about three years now. I love this job...

Unit 13　Business Service

Situational Conversations

Conversation 1　Booking Flight

(C: Clerk of Business Center　　G: Guest)

C: Good afternoon, Madam, can I help you?

G: Good afternoon. Is there any flight to Washington on September 24th?

C: Oh, let me see. There are three flights. The planes take off at about 9:00 a.m., 14:00 p.m. and 18:00 p.m..

G: I'll take 14:00 p.m. flight, then. Would you like to book a ticket for me?

C: Of course. Would you please fill in this form and present your passport?

G: OK. Here you are.

C: Which method do you want to fly, first class or economy?

G: First class, please.

C: To a window seat or an aisle one, which do you like?

G: An aisle seat, please. Can I pay cash now?

C: Yes, please pay 800 Yuan in advance.

G: OK, and when can I get the ticket?

C: We'll have the ticket sent to you on the morning of September 23th. Would you give me your phone number and address?

G: I'm now staying in Room 305. My telephone number is 13688322135. Thank you very much.

C: My pleasure.

Conversation 2　Copying and Typing

(C: Clerk　　G: Guest)

C: Good evening, Sir. What can I do for you?

G: Oh, I'd like to make these materials copied.

C: OK. How many copies do you want?

G: Three copies for each.

C: Oh, but your original is not very clear, would you mind making it a little darker by me?

G: All right. And would you copy these on both sides to the paper?

C: Certainly.

G: I'll leave the original here. Please call me when the copies are ready.

G: OK.

(*Two hours later*)

C: Here you are, Sir.

G: Thank you very much. And can you type these materials for me?

C: Certainly. What font and size would you like?

G: Times New Roman, size 4, to A 4 paper.

C: I see. What time do you expect it?

G: The sooner, the better! I need it before 10 o'clock.

C: OK. I'll send it to your room as soon as I finish typing.

G: Thank you very much.

C: (*Bring the bill*) Please sign your name here!

G: OK.

Classroom Activities

__ *Listening Practice* __

I. Listen to the recording and complete the following conversation.

(C: Clerk   G: guest)

C: Good morning, Mr. Black. What can I do for you?

G: Yes. I'd like to know whether you provide internet service here. I have to answer an E-mail to my boss.

C: Yes. Internet access is available in all guest rooms. The access is just next to the standing lamp.

G: Yes. I know. But I forgot to bring my laptop with me. I just wonder whether I can send E-mail here.

C: Well, you can get on the internet here. the price for half an hour of connection is 20 Yuan.

G: That's good.

(*a few minutes later*)

G: Your computer is very quick. I've done everything I wanted.

C: Pleased to hear that. For 25 minutes, we charge you 20 Yuan. We charge it on half an hour basis.

G: I see. Can I sign it to my room?

C: Yes, Sir. May I look at your room card?

G: Here they are.

II. Listen to the recording and answer the questions.

1.

(C: Clerk   G: Guest)

C: Good afternoon. Can I help you?

G: Yes. I'd like to make a long distance call to France. Could you please tell me the rate for calling France?

C: Yes, of course. The standard rate for calling France is 0.7 Yuan for every 6 seconds, excluding service charge.

G: What's your service charge, then?

C: It's 15%。

G: I see. Thank you.

2.

(C: Clerk   G: Guest)

C: Good morning, Sir. Can I help you?

G: Good morning. I want to send a fax.

C: Where to, Sir?

G: To Taiwan. Here is the fax number, (886) 02-2396-9795.

C: OK. I will send this fax at once.

G: Thank you.

C: You're welcome. (after a while) All done, Sir. Here you are.

G: Thank you. How much does it cost?

C: Let me see. It's 15.5 Yuan in all. How would you like to make the payment, Sir?

G: I'd like to pay in cash. Here you are.

C: Thank you. Here's the change.

Unit 14   Shopping Arcade

Conversation 1   Selecting a Gift

(A: Assistant   G: Guest)

A: Good afternoon, Madam. Welcome to our arcade.

G: Good afternoon. I want to buy a gift for my daughter.

A: Have you got an idea?

G: I'm afraid not.

A: Can I give you some advice?

G: Of course!

A: Why not give her a gift with Chinese feature?

G: Surely that's a good idea. What are they?

A: Things such as a pearl necklace, a silk blouse, a paper fan or the traditional Chinese paintings.

G: I think I'd better give her a pearl necklace. Is that OK?

A: Certainly. Girls always like beautiful jewelry, especially given by their mothers.

R: But I have never bought pearls before. Could you give me some suggestions on how to select the pearl necklace?

A: No problem, natural pearls are of higher value and cultured pearls can be made into more colors and designs and they have equal luster.

R: In my mind cultured pearls are more beautiful. What about the price?

A: The label price is RMB 4200.

G: It's a little high.

A: If you really want, you can get a discount of 20 percent. It's RMB 3360.

G: Are they real pearls?

A: Of course. Everything sold here is real. In this business our Arcade has good reputation.

G: I'll take it.

A: So I'll wrap it for you with a beautiful ribbon.

G: Thank you very much.

A: My pleasure.

Conversation 2　About Chinese Arts and Crafts

(A: Assistant　G: Guest)

A: Good morning, Sir. What can I do for you?

G: Oh, yes. I want to select some presents for my friends.

A: What would you like? We have various traditional Chinese arts and crafts.

G: I have no idea about them. Could you give me some suggestion?

A: Surely, these are Chinese figure paintings. They are made with ink brushes, ink sticks, rice paper and ink slabs, which are called the Four Treasures of Study.

G: Excellent. Are they expensive?

A: The prices are from several hundred RMB to several thousand RMB.

G: What is the vase made of?

A: It is made of the traditional enamel ware cloisonné and the typical color is blue. But now we have all kinds of colors.

G: What about this tea set?

A: It is made by Jingdezhen, Jiangxi, which is the Porcelain Capital of China. From Tang Dynasty, the famous ware is tri-chromatic glazed ware.

G: On the tea sets, I can see so many beautiful pictures.

A: Not only tea sets, but also coffee sets and table wares are made by them. Celadon is more famous than white ware. Which one do you like?

G: So I choose a vase and a tea set.

A: OK. I will give them to you at a reasonable price.

Classroom Activities

_ Listening Practice _

I. Listen to the recording and complete the following conversation.

(A: Assistant   C: Customer)

A: Welcome to Robinson's Shoes. We're having a sale on dress shoes.

C: That's great. I need some dress shoes. What do you have on sale?

A: Well, we have Silver Queens and Cool Holidays.

C: What do you recommend?

A: Well, Silver Queens are more fashionable and with higher quality. Whereas, Cool Holidays are not as expensive and they're more comfortable.

C: What's the difference in price?

A: With tax, the Silver Queens come to $47.00 and the Cool Holidays come to $39.00.

C: So that's about an $8.00 difference.

A: That's right.

C: I'll take the Cool Holidays.

A: How would you like to pay?

C: I'll put it on my credit card.

A: All right, here's your receipt. Have a nice day.

C: Thanks.

A: My pleasure.

Unit 15   Recreation and Fitness

Situational Conversations

Conversation 1   At Night Club

(W: Waiter   G: Guest)

W: Good evening, Madam and Sir. Welcome to our night club.

G: Good evening. We'd like to relax completely.

W: Here is your ideal place. We have karaoke hall and KTV rooms. Which one do you prefer?

G: It is the first time that we come here. Could you give us some advice?

W: Surely. The karaoke hall is equipped with super stereo and lightning systems. In a fashion style the dancing stage is decorated. Many Fashion Shows have been held here. It's 15 Yuan to sing a song.

G: Not bad. How about the KTV room?

W: The big room accommodating over 8 persons is 80 Yuan per hour including drinks, the small room with or under 8 persons is 50 Yuan per hour excluding drinks.

G: Sounds great. We want a small room. What kind of songs do you have?

W: We have all kinds including folk songs, pop songs, and rock and roll, and so on. As for language, we have Mandarin songs, Cantonese songs, South Korean songs and English songs. You just name it.

G: OK. But how will we use this machine?

W: It's very easy. First, select the codes of the songs you choose; second, press the key "input", that's OK.

G: Thank you for your introduction.

Conversation 2   At Training Center

(C: Clerk   G: Guest)

A: Good evening, Sir. Can I help you?

G: Oh, yes. I want to do some exercises. Would you introduce your facilities to me?

A: Of course. We have a well-equipped gymnasium with the latest recreational sports apparatus. You can see that we have race apparatus, rowing machines, stationary bikes, muscle builder sets, chest expanders and spring-grips, and so on.

G: Great! Are they safe?

A: No Problem. They are all made by the famous sports apparatus company.

G: Excellent. I wonder how to use these machines.

A: Our coach will tell you, moreover he will supervise all the activities.

G: Are there any other exercises?

A: Yes, We have Yoga lessons and Taiji lessons from 7 p.m. to 9 p.m. every evening.

G: Do you have any other sports rooms?

A: Well, we have a ping-pang room on the third floor and a bowling center and a game center on the fourth floor.

G: Is there a swimming pool?

A: The swimming pool is on the second floor under ground. It is 50 meters long and 2 meters deep, with security men on the bank.

G: Very good. Thank you, I will go to swim there.

Classroom Activities

__ *Listening Practice* __

I. Listen to the recording and complete the following conversation.

(C: Clerk   G: Guest)

C: Good evening, what can I do for you?

G: My doctor advised me to keep in good physical condition. Could you tell me what facilities you have here?

C: Well, we have a well-equipped gym with all the latest recreational sports apparatus, and we also have several sports courts to play tennis, badminton and ping-pang ball.

G: That's very good.

C: There is a wonderful sauna in our club. You can have a try.

G: Really? That sounds interesting. Is here a swimming pool?

C: Yes, of course. Our swimming pool is excellent.

G: Why do you say it's excellent?

C: First, it's big enough. It's 25 meters long, 20 meters wide and 2.5 meters deep.

G: And then?

C: Second, It's a heated swimming pool. The water can keep a comfortable temperature all year round. You can swim in any season.

G: Anymore?

C: At last, you can relax with beer, juice and coffee beside the pool.

G: Oh, it seems that I must spend some money here tonight.

C: The charge is very reasonable, I promise.

G: OK. Thank you for your information.

C: My pleasure, Sir. Have a nice time.

Unit 16　Meeting Service

Situational Conversations

Conversation 1　Arranging a Conference

(P: Conference planer   M: Manager of the Meeting Service)

P: Good afternoon, Sir.

M: Good afternoon. Welcome to our hotel. Can I help you?

P: Our firm is going to hold a video-conference next month. Would you please give me an introduction about your conference facilities?

M: OK. Our hotel is one of the best convention hotels in the city. We have 20 meeting rooms with the most modern equipment, video-conference and simultaneous translation system. So what size of conference will you have?

P: There will be 300 guests attending the convention. And the conference lasts 4 days from 20th to 23rd in August.

M: I see. What kind of facilities would you need?

P: We need a large conference hall with video-conference facilities and eight smaller meeting rooms. How much are they?

M: 2000 Yuan for the large conference hall and 300 Yuan for each smaller room per day.

P: Great. Besides that, we also want to reserve one suite for our office and 150 double rooms for the guests to the convention. Could you give me the rate, please.

M: 650 Yuan per night for a standard suite and 350 Yuan for a double room.

P: Now shall we talk about the meals? We want to host the guests buffet every day.

M: Could you give me more details about your requirements for the breakfast and buffet, such as the meal time?

P: I think the breakfast's time is 7:00 a.m. and buffet is 12:00 at noon and 6:30 p.m.. Can I know the terms?

M: Yes. The cost for the breakfast is 30 Yuan per person and 120 Yuan each for the buffet. Would you like tea and some snacks to be served in the meeting rooms?

P: That seems fine. You're so considerate. And I don't think there's anything else.

M: OK. We're looking forward to your guests.

Conversation 2　Booking Meeting Facilities

(C: Clerk　　G: Guest)

C: Good afternoon. Can I help you?

G: Good afternoon. Because we're going to hold a meeting on next Sunday, I want to book some facilities and personnel for it.

C: Next Sunday… it is November 15th, isn't it?

G: Yes. We need a conference hall for 200 people and six smaller rooms for discussion.

C: I see. We have some multi-function halls that can accommodate from 100 to 400 guests at the meeting and for buffet and cock-tail parties. And we also have several smaller meeting rooms which can seat about 50 people.

G: Great. What basic equipment do you offer?

C: The basic equipment includes such as recorders, microphones, loudspeakers.

G: That's great.

C: By next Wednesday everything will be ready. And you can come and check it then.

G: OK. Thanks.

Classroom Activities

_ *Listening Practice* _

I. Listen to the recording and complete the following conversation.

Conveniently located in the heart of midtown New York City, the Roosevelt Hotel gives you the unique opportunity to plan an intimate meeting to a stunning gala by offering a vast choice of meeting rooms.

Meeting:

Wayport High Speed Internet access is available in all 30,000 square feet of our function and meeting space, as well as in all of our 1,015 guest rooms. Also, WiFi Wireless Internet access is available in all common areas of the hotel.

In addition, the flexibility of 19 well-appointed breakout rooms complete with direct phone lines and PC compatibility, our on-site audio visual company and outstanding video conferencing abilities, makes the Roosevelt Hotel the ideal location in New York City to hold your next corporate event of 10 to 500 people.

Accommodation:

Each of our 1,015 luxurious New York City guest rooms, including the 52 suites, combine the classic styling of yesterday with all the modern conveniences of today.

Each guest room has new HD flat screen TVs, wireless internet access, dual telephone lines with voice mail, dataport capabilities, individual climate control, cable television and hairdryers, and irons and boards to assure that you have all the comforts of home.

For New York City business travelers, each of our guest rooms has a sofa chair, desk lamp with Internet and DC plugs, an ergonomic desk chair and high-speed Internet access so you're able to be productive away from the office.

The Roosevelt Hotel Presidential Suite boasts a square footage of 3,900 with eight rooms. That includes two bedrooms, a complete kitchen, formal living and dining area, and an expansive wrap-around terrace with a panoramic city view.

Fill out our online request for proposal to schedule your next meeting.

II. Listen to the recording and answer the questions.

(M: Manager of the Meeting Service   G: Guest)

M: Good afternoon. What can I do for you?

G: Good afternoon. I am Robby Smith from Sony. Our company is going to hold a convention in next month. We need several meeting rooms for our convention.

M: We'd be greatly honored to host you. Our hotel is one of the most technologically advanced and functionally superb venues in the city. If you are free, I'd like to show you the facilities in our meeting hall.

G: That's good. Thank you very much.

M: This center can comfortably seat 400 guests. And this is the 200-square meter center stage.

G: Is it movable? There is to be an awarding ceremony. We need raised tiers for those prizewinners.

M: The center stage can be raised or lowered in tiers. Let me show you. Press this green button and the curtain is raised.

G: Oh, I see. Is the screen connected with projector?

M: Yes. It is also equipped with hi-fi AV.

G: What if some of the speakers will use laptop computers?

M: They can connect it with the rear screen projector over the lectern.

G: How can the audience participate in the discussion?

M: Don't worry. We have some wireless microphones come in handy.

G: That's good. By the way, is there a simultaneous translation system?

M: Of course. Each participant is provided with a cordless headset receiver.

G : That's great. May I know the terms?

M: 2000 for the multi-function hall. 800 for each small room per day.

Transcripts for Listening Practice

Unit 1   Hotel Basics

Listening Practice

I. Listen to the recording and complete the following passage.

Welcome to Holiday Inn DIAMOND BAR

With a breathtaking view overlooking the San Gabriel Mountains our hotel's location is near Anaheim, downtown Los Angeles and a number of attractions and businesses making it the premier place to stay for business and leisure travelers.

Leisure travelers love that our hotel is near Disneyland® and many other local attractions including the Big League Dreams sports park and outdoor activities like golf and tennis. In addition, we are close to a variety of shops at the Ontario Mills which easily can meet all of your shopping needs.

Corporate guests of our hotel enjoy being near Anaheim businesses and appreciate the 24-hour business center that has fax, copy Internet access and print services. In addition, over 5,000 square feet of meeting space is available for our guests. Feel free to reserve one of our 13 rooms and take advantage our technical amenities and helpful service staff who can ensure that your next meeting or social event is a success.

Whether you're looking for hotels near Disneyland and Los Angeles or those near local corporations, we are the perfect choice. You'll feel right at home here as you relax by our outdoor pool and soak up the sun or as you burn off some steam in the fitness center. And, when it's time for a meal, you can eat right on our property at the on-site restaurant, DB's Bar and Grill, where kids eat free! Choose us— the name you can trust.

II. Listen to the recording and answer the questions.

(M: Hotel training manager   G: George, a college student during his internship)

M: Good morning, Gorge. You're going to spend 6 months on having your operational and managerial internship in our hotel. Right?

G: Yes. If possible, I'd like to work and learn in every department of both the front of the house and the back of the house.

M: Why not? First of all, you'll be a Front Office clerk. You'll be a reservation agent, receptionist, bellman, informant, operator and cashier. You'll have the most direct contact with foreign guests.

G: Great! Thank you. What then?

M: Then, you'll be a room attendant, a laundryman, a PA cleaner in the Housekeeping Dept.. You'll have a section of 14 rooms every day. That might cause you quite some physical labor.

G: No problem. I'd love to.

M: After that, you'll be put at the Food and Beverage Dept..

G: Fine. I'd try my best to make every customer know better about Chinese cuisine.

M: In addition, you still have chance to work as a shop assistant in our hotel's Shopping Arcade, a clerk in our Recreational Dept., a sales representative in Sales Dept., and a maintenance man in our Engineering and Maintenance Dept. to learn something of everything.

G: Oh, that's a big challenge.

Unit 2   Room Reservation

Listening Practice

I. Listen to the recording and complete the following conversation.

(C: Clerk   G: Guest)

C: Room Reservations. May I help you?

G: Yes. I'd like to cancel a reservation, because the travel schedule has been changed.

C: That's OK. Could you tell me in whose name was the reservation made?

G: White. W-H-I-T-E.

C: And what was the date of the reservation?

G: From September 15th for 3 nights.

C: Excuse me, but is the reservation for yourself or for another party?

G: It's for my boss.

C: Well, may I have your name and phone number, please?

G: Yes, it's Ellen Green, and my number is 245-3971.

C: Thank you, Madam. I will cancel Mr. White's reservation for September 15th for 3 nights. My name is Wang Ying and we look forward to another chance to serve you.

C: Thank you the same. Miss Wang.

G: It's my pleasure.

II. Listen to the recording and answer the questions.

A Group Reservation.

Scene: The telephone rings. The Reservationist answers the phone.

R: Reservations, May I help you?

Client(C): Yes, The Australia New-way Education Delegation will be visiting Beijing at the end of this month. I'd like to reserve 10 double rooms with twin beds for five days.

R: For which dates?

C: For July 23rd, 24th, ...and 27th.

R: One more moment please, Sir.

(The reservationist checks to the list.)

    Yes, we can confirm 10 rooms for five days.

C: Thank you. Is there a special rate for a group reservation?

R; Yes, there is a 10 per cent discount.

C: That's fine.

R: By the way, how will they be getting to Beijing? Will they be coming by air ?

C: Yes.

R: Could you give me the flight number, please, in case the plane's late?

C: Oh, sorry. I don't know the flight number, but I'll let you know by phone tomorrow.

R: Thank you, Sir.

C: Oh, yes. According to the program, they'll have a meeting on the 25th. Have you got a big conference hall?

R: Yes, Sir. we have a very nice multi-function hall.

Unit 3　Bell Service

Listening Practice

I. Listen to the recording and complete the following conversation.

(B: Bellman　G: Guest)

B: Good afternoon, Sir! Welcome to the Lake View Garden Hotel.

G: Thank you.

B: How many pieces of luggage do you have?

G: Just two pieces.

B: Two suitcases and one briefcase. Is that correct?

G: Yes. That's all.

B: I'll show you to the Front Desk. This way, please.

G: I see. Thanks.

B: I will take care of your luggage when you do the check-in.

G: OK.

On the Way to the Room

B: Let me see your key card, Sir.

G: That's it. Room 1203.

B: Your room is on the 12th floor. Let's take the elevator over there.

G: OK. By the way, where is the bar?

B: It's on the third floor. It opens around the clock.

G: It's very kind of you. Thank you.

B: You are welcome. The elevators on the right are for the guests of the hotel. You can take it up to the 12th floor. The elevators on the left are for the staff and luggage. I will take the elevator on the left up to your floor with your luggage. Your elevator is right here. Watch your step, Sir.

G: Thank you.

B: See you later!

G: Sure.

II. Listen to the recording and answer the questions.

(*A guest has already checked out but she suddenly remembers that she has something important to do. So she wants to leave the luggage at the Porter Section and get it back an hour later.*)

(*A: Bellman   B: Guest*)

B: Excuse me.

A: Yes. What can I do for you?

B: I have already checked out. But I suddenly remembered that I have something important to do. I have to go to the post office to get some stamps for my best friend, Ann. She is a stamp collector. So I want to leave the luggage at the Porter Section and get it back an hour later. Is that okay?

A: Sure. We can take care of your luggage until you are back.

B: Great! Here is my luggage.

A: Would you please put this claim tag on your luggage, Madam? And this is your storage receipt.

B: Do I have to pay?

A: No. you don't have to.

B: Thank you very much.

A: You are welcome.

Unit 4   Reception

Listening Practice

I. Listen to the recording and complete the following conversation.

(*A: Receptionist   B: Guest*)

A: Good morning! Can I help you?

B: I want a double room with a bath. How much a day do you charge?

A: It is a hundred Yuan a day including breakfast but excluding service charge.

B: It's quite reasonable.

A: How long do you intend to stay in this hotel?

B: I shall leave in a fortnight.

A: Have you got through with the check-in procedure?

B: Oh，yes，I'm going to fill in the form of registration right now. By the way, I'd like check in a suite room for my friend tomorrow morning.

A: Sorry，we have no vacant room for your friend tomorrow morning. But tomorrow afternoon is OK.

B: That sounds very good! Can I book the air ticket here?

A: Please go to the CAAC office to book your air ticket. If you want to book train ticket or ship ticket，you'd better go to the Shanghai International Travel Service.

(Next afternoon)

B: Can I check in a suite room for my friend beforehand as he will arrive in Shanghai this evening?

A: Sure. Here is the form for you, Sir. Would you mind filling in this form and paying 100 Yuan in advance for him?

B: All right. This is five hundred Yuan to pay.

A: Thank you. This is a receipt for paying in advance. Please keep it.

B: Could you tell me how many kinds of rooms do you have?

A: There are single rooms, double rooms, suites and deluxe suites in our hotel. Every room is equipped with a telephone and a TV set.

B: Oh, I see. Thanks.

A: You are welcome.

II. Listen to the recording and answer the questions.

(R: Receptionist   G: Guest)

R: Good morning, Sir. May I help you? Are you checking out now?

G: Yes. Sorry, I know we're a few minutes late. My name is Mr. Bell and I was in room 1111.

R: That's no problem. It's always really busy at check out time anyway.

G: Oh, really. The last hotel we stayed in charged us for a late check out.

R: The room isn't booked this week, so it's not a problem. How was everything?

G: The room was great. The beds were really comfortable, and we weren't expecting our own fridge.

R: I'm glad you liked it.

G: The kids were disappointed that the pool wasn't open this morning, though.

R: I apologize for that. We often have the water changed in the swimming pool on Monday morning until 10 a.m..

G: Well, we had a nice swim last night.

R: Will you be putting this on your credit card?

G: No. I'll pay cash.

R: Have you used any hotel services since breakfast?

G: No, we haven't.

R: OK. So the total comes to ￥986.78, including tax.

G: I thought it was ￥880. That's what they said yesterday when we checked in...Oh, I forgot. My husband ordered a plate of nachos. Sorry.

R: No problem. So...from ￥1000, here's your change. Now, I'll just need to ask you for your room key.

G: Here you are!

R: Thank you for your coming. Please drop in again. Good-bye.

Unit 5   Switchboard

Listening Practice

I. Listen to the recording and complete the following conversation.

(A: Operator   B: Guest)

A: Good afternoon, International Hotel. May I help you?.

B: Good afternoon. I have made an appointment with Mr. Brookman Wood from the America. He is staying in this hotel.

A: Oh, do you know his room number?

B: Yes, Room 2122.

A: Let me try his extension for you. … Sorry, there is no answer form Room 2122. May I take a message for him?

B: Yes, please tell him that my name is Grace Wang and I'm from the Business Center General Electric China. I'd like to meet him tomorrow evening in the coffee bar at this hotel around 7:30. Ask him to phone me at this number 55219181.

A: Yes, I'll make sure that Mr. Brookman Wood gets your message.

B: Thank you so much.

II. Listen to the recording and answer the questions.

A: Good morning. Operator. May I help you?

B: Morning. This is Billy calling from Room 1208. I've tried to ring my boss in London twice this morning and both times I was cut off.

A: I am sorry to hear that. Did you actually speak to the person in London, Mr. Billy?

B: Yes, it was the same both times. We spoke for about thirty seconds and then the connection was broken.

A: I am awfully worried for that, Mr. Billy. That certainly should not have happened. May I have his number?

B: Yes, the number is 0044-020-5556728.

A: All right, Mr. Billy. Let me try the number again and see if the fault is in their equipment or in ours. I'll call back as soon as I can.

B: Good. Thank you very much.

A: You are welcome.

Unit 6　Information Service

Listening Practice

I. Listen to the recording and complete the following conversation.

Conversation 1　Introducing restaurants

(C: Clerk　G: Guest)

C: Good morning. What can I do for you?

G: Good morning. I'm planning to take a friend of mine to dinner. You see, we both love Beijing Roast Duck. I'm wondering if you could recommend to me a good local restaurant where I can taste Beijing Roast Duck.

C: I'd love to, if Beijing Roast Duck is what you are looking for, there is no other place in the whole city that will please your appetite better than Qian Men Roast Duck Restaurant. The restaurant serves very good Roast Duck. You might want to try there.

G: How far is it from here?

C: It is on Qian Men Street, near Tian'anmen Square. I would suggest that you'd better take a taxi there.

G: Thank you very much. One more thing, could you write down the name of the restaurant on this piece of paper so that I can show it to the taxi-driver?

C: Yes, here you are.

G: By the way, do you know how much we should pay the taxi-driver for the trip?

C: Perhaps 50 Yuan is OK.

G: Thank you for your information. Good bye.

C: You are welcome. Bye-bye.

Conversation 2　Searching for guests

(C: Clerk　G: Guest)

C: Good afternoon. What can I do for you?

G: Good afternoon. I'm looking for a friend, Mr. Black. Could you tell me if he is in the hotel?

C: Mr. Black? Just a minute, please. I'll see if he is registered.

G: Ok, thank you.

C: Black, Mr. Black? There are a lot of Blacks here today…Mr. David Black, Mr. Charles Black…

G: Mr. David Black from Canada. Isn't he staying at this hotel?

C: Oh, yes, here's his name Mr. and Mrs. David Black and family. They are in Room 203. Please wait a moment, let me phone him… Mr. Black said he's waiting for you in his room.

G: OK. Step this way, please. Here it is.

C: Thank you.

G: It's my pleasure.

II. Listen to the recording and answer the questions.

(C: Clerk　G: Guest)

C: Good afternoon, Sir. Can I help you?

G: Yes. I'd like to make an international call to Beijing, China. But I don't know what time it is in Beijing now. Could you tell me, please?

C: Of course, Sir. The time difference between Beijing and New York is 13 hours.

G: Is New York time earlier or later than Beijing time?

C: Sorry, Sir. Beijing time is 13 hours earlier than New York time. You see, the local time in New York now is 14: 30. Then the time in Beijing should be 3:30 in the morning. Have you got it?

G: Yes, Madam. That means now is people's sleeping time in Beijing. I'd better wait for half day to call.

C: If it is not urgent, you can make the call after 19:00.

G: Ok, thank you very much.

C: You are welcome.

Unit 7　Foreign Exchange and Cashier's

Listening Practice

I. Listen to the recording and complete the following conversation.

(C: Clerk　G: Guest)

C: Good evening, Madam. May I help you?

G: Yes, I'd like to change some money.

C: How much would you like to change?

G: Let me see. I'll need about 700 dollars.

C: I'm afraid we have a change limit of 500 dollars between 9 pm and 8 a.m..

G: Well, I'll be leaving at 7:00 a.m. on an all day tour tomorrow and I'll need at least that money. Can't you make an exception for me?

C: I'm afraid that we have to place a limit on exchange for the benefit of all our guests. If we change large amounts, our cash supply runs out and we are unable to oblige our other guest.

G: Why do you keep a change limit?

C: We restrict the amount of cash kept at night for security reasons.

G: Well, I suppose it can't be helped.

II. Listen to the recording and answer the questions.

C: Good morning. May I help you?

G: I'm Peter Lee in room 102. I'm checking out now. But my flight will leave at five thirty and I don't want to wait around at the airport all day. Could I keep the room this afternoon?

C: Certainly, but it's the hotel policy. The check-out time is twelve at noon. You'll have to pay half of the rate more, if you leave after twelve.

G: Never mind, then. Can I just leave my luggage somewhere until three?

C: Certainly, Sir. Please leave it to our Bell Captain's Desk over there. He'll take care of it.

G: Thank you.

C: It's my pleasure.

Unit 8 Housekeeping （*9*）

Listening Practice

I. Listen to the recording and complete the following conversation.

(A: Clerk   B: Guest)

A: Good afternoon. Welcome to the tenth floor.

B: Good afternoon, I have just checked in. My room number is 1016.

A: Let me show you to your room ... Here we are.

B: Thank you very much.

A: Now, Sir. May I introduce the room facilities to you? Here is the light switch and this is the temperature adjuster. The wardrobe is here and the cotton bathrobes are inside of it. Beside the wardrobe is the minibar, and there is a mini safe in the wardrobe.

B: Great. Now can you tell me something about the TV programs?

A: Well, the television provides satellite channels plus pay movies, with TV channels in Chinese and English. You can watch news from CNN and BBC. By the way the panel on the night stand between the beds controls the facilities.

B: It's amazing. Oh, by the way, I need a shower after such a long flight.

A: The bathroom is over there with hot water supplied round the clock. You can find all you may need: soap, shampoo, toothpaste and toothbrush, shower cap, comb, razor and shaving cream. If you have any laundry, just put it in the laundry bag. It will be picked up every morning.

B: Thank you very much. You have made me feel welcome.

II. Listen to the recording and answer the questions.

(A: Clerk   B: Guest)

A: Good afternoon. May I help you?

B: Yes, This is Room 1102 and I checked in about 15 minutes ago.

A: Yes, Sir. What can I do for you?

B: My room is in a mess. The bed sheets need changing and the bathroom is in a terrible mess. The bathtub is full of water, there is no soap and the tower is dirty.

A: I'm sorry to hear that. How come that happened? Room 1102, let me check…

B: OK.

A: Well, Sir. I do apologize for that. We have made a mistake. Room 1102 is not ready for new guests. The housekeeping should have checked the room. Would you please move to Room 903. That room is clean and neat.

B: All right.

A: Please get your luggage ready and the porter will help you to move.

B: That's very kind of you.

Unit 9   Housekeeping   (99)

Listening Practice

I. Listen to the recording and complete the following conversation.

(F: Floor attendant   G: Guest)

G: Good morning. Would you please do me a favor?

F: Yes, Sir. I'm always at your service.

G: My friend is coming here tonight for two days. Could I have an extra bed?

F: Please contact the Front Office first. I'll get you the extra bed with their permission.

G: Have you any idea how much an extra bed costs?

F: It's $30 for one night.

G: By the way, could you get us a few more hangers? I have so many clothes. I am long-staying guest, as you know.

F: Yes, Sir. We are happy to have you. We do hope you are enjoying your stay with us.

G: Thanks. Could you change a pillow for me? This one is too thin, and with a stain on it.

F: Certainly, Sir. I'll see to it right away. I do wish we had known earlier.

G: How nice of you to say so!

F: It's my pleasure. I'll be back in a minute, Sir.

II. Listen to the recording and answer the questions.

(A: Guest   B: Clerk)

A: Excuse me. My room number is 201.

B: Yes, Sir. What can I do for you?

A: I don't mean to make trouble, but I have to say that it was so noisy during the night that I kept awake last night.

B: Oh, I'm very sorry to hear that.

A: There is a lot of noise from the street and a construction site nearby.

B: Yes, I'll see if I can find another quieter room for you… Got it! You may move to room 812. It's higher up and at the backside.

A: That would be better. Thank you for your kindness.

B: Please bring your key card to the reception and the receptionist will help you to make the change.

A: Thank you very much.

B: You are welcome. Just let me know if there is anything I can do for you?

Unit 10 Maintenance and Safety

Listening Practice

I. Listen to the recording and complete the following conversation.

(H: Housekeeper   G: Guest   E: Electrician)

G: I have locked myself out of my room? May I borrow a duplicate key.

H: Don't worry, Madam. I'll open the door for you.

G: Thank you very much indeed. Sometimes I'm quite absent-minded.

H: It doesn't matter, Madam. What else can I do for you?

G: Well, I'm afraid there's something wrong with the TV. The picture is not clear.

H: I'm sorry. May I have a look at it?

G: Sure. Come on in.

(The housekeeper tried to fix it but in vain)

H: I'll send for an electrician from the maintenance department. Please wait just a few minutes, Madam.

G: That's very kind of you.

E: (Knocking at the door) Maintenance. May I come in?

G: Come in, please.

E: Thanks, Madam. I'm here to check and fix your TV.

G: By all means.

E: Let me have a look. …Madam, everything is OK. Please have a try. Here is the remote.

G: What efficiency! Thanks a lot. (Taking out some money) This is for you.

E: Oh, no. We won't accept tips but thank you anyway. We wish you a nice stay with us, Madam.

II. Listen to the recordings and then fill in the form.

Conversation 1

(H: Housekeeper   G: Guest)

H: Housekeeping. May I come in?

G: Yes, what's the matter?

H: Your smoke detector is flashing, Sir. Is there anything burning in your room?

G: No. I've been smoking. That's all.

H: May I look around?

G: Go ahead.

H: Thank you very much. But I have to tell you our hotel is "Green" hotel. Our policy is whoever smoking inside hotel will be fined…

Conversation 2

(H: Housekeeper   G: Guest)

H: Maintenance. May I come in?

G: Come in.

H: What's the trouble?

G: The water tap drips all night long. I can hardly sleep.

H: I'm so sorry. Some parts need to be replaced. I'll fix it as soon as possible. It will not take too much time.

Conversation 3

(H: Housekeeper   G: Guest)

H: Good evening. Did you call for service? What can I do for you?

G: Yes. The light in this room is too dim. Please get me a brighter one.

H: Certainly, Sir. I'll be back right away.

Conversation 4

(H: Housekeeper   G: Guest)

G: My air conditioner is out of order and it makes too much noise.

H: I'm sorry, Sir. Let me take care of it.

G: Go ahead.

H: Excuse me, Sir. The filter of the machine is too dirty. We have to clean it.

G: Then how long shall I have to wait? It's so hot in the room.

H: If you like, we can help you to move to a new room.

Unit 11　Restaurant Service

Listening Practice

I. Listen to the recording and complete the following conversation.

(W: Waiter　　G: Guest)

W: Good afternoon, how can I help you today?

G: I'd like a table for one, please.

W: Right this way. Here you are.

G: Thank you. Can I have a menu?

W: Here you are. My name's Alan and I'm your waiter today. Would you like to hear today's specials?

G: Certainly.

W: Well, we have a wonderful mushroom soup to start off with. Today's main course is fish and chips.

G: Fish and chips? Is the fish fresh?

W: Certainly, Madam. Fresh off the docks this morning.

G: Alright, I'd like the fish and chips.

W: Would you like to have a starter?

G: Hmmm, I'm not sure.

W: Our salads are excellent, Madam.

G: I'd like a green salad.

W: Very good. Would you like something to drink?

G: Oh, I'd like some mineral water, please.

W: OK. So that's a green salad, fish and chips and mineral water.

G: Yes, that's right.

W: Thank you and enjoy your lunch.

G: Thank you.

II. Listen to the recording and answer the questions.

(W: Waiter　　G: Guest)

G: Waiter.

W: Yes, Madam?

G: This coffee is too weak.

W: I'm sorry, Madam. I'll get you another one. Is everything all right?

G: No, this fish was recommended, but it is not fresh.

W: Oh! Sorry to hear that. This is quite unusual as we have fresh fish from the market every day.

G: Who knows? It is not fresh and I am not happy about it.

W: I'm terribly sorry, Madam. I'll look into the matter. I can give you something replaced, if you'd like a change. That would be our treat, of course.

G: It is very kind of you, but I suffered too much here. All that I need is fresh and healthy food. I don't want to trouble anyone. No more, thanks.

W: Just feel ease, Madam. Please give us another chance. I'm sure everything will be all right again the next time you come.

G: I hope so.

W: Thank you very much, Madam.

Unit 12　Bar Service

Listening Practice

I. Listen to the recording and complete the following conversation.

(B: Barman　　J: Jack　　S: Sally)

B: Good evening, Sir and Madam. What may I offer you tonight?

J: Sally, what do you prefer?

S: I don't know what I want. I'm not really a drinker.

J: It doesn't matter. I would like to look through the drink list.

B: Ok, Sir. Here is the drink list.

J: An aperitif or some white wine?

S: Sorry, I don't drink at all.

J: Man, what would you recommend for the lady?

B: How about our special cocktail? It is usually popular with ladies.

S: Is it non-alcoholic?

B: Certainly, Madam. It is a kind of soft drink.

S: It sounds interesting. I'll take that.

B: Okay, Madam. What can I make for you, Sir?

J: I'm very thirsty. I'll have some beer.

B: Any special brand, Sir?

J: What about your local brew? I hear it's good.

B: It is Yan Jing Beer. Bottled or draught?

J: Let me try the draught.

B: Fine. One non-alcoholic cocktail for the lady and one draught Yang Jing Beer.

J: Yes, that's right. By the way, could we have some snacks?

B: Certainly, I'll get a fresh supply.

J: Thank you. How much do I owe you?

B: 86 Yuan. You can hold the payment of the bill until you decide to leave if you like.

J: That's great.

II. Listen to the recording and choose the best answer with the questions.

(J: Mr. Jackson   B: Bartender)

J: Bartender, could I have a drink? What's taking so long?

B: Excuse me, Sir. Yes, what can I get you?

J: I'd like a whiskey sour.

B: Certainly Sir, I'll get that straight away.

J: What a day! My feet are aching! Where's an ashtray?

B: Here you go, Sir. Did you have a busy day?

J: Yes, I had to walk all over town to get to meetings. I'm exhausted.

B: I'm sorry to hear that, Sir. Here's your drink. That should help.

J: (takes a long sip)

   That's what I needed. Much better. Do you have any snacks?

B: Certainly, here are some peanuts and some savory crackers, and a napkin.

J: Could I have a stir stick?

B: Coming up... Here you are.

J: Thanks. You know, I'm sorry to say this, but these snacks are awful.

B: I'm terribly sorry about that, Sir. What seems to be the matter?

J: The peanuts are stale!

B: I apologize, Sir. I'll open a fresh can immediately.

J: Thanks. Sorry to be in such a bad mood.

B: That's quite alright. Can I get you another drink? This one's on the house.

J: That's kind of you. Yes, I'll have another whiskey sour.

B: Right away, Sir. Do you have any preferences on the whiskey?

J: Hmmm, what's that bottle over there?

B: That's Jack Daniel's - aged 12 years.

J: That sounds good. I'd like to smoke...

B: Just a moment, here's an ashtray.

J: Thanks. So how long have you worked at this bar?

B: It's been about three years now. I love this job...

Unit 13   Business Service

Listening Practice

I. Listen to the recording and complete the following conversation.

(C: Clerk   G: Guest)

C: Good morning, Mr. Black. What can I do for you?

G: Yes. I'd like to know whether you provide internet service here. I have to answer an E-mail to my boss.

C: Yes. Internet access is available in all guest rooms. The access is just next to the standing lamp.

G: Yes. I know. But I forgot to bring my laptop with me. I just wonder whether I can send E-mails here.

C: Well, you can get on the internet here. the price for half an hour of connection is 20 Yuan.

G: That's good.

(*a few minutes later*)

G: Your computer is very quick. I've done everything I wanted.

C: Pleased to hear that. For 25 minutes, we charge you 20 Yuan. We charge it on half an hour basis.

G: I see. Can I sign it to my room?

C: Yes, Sir. May I look at your room card?

G: Here they are.

II. Listen to the recording and answer the questions.

1. (*C: Clerk   G: Guest*)

C: Good afternoon. Can I help you?

G: Yes. I'd like to make a long distance call to France. Could you please tell me the rate for calling France?

C: Yes, of course. The standard rate for calling France is 0.7 Yuan for every 6 seconds, excluding service charge.

G: What's your service charge, then?

C: It's 15‰。

G: I see. Thank you.

2. (*C: Clerk   G: Guest*)

C: Good morning, Sir. Can I help you?

G: Good morning. I want to send a fax.

C: Where to, Sir?

G: To Taiwan. Here is the fax number, (886) 02-2396-9795.

C: OK. I will send this fax at once.

G: Thank you.

C: You're welcome. (after a while) All done, Sir. Here you are.

G: Thank you. How much does it cost?

C: Let me see. It's 15.5 Yuan in all. How would you like to make the payment, Sir?

G: I'd like to pay in cash. Here you are.

C: Thank you. Here's the change.

Unit 14　Shopping Arcade

Listening Practice

I. Listen to the recording and complete the following conversation.

(A: Assistant　　C: Customer)

A: Welcome to Robinson's Shoes. We're having a sale on dress shoes.

C: That's great. I need some dress shoes. What do you have on sale?

A: Well, we have Silver Queens and Cool Holidays.

C: What do you recommend?

A: Well, Silver Queens are more fashionable and with higher quality. Whereas, Cool Holidays are not as expensive and they're more comfortable.

C: What's the difference in price?

A: With tax, the Silver Queens come to $47.00 and the Cool Holidays come to $39.00.

C: So that's about an $8.00 difference.

A: That's right.

C: I'll take the Cool Holidays.

A: How would you like to pay?

C: I'll put it on my credit card.

A: All right, here's your receipt. Have a nice day.

C: Thanks.

A: My pleasure.

Unit 15　Recreation and Fitness

Listening Practice

I. Listen to the recording and complete the following conversation.

(C: Clerk　　G: Guest)

C: Good evening, what can I do for you?

G: My doctor advised me to keep in good physical condition. Could you tell me what facilities you have here?

C: Well, we have a well-equipped gym with all the latest recreational sports apparatus, and we also have several sports courts to play tennis, badminton and ping-pang ball.

G: That's very good.

C: There is a wonderful sauna in our club. You can have a try.

G: Really? That's sound interesting. Is here a swimming pool?

C: Yes, of course. Our swimming pool is excellent.

G: Why do you say it's excellent?

C: First, it's big enough. It's 25 meters long, 20 meters wide and 2.5 meters deep.

G: And then?

C: Second, It's a heated swimming pool. The water can keep a comfortable temperature all year round. You can swim in any season.

G: Anymore?

C: At last, you can relax with beer, juice and coffee beside the pool.

G: Oh, it seems that I must spend some money here tonight.

C: The charge is very reasonable, I promise.

G: OK. Thank you for your information.

C: My pleasure, Sir. Have a nice time.

Unit 16   Meeting Service

Listening Practice

I. Listen to the recording and complete the following conversation.

Conveniently located in the heart of midtown New York City, the Roosevelt Hotel gives you the unique opportunity to plan an intimate meeting to a stunning gala by offering a vast choice of meeting rooms.

Meeting:

Wayport High Speed Internet access is available in all 30,000 square feet of our function and meeting space, as well as in all of our 1,015 guest rooms. Also, WiFi Wireless Internet access is available in all common areas of the hotel.

In addition, the flexibility of 19 well-appointed breakout rooms complete with direct phone lines and PC compatibility, our on-site audio visual company and outstanding video conferencing abilities, makes the Roosevelt Hotel the ideal location in New York City to hold your next corporate event of 10 to 500 people.

Accommodation:

Each of our 1,015 luxurious New York City guest rooms, including the 52 suites, combine the classic styling of yesterday with all the modern conveniences of today.

Each guest room has new HD flat screen TVs, wireless internet access, dual telephone lines with voice mail, dataport capabilities, individual climate control, cable television and hairdryers, and irons and boards to assure that you have all the comforts of home.

For New York City business travelers, each of our guest rooms has a sofa chair, desk lamp with Internet and DC plugs, an ergonomic desk chair and high-speed Internet access so you're able to be productive away from the office.

The Roosevelt Hotel Presidential Suite boasts a square footage of 3,900 with eight rooms.

That includes two bedrooms, a complete kitchen, formal living and dining area, and an expansive wrap-around terrace with a panoramic city view.

II. Listen to the recording and answer the questions.

(*M: Manager of the Meeting Service   G: Guest*)

M: Good afternoon. What can I do for you?

G: Good afternoon. I am Robby Smith from Sony. Our company is going to hold a convention in next month. We need several meeting rooms for our convention.

M: We'd be greatly honored to host you. Our hotel is one of the most technologically advanced and functionally superb venues in the city. If you are free, I'd like to show you the facilities in our meeting hall.

G: That's good. Thank you very much.

M: This center can comfortably seat 400 guests. And this is the 200-square meter center stage.

G: Is it movable? There is to be an awarding ceremony. We need raised tiers for those prizewinners.

M: The center stage can be raised or lowered in tiers. Let me show you. Press this green button and the curtain is raised.

G: Oh, I see. Is the screen connected with projector?

M: Yes. It is also equipped with hi-fi AV.

G: What if some of the speakers will use laptop computers?

M: They can connect it with the rear screen projector over the lectern.

G: How can the audience participate in the discussion?

M: Don't worry. We have some wireless microphones come in handy.

G: That's good. By the way, is there a simultaneous translation system?

M: Of course. Each participant is provided with a cordless headset receiver.

G : That's great. May I know the terms?

M: 2000 for the multi-function hall. 800 for each small room per day.

Terminology of Hotel Service

Hotel Basics

hotel personnel	酒店员工	"Green" Hotels	绿色环保饭店
late check out	延迟退房服务	a full ocean view room	海景房
concierges	酒店礼宾部	an extended stay hotel	公寓式酒店
eco-friendly	环保	environmentally friendly	环保
rack rate	门市价	hospitality industry	酒店业
hotel amenities	酒店设施	hotel room upgrade	酒店客房升级
valet park	代客泊车	hotel rating system	酒店等级评定系统
hotel renovation	酒店改造	lodging industry	酒店业
energy-efficient	节能	hotel room cancellation policy	酒店房间预订取消政策

Room Reservation

accommodation cost	住宿费	accommodation	住宿
adjoining room	相邻的房间	advanced deposit	预定押金
banquet hall	宴会厅	bay suite	湾景套房
complimentary	（给入住客人）优惠的	connecting room	相通的房间
continental breakfast	大陆早餐	deduction	折扣
deluxe ocean view suite	豪华海景套房	deluxe suite	豪华套房
diplomatic suite	外交套房	double room	双人间
executive room	商务客房	executive deluxe suite	行政豪华套房
executive suite	行政套房	family suite	家庭套房
guarantee	担保	junior suite	小套间
presidential suite	总统套房	registration	登记，注册
room rate	房价	salon suite	沙龙套房
senior suite	大套间	sitting room	客厅
standard room	标准间	standard suite	标准套房
superior suite	高级套房		

Bell Service

backpack	背包	bath tub	浴缸
bedclothes	床上用品	bedside lamp	床头灯

bedspread	床罩	bell service	送行李服务
blanket	毯子	briefcase	公文包
carpet	地毯	central heating	中央供暖
clothes-hanger	衣架	cold and hot water taps	冷热水龙头
curtain	窗帘	dressing table	梳妆台
food delivery	送餐	handbag	手袋
laundry service	洗衣服务	luggage /baggage	行李
mini-bar	迷你酒吧（房间里的小冰箱）	parcel	包裹
pillow	枕头	remote control	电视遥控
sheet	床单	stool	床榻
suitcase	手提箱	thermos	热水瓶
towel	毛巾	toilet paper	厕纸
TV set	电视机	Wardrobe	衣柜

Reception

banquet facilities	宴会设施	beauty salon	美容院
business centre	商务中心	cocktail bar	鸡尾酒吧
conference facilities	会议设施	currency exchange	货币兑换
designated hotel	指定酒店	dining hall	饭厅
elevator	电梯	gymnasium	体育馆
holiday village	度假村	King -Size / Queen -Size bed	特大号和大号床
Ladies' room	女洗手间	Men's room	男洗手间
lobby	大堂	lodge	山间客栈
lounge	休息室	massage room	按摩室
reception desk	接待处	State guest house	国宾馆
Villa hotel	别墅宾馆	youth hotel	青年旅馆

Switchboard

central exchange	电话总局	city phone	城市电话
collect call	对方付款长途电话	DDD=Domestic Direct Dial	国内直拨
dial a number	拨号码	dial tone	拨号音
external call	外线电话	extension	分机电话
house phone	内部电话	inland telegram	国内电报
internal call	国内电话	IDD=International Direct Dial	国际直拨
international prefix	国际字冠	long distance	长途电话
ordinary mail	平信	ordinary telegram	普通电话
person-to-person	（长途）叫人电话	station-to-station	（长途）叫号电话
postcard	明信片	receiver	听筒

registered fee	挂号邮资	special line	专线
switchboard	交换台	telegram(cable)	电报
telephone directory	电话簿	wake-up call/morning call	叫醒电话

Information Service

check-in	登记入住	complaint	投诉
confirmation	确认	corridor/hallway	走廊
entrance	入口	escalator	扶梯
Front desk	前台	hotel sign	饭店字标
hotel uniform	饭店制服	message	留言
Parking lot	停车场	Registration card	登记卡
Room status report	房间状态报告	temperature	温度
time lag	时差	city tour	城市观光
weather report	天气预报		

Cashier's

account	账户	bad check	空头支票
blank check	空白支票	cash	现金
Cashier	出纳	certificate check	保付支票
Change	零钱	check/cheque	支票
Credit card	信用卡	debit	借方
debt	欠款	debt notice	欠款通知
denominations	面值	deposit	押金
Diners Club	大来信用卡	discount	折扣
exchange rate	兑换率	extra charge	附加费用
fee, charge	费用	gift certificate	礼券
imprint	刷卡	merchandise	商品
payment	付款	payroll check	工资支票
peak time	高峰期	personal check	个人支票
receipt	收据	rental	租金
service charge	服务费	tip	小费
traveler's check	旅行支票	treasurer's check	银行本票

Housekeeping   (I)

ashtray	烟灰缸	bath tub	浴盆
bedside lamp	床头灯	detergent	清洁剂
floor lamp	落地灯	Food and Beverage Department	餐饮部
Housekeeping Department	客房部	Laundry Department	洗衣部

Occupied Dirty	占用脏房	Occupied Room	占用房
Out Of Order	坏房	pillow	枕头
pillowcase	枕套	Public area	公共区域
quilt	被子	toilet	马桶
Vacant Dirty	空房脏房	Vacant Ready	空净房
vacuum cleaner	吸尘器	wall lamp	壁灯
wash basin	盥洗池		

Housekeeping (II)

baby-sitting service	照看婴儿服务	clothes-hanger	衣架
complimentary	免费	electric iron	电烫斗
hair dryer	电吹风	outside call	外线电话
rollaway	折叠床	room service	客房送餐服务
transformer	变压器	valet service	洗烫服务

Maintenance and Safety

Backup Generators	备用发动机	breakdown	故障
carpentry	木工活	Central Air Conditioning system	中央空调系统
Central heating system	中央暖气系统	deadbolt	（门窗的）插销
extinguisher	灭火器	fire exit	消防通道
Fire fighting network	灭火系统	furnishings	室内陈设
indemnity	补偿、赔偿	infrastructure	基础设施
lighting fixtures	灯光装置	lubrication	润滑油、润滑
mechanical rating	技术等级	minor adjustment	微调
on a regular schedule	定期地	out of service	不能使用
performance	性能	plumbing	管道系统
repainting	重新油漆	replacement	替换
steel welding	焊接	the established standards	现有的标准
upholstery	室内装潢、家具装饰	utility	水电煤等能源
wear	磨损		

Restaurant

à la carte	按菜单点菜的（与套餐相对）	à la mode	加有冰激凌的
alcohol （liquor）	酒，烈性酒	appetizer	开胃菜
appetizing	有食欲的	apron	围裙
awful (taste)	难吃的	barbeque	烤肉
beverage	饮料	bitter	苦的
bland	淡而无味的	boil	煮

booster seat	幼儿座椅	booth/bench	（餐馆中的）火车座，高背座
booze	酒，烈性酒	breaded	裹面包屑后烹制的
broiled	烤的	buffet	自助餐
burnt	烧焦的	busboy	（美）餐馆工，特别负责清洁
cash out	收银每天最后清账，结账	chef	主厨
clear	清理（餐桌）	comment card	意见簿
condiments	调味品	cook	烹调
coupon	优惠券	creamer	奶精
cutlery /silverware / utensils	餐具（刀具、银器、器皿）		
deep fried	油炸的	defrost	解冻、化冻
delicious	美味的	dessert	甜食
dirty dishes	客人使用过的餐具	dishwasher	洗碗工、洗碗机
doggie bag	打包袋	dressing	（拌沙拉的）调料
dry	不加黄油（或果酱）的	entrée / main course	主菜
fast-food	快餐	fine dining	高级餐馆
float	（收银的）备用零钱	fry	油炸
gratuity /tip	小费	grill	烧烤
highchair	餐馆中的儿童专用椅子	homemade	自制的
hot	烫的，辣的	ingredients	配料、成分
menu	菜单	microwave	微波炉
mild	味道不重的，不辣的	notepad	餐馆服务生用的记事簿
over charge	多收钱	pack up	打包
pickled	腌制的	rare	生的，三成熟
recipe	菜谱	regulars	常客
restrooms	洗手间	rich	油腻的
salty	咸的	sauce	调味汁、酱汁
seasoning	佐料、调味料	self-serve	自助的
serve	招待、照顾（客人）	set (tables)	摆放餐具
side dish	配菜	sour	酸的
specials	特价菜	specialty	特制品，特产
spicy	辣的	sweet	甜的
take-out /take-away	外卖	waiter /waitress	男女服务生
warm up	加热	well- done	全熟的
yummy	好吃的	yucky	难吃的

Bar

bar	酒吧	barstool	酒吧高脚凳
bartender	酒保	black coffee	不加牛奶的咖啡

bottle opener	启瓶器	cocktail	鸡尾酒
coffee maker	咖啡机	corkscrew	开塞钻
counter	吧台	cut off	停止卖酒给醉酒的人
designated driver	因开车而不能饮酒的司机		
double	双份	draft	生啤酒
free refills	免费续杯的饮料	glassware	玻璃器皿
happy hour	特指每天下午 5 点至 7 点某些酒吧买一送一指定的啤酒，鸡尾酒及软饮料活动		
Highball	加冰威士忌	last call	酒吧打烊前最后卖出的酒
liqueur	烈性酒	nightclub	夜总会
non alcoholic beverage	非酒精饮料	on the rocks	加冰
pitcher	装啤酒的罐子	pour	沏（茶），倒（水、酒）
pub	酒馆	shot	少量饮料；（尤指）少量烈酒
shooter	酒精与果汁混合的饮料	stir /mix	搅拌
straw	吸管	straight up	纯酒精饮品（不兑任何饮料）
wine list	酒水单	winery	葡萄酒酿造厂
wine tasting	品酒		

Business Service

air mail	航空邮件	broadband service	宽频服务
business class	商务舱	care of (C/O)	由……转交
Day ticket	一日票	economy class	经济舱
Express	快递	first class	头等舱
group booking	团体订票	hard berth	硬卧
hard seat	硬座	information booth	信息中心，服务中心
Internet access	互联网接入	International communication facilities	国际通信设备
lower berth	下铺	luxurious class	豪华舱
middle berth	中铺	one way ticket	单程票
ordinary mail	平邮	paper clip	回形针
PC rental	电脑出租	Professional secretarial service	专业秘书服务
registered letter	挂号信	round trip ticket	往返票
soft berth	软卧	soft seat	软座
upper berth	上铺	wireless Internet	无线上网
word processing	文字处理	Zip code/postal code	邮编

Shopping Arcade

artificial	人工的	bargain	讨价还价

Beijing opera masks	京剧脸谱	Beijing Roast Duck	北京烤鸭
blue and white porcelain	青花瓷	bracelets	手链
chinaware	瓷器	cloisonné	景泰蓝
crystal ornaments	水晶饰品	earring	耳环
exhibiting	展示	gift shop	礼品店
hair pin	发卡	hotel shop	商场部
imprint	刷卡	jade	玉
medium-sized	中号的	natural	天然的
necklace	项链	pearl	珍珠
preserved fruit	果脯	scarf	围巾，披肩
silk stuff	丝绸制品	souvenir shop	纪念品店
window	橱窗		

Recreation and Fitness

ball room/ dancing hall	舞厅	barber	理发师
billiard room	台球室	bowling alley	保龄球场
cleaning milk	洗面奶	coffee house	咖啡厅
cream-based mask	乳脂面膜	D.J.	调音师
disco hall	迪斯科舞厅	eye shadow	眼影
eye-cream	眼霜	facial mask	面膜
gymnasium	健身房	hairdresser	美发师
make-up	化妆粉	massage parlor	按摩房
moisturizing lotion	保湿霜	multifunctional hall	多功能厅
orange juice	橘子水	sauna	蒸汽浴室
Saxophone	萨克斯管乐器	Seven up	七喜
soft drinks	软饮料	song order slip	点歌单
songs lyric	抒情歌曲	tonic	营养素
Waltz	华尔兹舞		

Convention Service

annual convention	年会，年度大会	breakout	分会室
colloquium	学术讨论会	conference center	会议中心
conference venue	会议地点		
cordless headset receiver	无绳头戴式接收机	convention center	会展中心
convention facility	会议设施，会议举办场所		
convention service manager	会议服务经理	debate	辩论会
drop curtain	垂幕	forum	论坛
hotel accommodation	酒店膳宿	incentive travel	奖励旅游

keynoter	主要演说人	meeting planner	会议策划人
meeting room	会议室	meeting professional	会议专业人员
meeting prospectus	会议计划书	multifunction Meeting-room	多功能会议室
panel	座谈小组	plenary session	全体会议
rear screen projector	幕后电子投影仪	seminar	研究会
site selection	挑选会址	sponsor	主办单位，赞助商
symposium	座谈会	theater	舞台式会议厅
tier	升降台	venue	会场位置
workshop	研讨会		

Reference

1. 陈克成. 旅游交际英语通[M]. 上海：华东师范大学出版社，1992
2. 王逢鑫. 汉英旅游文化词典[M]. 北京：北京大学出版社，2001
3. 程中锐. 饭店工作英语[M]. 北京：中国旅游出版社，2002
4. 郭兆康. 宾馆英语[M]. 北京：高等教育出版社，2003
5. 刘海霞. 旅游饭店职业英语（初，中，高）[M]. 北京：旅游教育出版社，2005
6. 邹晓燕. 旅游专业英语实用教程[M]. 北京：清华大学出版社，2005
7. 肖璇. 现代酒店英语实物教程[M]. 广州：世界图书出版公司，2006
8. 新世纪高等职业教育教材委员会. 实用酒店英语[M]. 大连：大连理工大学出版社，2006
9. 吴云. 旅游实践英语[M]. 北京：旅游教育出版社，2007
10. 李佳. 饭店英语[M]. 北京：化学工业出版社，2007
11. 饶莉. 饭店英语[M]. 武汉：武汉大学出版社，2007
12. 魏国富. 实用旅游英语教程[M]. 上海：复旦大学出版社，2007
13. 陈的非. 饭店实用英语[M]. 北京：机械工业出版社，2008
14. 赵丽. 新编饭店实用英语听说教程[M]. 北京：清华大学出版社，2009
15. 郭兆康. 饭店实用英语. 大连：东北财经大学出版社，2009
16. 谢关平. 旅游英语[M]. 合肥：中国科学技术大学出版社，2009
17. 赵丽. 餐饮英语[M]. 北京：北京大学出版社，2009
18. 林群. 旅游服务英语[M]. 北京：清华大学出版社，2010
19. 黄中军. 实用旅游英语[M]. 北京：清华大学出版社，2010
20. 杨义德，李斌. 旅游英语教程[M]. 北京：北京大学出版社，2012
21. 莫红英. 旅游英语[M]. 北京：旅游教育出版社，2013
22. 李燕，徐静. 旅游英语[M]. 北京：清华大学出版社，2013

推荐网站：
1. http://www.therooseveldthotel.com/About/
2. http://www.fourseasons.com/business_services/
3. www.bls.gov/oco/ocos296.htm#nature
4. www.collegegrad.com/careers/servi19.shtml#con
5. www.bogglesworldesl.com
6. http://www.englishformyjob.com/ell_politeness.html
7. http://www.education-online-search.com/articles/careers/hospitality_careers
8. http://www.englishclub.com/english-for-work/
9. http://www.englishformyjob.com/ell_hotelindustry.html
10. http://www.englishclub.com/english-for-work/airline-announcements.htm
11. http://educare.intnet.mu/front_off.html
12. http://www.associatedcontent.com

教师服务

感谢您选用清华大学出版社的教材！为了更好地服务教学，我们为授课教师提供本书的教学辅助资源，以及本学科重点教材信息。请您扫码获取。

≫ 教辅获取

本书教辅资源，授课教师扫码获取

≫ 样书赠送

旅游管理类重点教材，教师扫码获取样书

 清华大学出版社

E-mail: tupfuwu@163.com
电话：010-83470332 / 83470142
地址：北京市海淀区双清路学研大厦 B 座 509

网址：http://www.tup.com.cn/
传真：8610-83470107
邮编：100084